AMERICAN HISTORY IN FOCUS SERIES

Under the Editorship of
William H. Goetzmann

THE COLONIAL HORIZON:
AMERICA IN THE SIXTEENTH AND SEVENTEENTH CENTURIES
William H. Goetzmann, University of Texas

THE AMERICAN REVOLUTION:
THE ANGLO-AMERICAN RELATION, 1763–1794
Charles R. Ritcheson, Southern Methodist University

YEARS OF TURMOIL:
CIVIL WAR AND RECONSTRUCTION
John Niven, Claremont Graduate School

THE GILDED AGE: AMERICA, 1865–1900
Richard A. Bartlett, The Florida State University

THE AGE OF INSECURITY: AMERICA, 1920–1945
Robert A. Divine, University of Texas

THE GILDED AGE: AMERICA, 1865–1900

Interpretive Articles and Documentary Sources
Edited by
RICHARD A. BARTLETT
The Florida State University

▲▼ ADDISON-WESLEY PUBLISHING COMPANY
Reading, Massachusetts / Menlo Park, California / London / Don Mills, Ontario

To M. C. B.

PREFACE:
THE AMERICAN HISTORY IN FOCUS SERIES

History is the recorded deeds, ideas, and emotions of men. Living history is the re-recording of these deeds, ideas, and emotions by interpreters in each new generation. *The American History in Focus Series* seeks to provide the student with what might be called "the varieties of living historical experience," from a mid-twentieth century point of view. Each of the major historical epochs in American history is brought into focus by means of modern interpretive articles written by major scholars in the field, scholars who may be said to be on "the growing tip" of historical knowledge. Their interests span a vast range of historical methods and commitments. Collectively, they represent the multiple points of view of political, social, economic, diplomatic, military, and intellectual historians —historians who are nonetheless very much products of our own times and affected by current interests. These selections are concerned in almost every instance with answering that simple but all-important question— "so what?"—as it relates to our historical heritage. Of what relevance has past American historical experience been to the total course of human development, to the emergence of American values, achievements, problems, and predicaments? How did I, a citizen of the United States, get to be where and what I am today with all the privileges, burdens, and responsibilities that are entailed? What experiences of quality and nobility of conduct can be noted in the past against which we can measure our own aspirations and behavior—for we can the better recognize quality in our own lives for having seen it somewhere before in the recent or distant past?! By portraying realistically the complexities, relativisms, and ambiguities in the interpretations of time past, the editors and authors represented in these volumes provide new perspectives for determining our cultural identity.

Each of the volumes concentrates on a major period in American history, from colonial times to the present. Each is structured around focal, interpretive articles of modern historians with several varieties of history represented. These focal articles are supplemented by important and revealing historical documents of the particular era with which the historian is concerned. These are samples of the kinds of materials out of which he has constructed his interpretation. They are intended to serve two purposes: first, to give today's student a "feel" for the language and perspectives of the people of earlier generations; second, to provide materials with which to *test* the generalizations of the modern interpreters—to provide a laboratory situation whereby the student may critically examine some of the interpreter's answers and hopefully even some of his questions. For serious historical study requires constant criticism of historical generalizations, and it is too little recognized that such criticism might properly begin with the question, "did the historian ask the right questions of the period?"

Given the above, it should be obvious that these are experimental books especially designed as tools for learning. They are neither exercises in belletristic virtuosity, nor are they "canned" problems where the rules are clear and for the clever, the answers pat. Rather they are intended to be sophisticated, broad-based springboards to future discussion. As an added dimension we have experimented with the addition of pictorial materials which are not intended as idle embellishment but should rather serve as integral parts of the text—as further documents of the time. These, too, when examined with care, afford points of focus.

In attempting to draw a distinction between the nature of science and the nature of history, an historian of science, Derek de Solla Price, makes a striking analogy. He sees science as a "many-brained" machine into whose circuits all of the latest "growing tip" discoveries, however limited, can be wired so that advances in knowledge can result without the necessity for retracing in detail the historical steps involved in previous discoveries. History, on the other hand, is a "single-brained" enterprise in which each historian has to go back over all the sources and interpretations of the past before making his own generalization.* The *American History in Focus Series* attempts to draw upon the advantages of both. For the individual student it is clearly a "single-brained" experience. But in assembling between two covers modern interpretations, along with documents from the past, both written and pictorial, we have attempted to provide the advantages of a "many-brained" approach as well, so as to encourage the student to examine the nature of historical enquiry as a process of thought, and to address himself to the problem of cultural identity in a changing world.

William H. Goetzmann, General Editor

* Derek D. Price, "Two Cultures and One Historian of Science," *Teachers College Record,* **64,** 7, April 1963, pp. 528–531.

CONTENTS

GENERAL INTRODUCTION

GENERAL INTRODUCTION

In the years between 1865 and 1900 the face of America changed. Five transcontinental railroads linked the East with the West, more virgin land was put to the plow than in all the years of American history prior to 1865, the land frontier came to an end, immigration from Europe attained the proportions of a tidal wave of humanity, great cities arose, and a discontented working population began to suffer under the burden of expanding, unregulated industry.

Any period that embraces such massive changes in the life of a nation will probably be given a name. And so it was with the post-Civil War period. Mark Twain called it the Gilded Age, and, with Charles Dudley Warner, wrote a novel about it. Although Twain's Gilded Age was primarily the Grant years, the phrase has come to apply to the entire post-Civil War era, 1865–1900.

And why is it known by such a name? It was an age of quick riches, and the nouveaux riches left an unduly deep impress upon the American memory, just as the superficial "jet set" of today will retain its undeserved fame for decades to come. The Gilded Age represented to the popular mind an era in which thousands of families arose from humble origins to positions of great wealth. These people, these nouveaux riches, put on airs. They overdressed, built garish mansions, gave incredibly expensive parties. Yet everyone knew that beneath the veneer of gentility was a humble or middle-class background, a farmer's or a small businessman's vocabulary. Beneath the thin coating of gilt was plain iron. And so the name: the Gilded Age.

The phrase proved harmful for the history written of the age. Historians proceeded to take the term at its face value; they considered those thirty-five years as inconsequential to the American story and went on to the exciting twentieth century. Business was presented simply as a matter of robber barons stealing from the public domain and forming monopolies. Labor was viewed as incendiary and radical. The West was noted because of the end of the frontier. Politics was considered a matter of Tweedledum and Tweedledee (Republicans and Democrats both essentially alike), and foreign relations were thought to be minor and unimportant.

Only recently have historians begun a reappraisal of the Gilded Age. They have discovered this first era of modern America to be complicated, fascinating, and important as a seedbed of the American civilization of the twentieth century. They have found the age a mirror of the present, with

1

the primary theme being *change*. The great problems were the result of the failure of all facets of the civilization to change and adjust at the same pace. Business moved reluctantly toward regulation and a social philosophy. Labor ended the era frustrated, with its victories still ahead. The agricultural West already felt the enigma of hardship in the midst of plenty. By the end of the age the farmer was asserting his political power, however, and he still retains it. Politics had a seamy side and was perhaps too close a parallel to the politics of today, still unable to cope adequately with rapid new developments. Only in the realm of foreign relations was the age wanting, for until the mid-1890's that realm of governmental concern, so predominant today, was a matter of mere routine. When, toward the end of the Gilded Age, the United States took steps into the world arena as a major power, philosophical questions were raised that are still being debated. Two short readings at the end of Part IV present the foreign-policy dilemma.

It is clear that dynamic changes took place in this thirty-five year period, transformations that established patterns of action that are still followed today. This is true for business, labor, the West, politics, and, at the very end of the era, for the realm of foreign relations. It is hoped that the following interpretive essays, along with the accompanying documents, will help bring about a greater understanding of those complex, changing years, 1865–1900: the Gilded Age.

I/BUSINESS:
SINE QUA NON OF THE AGE

INTRODUCTION

When the Gilded Age began, there was no opposition to the prevailing business structure. Taxless and regulationless, the expanding economy changed its dimensions almost as rapidly as a balloon inflating before one's eyes. Men of courage, audacity, and vision built enormous corporate structures to serve an expanding economy, an expanding population, and an expanding country. Their world of 1865 was full of promise and opportunity, and they made the most of it.

One transcontinental railroad, completed in 1869, spurred the completion of four more by 1900, and by that year the tracks of the iron horse made a gridwork across America. The bison were virtually eliminated, and replaced by beef cattle, to be raised on the Great Plains, carried by rail to a central processing plant, there prepared and canned, preserved, or refrigerated, and then sent to the far corners of America in freight cars or the new refrigerator cars. The grasslands of the Middle Border (western Minnesota, Dakota, Nebraska, Kansas, and down into Texas) inspired vast bonanza wheat farms; rails carried the golden grain to the central flour mills, as at Minneapolis and St. Paul, where the snow-white product was bagged and then carried by rail to Maine and California. The demand for oil prompted shrewd men to gain control of oil fields, refineries, railroads that carried the product, or pipe lines.

In all major facets of production and consumption, business was nationalized, products standardized, and monopolies extended. Competition was bitter. No one was around to halt the successful or protect the unsuccessful, or the consumer either. The unscrupulous capitalist was a product of his age, and he measured his success by his power and control. No one taxed his wealth. No one told him how to run his business. No one protected his labor force.

Such unrestrained business activities changed the face of America in the Gilded Age. Drab, cheerless, soot-encrusted, red-brick factories sprouted across the land, and sulfurous-smelling burning coal, used to produce steam power, tossed out clouds of black smoke from the tall chimneys. Chugging steam locomotives made an additional contribution to the grime. From those factories, carried by those railroads, came more and more consumer goods. Advertising helped create the demand for thousands of products. The American people entered the twentieth century in full accordance with the oft-heard phrase, that they had "the highest standard of living in the world."

And they had the most millionaires, the worst slums, brutal class inequities, recurring panics and depressions, and restless workingmen and agriculturalists. Yet the callousness, crassness, and frank dishonesty which accompanied this nationalizing of business resulted in protests that were eventually translated into governmental action.

Within about two decades after the dim realization of need, governmental regulations began. The Interstate Commerce Act came in 1887, and the Sherman Antitrust Act followed three years later. Although both of these Acts were admittedly weak, they were signs of official recognition of need, and they indicated that our democracy was not insensate to the problems of a changing civilization. The two-decade lag between realization of need and governmental action was not an undue length of time. The process of trust formation was not yet complete, and, we might add with a measure of pride, no other nation had such legislation before the turn of the century.

The Gilded Age was indeed dominated by business, but well before the century's end the other sections of American society were being heard. The basic morality of Americans insisted upon it, and even many elements of the business community came to acknowledge the need, and accept the governmental restrictions.

INTERPRETATION

Professor Sidney Fine of the University of Michigan is an authority on labor history and the United States since 1876. In the reading given below, he analyzes the crystallizing attitudes of the American businessman, and his professional compatriots in the clergy and the learned professions, toward the business system.

A few business historians, Professors Kirkland and Miller, for example, have questioned some of Professor Fine's observations on the impact of Darwinism on businessmen. They suggest that most American entrepreneurs never knew who Darwin was. This is a controversial point, however, and in no way harms the high quality of the essay given below.

SIDNEY FINE, *Laissez Faire and the American Businessman*

It is, of course, extremely difficult to speak in general terms of the business community as a whole with respect to the functions of government. Manufacturers, merchants, bankers, railroad entrepreneurs, and small businessmen in the period after the Civil War did not necessarily regard the problem all in the same light, nor were individuals within these groups equally articulate in the expression of such opinions as they did entertain. One finds among the businessmen protectionists and free traders, friends of hard money and of soft money, opponents of any real government control of corporate enterprise and advocates of government regulation of corporations as creatures of the state. What follows, therefore, is largely an attempt to focus upon what appear to have been some of the dominant elements in the thought of the business community regarding the role of the state and, particularly, although by no means exclusively, the thought of the industrial capitalists.

With the triumph of the North in the Civil War the industrial capitalist became for the first time the regnant figure in American life. No longer did he have to contend with the slaveholding aristocrat for control of the state. The policies he favored—a national banking system, a high protective tariff, generous land grants to railway corporations, and the authorized importation of contract labor—were put into effect during the war years by a government amenable to his will, and after Appomattox the national administration remained responsive to his wishes. As the *Nation* caustically pointed out, what the national government interpreted as the common good was, in actuality, "the good of those . . . rich and powerful enough to make their influence felt at Washington."

Since the businessman was the admired social type of the Gilded Age, large sections of the American public acquiesced in his views. Warren Miller, a former United States senator from New York, expressed a desire to see more businessmen in American legislatures because he regarded them as "more competent to deal with the live questions of the hour than any other class"; and Godkin noted that Americans had "an inordinate respect for the opinions on all subjects of 'successful business men.' " A critic of the contemporary business scene, Henry Demarest Lloyd, thought the popular support given the businessman was less a matter of "respect" than of selfishness. "Every man," he confided to his notebook, "winks at the practice of the business world because he is in the race, and hopes to 'get there,' or hopes as preacher, editor, superintendent of charity to share in the gains."

Not content merely to be the most influential figure on the American scene, the businessman felt the need for a philosophy to explain and to justify his preëminent position. To a great extent, he found what he sought in the precepts of social Darwinism and laissez-faire economics. The businessman, to be sure, did not accept the doctrines of Spencer and the economists *in toto*: he took from their thought only what suited his needs. His version of laissez faire, unlike theirs, was essentially a rationalization of the *status quo*. The theorists of laissez faire were, after all, reformers in their own manner and were opposed to the use of government for the benefit of any particular class. They denounced evidences of governmental favoritism, such as the protective tariff, that were dear to the heart of the businessman. The businessman, for his part, saw no wrong in government activities that were conducive to his welfare: he did not ordinarily object to the use of state power to promote business enterprise. He tended to become an opponent of the state only when it sought to regulate his economic endeavors or to cater to the needs of other economic groups. Laissez faire to him meant, "Leave things as they now are." "If asked what important law I should change," Andrew Carnegie declared, "I must perforce say none; the laws are perfect."

One element of the businessman's defense of the *status quo* was a formula for success. The success of the businessman, it was explained, was the result of his possessing certain simple virtues and abilities; the failure of the poor man resulted from his lack of these same virtues and abilities. In his book *The Successful Man of Business,* Benjamin Wood explained that success was "nothing more or less than doing thoroughly what others do indifferently." In a lecture delivered at Cornell University in 1896, Carnegie gave it as his opinion that success "is a simple matter of honest work, ability, and concentration." Another businessman asserted that "wealth has always been the natural sequence to industry, temperance, and perseverance, and it will always so continue." Why did poverty still exist in society? To S. C. T. Dodd, solicitor for Standard Oil, the answer was simple. Poverty exists, said Dodd, "because nature or the devil has made some men weak and imbecile and others lazy and worthless, and neither man nor God can do much for one who will do nothing for himself."

Not only did the businessman equate success with virtue and concentration, but he sought to impress upon one and all the view that there was ample room at the top for those who were willing to make the effort. "The storehouse of opportunity is open to all," proclaimed Benjamin Wood. Henry Wood thought that "examples on every hand" proved how simple it was to move into the "independent class." This was not a matter of theory, but of "universal experience." Wall Street's Henry Clews also emphasized the numerous opportunities for acquiring wealth in the United States. It required neither genius, education, breeding, nor even luck to gather "the nimble dollar"; it was necessary for one only to begin "aright."

The businessman's interpretation of success found popular literary expression in the biographies of William Makepeace Thayer and the novels of Horatio Alger. These two authors were among the chief representatives of a veritable "cult of success" that glorified the self-made man and trumpeted the idea that the road to the top lay open to those with the requisite qualities. The implications of such a version of success were obvious—it would be fatuous to interfere with an economic system that so readily rewarded ability and that provided an opportunity for all to gain riches. This, indeed, was the theme of Carnegie's paean of praise to the system that had made his rise to fame possible, *Triumphant Democracy,* published in the year of the Haymarket Affair. "The publication of it is very timely," George Pullman wrote to Carnegie, "as owing to the excesses of our turbulent population, so many are uttering doubts just now as to whether democracy has been a triumph in America." The St. Paul real-estate and loan agent H. S. Fairchild thought the book "better than a direct argument" against the principles of the discontented. It "makes them hesitate to engage in wild legislation or revolutionary schemes that might endanger a government that offers such opportunities, that has accomplished so much, and on whose success the hopes of humanity rest."

In further support of his position and of the *status quo,* the man of wealth pointed to the teachings of Spencer. That part of Spencer's thought that dealt with the struggle for existence, the survival of the fittest as the result of natural selection, and the inevitability of progress was readily adaptable to the pattern of American economic life and to the needs of the businessman. It took no great imagination to see that Spencer offered a rationale for the business triumphs of the industrial leaders and for opposition to all proposals of state intervention on behalf of the unsuccessful. Upon reading Darwin and Spencer, Carnegie remarked, "I remember that light came as in a flood and all was clear."

Competition, the success of some and the failure of others, and the consolidation of industry into ever larger units were all readily explainable by the businessman in the terms that Spencer had made popular. "Competition in Economics," the publisher Richard R. Bowker proclaimed, "is the same as the law of the 'survival of the fittest,' or 'natural selection,' in nature." The great Southern textile manufacturer Daniel A. Tompkins informed an audience that "in a businessman's every-day life he sees this law of the survival of the fittest at work, thinning out the ranks of his competitors, introducing new material." "Competition, the very essence of business life," Tompkins continued, "puts down some and elevates others. The fittest survive. It must be so, else there is no life, no progress. Whatever the socialist and other sentimentalists may think, the survival of the fittest is, has been, and will always be the law of progress in national affairs, in business and in all other walks of life." It would be "the silliest kind of sentimentalism" to fret about those who were "defeated" in this struggle for existence. "The poor and the weak," the general manager of the Atlas Works informed a committee of Congress, "have to go to the wall to some extent, of course. That is one of the natural laws that we cannot get over except by providing for them by charity."

Not only did the businessman describe the success of individuals in Darwinian terms, but he was able to explain and justify the consolidation of industry in similar terms. The concentration of capital, Carnegie declared, "is an evolution from the heterogeneous to the homogeneous, and is clearly another step in the upward path of development." Carnegie was, moreover, quite certain that "this overpowering, irresistible tendency toward aggregation of capital and increase of size ... cannot be arrested or even greatly impeded." Rockefeller, too, explained the growth of the "large business" as "merely a survival of the fittest ... the working out of a law of nature and a law of God." It was obviously futile, in the view of business advocates of social Darwinism, for the state to attempt to interfere with the process that brought the fittest individuals and concerns to the fore. "Yes; they are very shrewd men," William Vanderbilt said of the Standard Oil leaders to a committee of the New York legislature. "I don't believe that by any legislative enactment or anything else through any of the States or all of the States, you can keep such men as them down; you can't do it; they will be up on the top all the time; you see if they are not." "If I were able," declared the president of the Chicago, Burlington and Quincy, "I would found a school for the study of political economy in order to harden men's hearts!" And it is clear that, just as the theories of the social Darwinists were readily adaptable to the needs of the captains of industry, so was there much in the doctrines of the laissez-faire economists that fitted the specifications of a businessman's philosophy. Like the economists, the businessman was prone to talk of the inexorable natural laws that governed the economic order of competition as the great regulator, and of the virtues of self-interest.

The doctrine of self-interest was particularly attractive to the business-man, for it supplied him with a truly potent argument with which to defend the existing order. If each individual in his pursuit of wealth un-consciously promoted the general good, did not those who were most successful in the quest for economic gain promote the general welfare more effectively than all others? The millionaires, declared Carnegie, "are the bees that make the most honey, and contribute most to the hive even after they have gorged themselves full." The millionaire "cannot evade the law which ... compels him to use his millions for the good of the people." What need was there then for the state to seek by positive action to promote the well-being of the mass of the people. The captains of industry, said John F. Scanlan, of the Western Industrial League, "are fathers to guide the masses to higher conditions."

Like the laissez-faire economists and the social Darwinists, whose views they found so palatable, businessmen generally cautioned the state to pursue a hands-off policy with respect to economic matters. The Chicago banker Lyman Gage, eventually to become McKinley's secretary of the treasury, informed a committee of Congress that insofar as the industrial affairs of the country were concerned, the legislature should "simply ... define the obligations of citizens to each other, and ... secure the en-forcement of individual rights." The state, businessmen thought, should protect property and enforce contracts, but they did not wish it to inter-fere with prices, wages, or profits. "The more the legislature and the people let these things alone, the better they will work out their own solution," asserted the president of the Wholesale Grocers' Association of New York City. If trade were untrammeled, the head of the sugar trust informed the United States Industrial Commission, no economic group would enjoy any special advantage, and the country would benefit. Of course, if one concern managed to get rid of its competitors in the process, that was trade, and nothing could be done about it.

The businessman was prone to contrast the beneficent natural laws which, in his view, governed the economic order with the clumsy, artificial laws devised by man. "Oh, these grand immutable, all-wise laws of natural forces," exulted Carnegie, "how perfectly they work if human legislators would only let them alone! But no, they must be tinkering." The president of the American Exchange Bank and the onetime president of the American Bankers Association, George S. Coe, thought the laws of economics "as sacred and as obligatory as . . . those of the decalogue." He spoke of the "impotence and limitations of human law" and insisted that "all material values are governed by influences far beyond the reach of human vision and legislation." In Charles Flint's view, industrial progress was assured so long as "natural conditions" were undisturbed. However, if legal restraints were imposed, then, Flint warned, the "wheels which have been driving all this vast machinery will come to rest." The nation was already "overwhelmed . . . by useless legislation," according to J. G. Batterson, the president of the New England Granite Works, and more was to be gained by the repeal than from the enactment of any law. "The universal law of supply and demand," he averred, "is superior to any law which can be enacted by Congress or any other power on earth."

Not only did the businessman compare man-made law unfavorably with natural law, but he also found virtue on the side of private enterprise as contrasted to government enterprise. "It is better always," said the merchant Danford Knowlton, "to leave individual enterprise to do most that is to be done in the country." Even the Post Office, Jay Gould thought, should be in private hands, "because individual enterprise can do things more economically and more efficiently than the Government can."

In his approach to such problems of the day as labor relations, money, railroads, and trusts, the businessman generally adhered closely to the laissez-faire doctrine. He naturally looked with disfavor on attempts by workers to interfere with the *status quo*. Regarding himself as the benefactor of the community in general and of the laborer in particular, the industrialist exhorted the workingman to remain quiescent and to trust to his employer and to natural law to improve his position. The entrepreneur, he informed the worker, was entitled to a large share of the total product because he was "the most important factor in the modern economy" and made the major contribution to production. It was altogether proper for him to earn more than the laborer because he possessed "superior judgment, skill, and sagacity." Moreover, since the efforts of the few had served to raise wages and increase purchasing power, the laborer had no cause for complaint. If the worker succeeded somehow in reducing the margin of profits, the capitalist would be unable to put forth his best efforts, and the total product would be diminished, to the detriment of all. Trade unions that sought to reduce the hours of labor or to improve wage rates were reminded that matters of this sort were determined by inexorable laws of supply and demand that unions, as well as employers, were powerless to set aside. Some businessmen, indeed, insisted that trade unions not only were an "intrusion" upon the domain of natural law, but that they were withal destructive of the rights of the individual laborer and, in effect, subversive of the existing order. One manufacturer referred to unions as "fierce, cruel, arbitrary, dictatorial—in a word, tyrannical!" The *Portage Lake Mining Gazette,* reflecting the views of employers in Michigan's copper country, declared that "nothing more thoroughly un-American, in practice and in principle, can well be conceived than trades unionism." The secretary of the Southern Industrial Convention contended that "labor organizations are . . . the greatest menace to this Government that exists inside or outside the pale of our national domain." Henry Clews thought the demands of the Knights of Labor "utterly revolutionary of the inalienable rights of the citizen" and "completely subversive of social order." When Carnegie's lieutenant, Henry Clay Frick, broke the Amalgamated Association of Iron and Steel Workers in the famous Homestead Strike of 1892, the Pittsburgh employer Thomas Mellon applauded this action as one that all employers would sooner or later have to repeat. Employee "usurpation" of the control of business "had to be checked," he wrote Carnegie, "or industry requiring the employment of labor would have to cease."

The state as well as the trade union was cautioned by employers to entrust the labor contract to the bargaining of the individual worker and his employer. "I say the legislature has no right to encroach upon me as to whether I shall employ men eight hours, or ten, or fifteen," the clothing manufacturer Henry V. Rothschild informed a committee of the House of Representatives. "It is a matter of mutual agreement, and the legislature has no right, according to the principles of our government, according to the principles of the Declaration of Independence, to impose upon me what hours of labor I shall have between myself and my employees." Jane Addams has informed us that the Illinois labor legislation of the 1890's "ran counter to the instinct and tradition, almost to the very religion of the manufacturers of the state."

With respect to the great currency problems that troubled the nation in the three and one-half decades after the Civil War, the business community was in essential agreement with the laissez-faire economists. Although some businessmen were sympathetic to the cause of greenbacks, businessmen in general and the banking community in particular favored specie resumption. The battle of the standards found business leaders generally arrayed on the side of gold and using the conventional arguments as to the limited role government should play in this sphere.

The advent of the railroad and the practices which railway managers found it necessary to employ raised doubts in the minds of some business-men regarding the virtues of a completely unregulated economic order. Merchants and shippers disadvantageously affected by personal or place discrimination or by railway-rate agreements decided that the railway business was not one that could be safely entrusted to the free play of economic forces and that in this field at least the power of the state would have to be invoked. The pro-rata movement in the East during the 1850's and 1860's was led by members of the business community; merchants and shippers played the crucial role in the framing of the so-called Granger laws in Illinois, Iowa, Wisconsin, and Minnesota; and commercial elements in New York City were instrumental in securing the Hepburn investigation of the New York State Assembly and the railway legislation that the state subsequently adopted and were, according to one scholar, "the single most important group" behind the passage of the Interstate Commerce Act.

Railroad officials sought for a time to stave off state and federal railroad regulation and were not at all pleased with the regulatory legislation that was enacted. Charles Elliott Perkins, of the Chicago, Burlington and Quincy, expressed the wish that the "intelligent people" could "be made to see that the let alone policy as regards railroads is the safe one and that any other policy is full of danger." Confronted by the Hepburn investigation, Presidents William H. Vanderbilt of the New York Central and H. J. Jewett of the New York, Lake Erie and Western Railroad spoke of the attack on the railroads as evidence of the "growth of a disregard to the rights of property in this country." "This growing tendency to socialistic principles," they declared, "is one of the most dangerous signs of the times, and if not checked, will produce scenes of disaster that would now appal the country." This was not, Vanderbilt and Jewett thought, a matter with which individual states might cope, and unless Congress could some-how interpose its authority, all concerned would have to "wait for time either to furnish a remedy or permit the great laws of trade, now tram-meled by destructive competition, to work out the result." When Congress finally did "interpose its authority" by enacting the Interstate Commerce Act, railroad officials were not, however, altogether satisfied with the result. The great railroad entrepreneur John Murray Forbes branded the measure "a cross between socialism and paternalism," and other railroad leaders were equally critical of the statute.

Persuaded, however, to recognize the folly of unlimited competition in an industry in which fixed costs are so prominent a factor, railroad presidents became eager for federal legislation that would legalize the pooling arrangements that the roads might themselves devise. Railroad officials, nevertheless, made it clear to the United States Industrial Commission at the turn of the century that although they were prepared to accept legislation of this sort, they, like the laissez-faire economists, were firmly opposed to the grant of full rate-making authority to the Interstate Commerce Commission and to the "sublime folly" of government ownership. President E. B. Thomas of the Erie Railroad was doubtless giving expression to the thought of many of these officials at this time when he asked the Commission why public authorities did not permit the railways, which had done so much for the country, "to work out their own solution instead of hampering them so much with investigation, legislation, and all that line of procedure."

Like the advent of the railroad, the trend toward business consolidation and the growth of trusts and industrial combinations in the last decades of the nineteenth century caused many persons to question the validity of the businessman's argument that competition equitably regulates the economic life of the nation and that state intervention is therefore unnecessary. Since one of the chief reasons for the formation of trusts was the desire of the interested parties to avoid the rigors of competition, there was some difficulty in fitting these combinations into the businessman's picture of the self-regulating economic order. Many merchants and small businessmen, indeed, frightened by the implications of the consolidation movement, advocated anti-monopoly action that would have as its objective the destruction of the trusts and the restoration of competitive conditions that would be more favorable to them and more in consonance with the American ideal of equality of opportunity. Other businessmen, however, and particularly those associated with the larger concerns, insisted that the trusts were a natural and inevitable product of industrial progress and a source of benefit to the community. Most of the businessmen who argued in this fashion maintained that the trusts did not interfere with competition in any essential way. Some, however, averred that competition had served its purpose and that the era of competition was being replaced by a new era of coöperation.

Those who maintained that the trust in no way violated the principles of competition generally pointed to the factor of potential competition. It was alleged that if a trust should attempt to secure more than the average return from capital, new competition would invade the field, and this would force prices down. Competition and the natural laws of supply and demand could therefore be relied on to secure to the consumer a fair price even in areas of the economy that were dominated by industrial combinations. S. C. T. Dodd, of Standard Oil, and Hermon B. Butler, of Ryerson and Son, insisted that the formation of business consolidations had actually improved the quality of competition and that any antitrust action would constitute an unwarranted restraint of trade. In similar fashion, Charles Elliott Perkins argued that the experience of many industries had demonstrated that combination was "a necessary part . . . of the natural law of competition" and that its results were of benefit to the public at large.

A few businessmen, however, spoke of the "debauch of competition" and extolled the trust as the harbinger of a new era of coöperation and industrial peace. The virtues of competition, these businessmen contended, had been exaggerated, and all should rejoice that industry was moving on to a higher level. The vice president of the National Bank of the Republic informed the American Bankers Association in 1896 that competition was the life of trade "within well defined limits, but beyond those limits it [was] far from profitable and wise." With trusts well established, the manufacturer Otis Kendall Stuart argued, the "geniuses of commerce and finance" would be able to direct industry so as to secure something better and more ethical than mere individual success. "The trust," Stuart contended, "is not only the next natural step in business, it is a step in social evolution; the trust is not only a conservator of energy and of wealth, it is a conservator of morals and religion."

Though businessmen who defended the trusts differed in their views as to the vitality of competition, the vast majority of them were agreed that industrial combinations were not properly the concern of the state. If a particular çombination effectively served the needs of the people, they maintained, it would survive; if not, it would perish. Legislation, at all events, could in no way affect the survival of the fittest business concerns. Henry O. Havemeyer, president of the American Sugar Refining Company, summed up the views of many businessmen in this matter when he informed the United States Industrial Commission that "the Government should have nothing to do with them [trusts] in any way, shape, or manner." The public, he argued, needs no information about monopoly. "Let the buyer beware; that covers the whole business. You cannot wet nurse people from the time they are born until the time they die. They have got to wade in and get stuck, and that is the way men are educated and cultivated."

Although the businessman was prone to argue the virtues of the negative state, he was hardly consistent in his application of laissez-faire theories. To be sure, he criticized state action that might circumscribe his activities or that would aid other groups in the community, but he did not oppose such activities of the state as served to promote business enterprise or to enhance business profits. Andrew Carnegie regularly denounced legislative tinkering but nevertheless advocated government construction of a Lake Erie and Ohio River Ship Canal that would lower ton-mile rates from the Lakes to the Carnegie works in Pittsburgh. The National Association of Manufacturers, organized in 1895, criticized the manufacture and free distribution to farmers by the Department of Agriculture of vaccine designed to combat blackleg but importuned the federal government to promote foreign trade by chartering an international American bank, subsidizing the merchant marine, enacting a protective tariff, and reforming the consular service so as to make it more solicitous of the export needs of American manufacturers. Railway officials who attacked rate-making as an improper exercise of legislative authority saw nothing amiss in legislation to prevent strikes from interfering with interstate commerce, to define liabilities in case of bankruptcy, and to require tests for color blindness; and many of them had perhaps forgotten that they were speaking for railroads that had benefited from federal land grants and from the largesse of state and local governments.

One of the most patent violations of the laws of trade in the period after the Civil War was the protective tariff; and yet most businessmen, and particularly industrialists, approved of this form of government bounty. Henry Clews, who told the workingman not to organize but to rely on the laws of trade, was not so convinced of the benign effects of natural law when it came to the tariff: he bitterly criticized Grover Cleveland's famous tariff message of 1887. Henry Wood and Charles Flint, who thought the state should do little more than protect property and provide for the enforcement of contracts, approved the enactment of tariff legislation that afforded protection to American industries. After declaring that he did not "believe in attempting to control the business of the citizen by legislative enactment," the banker E. R. Chapman went on to say that he was a high protectionist. Andrew Carnegie, although an acknowledged disciple of Herbert Spencer, was not disposed to interpret natural law in the same manner as the English philosopher when it came to the subject of the tariff. To the American ironmaster, the protective tariff was a necessary means of implementing the "evident law of nature" that many nations should enjoy "the blessings of diversified industries."

At the National Tariff Convention of 1881 representatives from virtually all the major industries of the country announced their adherence to the principle of protection. Laissez-faire economists were denounced at this convention because of their support of free trade, but words of praise were directed at Francis Bowen, who, although an advocate of laissez faire, was, at the same time, a friend to protection. Most of the witnesses connected with manufacturing industries who testified before the United States Industrial Commission spoke in favor of the protective tariff and yet denounced projects for regulating the trusts as contrary to the laws of trade. The businessman thus refused to carry laissez faire to its logical conclusion. He was quite willing to sanction state interference with the laws of trade when that interference offered hope of higher profits. But when the state sought to embark on programs of social reform, the businessman became an opponent of state action, an advocate of laissez faire. ...

Since the businessman was the dominant figure on the American scene during the years from 1865 to 1901, his views received strong support from most elements in American life. Nowhere, however, did the business spirit find greater favor than in the Protestant church. In the Gilded Age, "urban Protestantism cultivated the middle and upper classes who possessed the ultimate power in American society." Never before had wealth mattered so much to the church. Wealthy business figures were appointed to church boards in increasing numbers, and men of business ability were in demand to serve as church officials. Even the Baptists, who had prided themselves on being a poor man's denomination, ceased to express contempt for wealth and decided that the man of wealth was also "a man of talent." The churches were fast becoming "social and religious clubs for the privileged classes."

Ministers who resented the "aristocratic drift of Protestantism" denounced the alliance between church and market. "No Christian minister," charged the Reverend Franklin M. Sprague, "can deny that the church is crippled, yea, bound and gagged, because of her alliance with wealth." "The simple fact," said the Reverend Arthur T. Pierson, "is ... that the communion of saintliness is displaced by the communion of respectability. Our churches are becoming the quarters of a monopoly." The Reverend R. Heber Newton complained that the church had "accepted the anti-Christian dogmas of the older political economists, and in so doing, really turned traitor to the ethics of Jesus Christ." The poor man, he declared, has no use for "a church that has no better gospel than laissez faire, no better brotherhood than the selfish strife of competition, no kingdom of God for human society here upon the earth, but only one up in the skies."

The Protestant minister, like the businessman, gave his support to laissez faire and the status quo. He provided religious sanction for the businessman's views with respect to property, inequality, stewardship, state aid, and labor. Property was defended by churchmen as an exclusive right. The general well-being and progress of society was declared to be in proportion to the freedom of the individual to acquire property and to be secure in its possession. Love requires the acquisition of property, declared Mark Hopkins, the eminent Congregational minister and president of Williams College, "because it is a powerful means of benefiting others." Those who have done the most for our institutions have been men with "a strong desire of property." "As men now are," Hopkins concluded, "it is far better that they should be employed in accumulating property honestly . . . than that there should be encouraged any sentimentalism about the worthlessness of property." Princeton's clergyman-president James McCosh was no less certain of the virtues of property. No one, said he, is at liberty to deprive us of our property or to interfere with it. Attempts to do so are "theft." "The laws protecting it [property] have been one of the greatest boons that can be conferred on man." . . .

The majority of Protestant churchmen, like the businessmen, took a completely negative view of social reform and state action. They considered reform a matter of individual regeneration rather than of improved social conditions. Character, they said, determines conditions more than conditions determine character. Like their business friends, they were opposed to any significant legislative interference with the laws of trade. They advised the state to protect property and enforce contracts and, in effect, to ignore the general welfare.

The idea that "government should be paternal and take care of the welfare of its subjects and provide them with labor" was denounced by the eminent divine Henry Ward Beecher as "un-American." "The American doctrine," Beecher declared, "is that it is the duty of the Government merely to protect the people while they are taking care of themselves— nothing more than that. 'Hands off,' we say to the Government." Roswell D. Hitchcock looked on most types of state action as communistic in character. Although recognizing that social evils existed, Hitchcock thought that the remedies for these evils were not to be prescribed by the state. Government, he asserted, may not meddle with wages, limit the number of working hours (except for minors), set up labor exchanges, or run any industry. "The questions to be settled are questions of political economy, which ought, on every account, to be settled dispassionately. Men may vote as they please, but the laws of production and of trade are as inexorable as the laws of nature." . . .

The workingman received no more sympathy from most Protestant clergymen than he did from the businessman. Labor, in the view of conservative church leaders, was but a commodity and like all other commodities was to be "governed by the imperishable laws of demand and supply." "It is all right to talk and declaim about the dignity of labor," declared the *Watchman and Reflector*. "But when all has been said of it, what is labor but a matter of barter and sale?"

The advice offered to the laborer by clergymen was to remain passive. The Reverend W. D. Wilson told the workingman that Jesus' advice was that he be content with his wages. If he were entitled to higher wages, in the Lord's good time he would receive them. What injustice he suffered in this world would be turned to his account in the hereafter. "Be quiet," declared Wilson. "Whatsoever your hands find to do, do it, and be content with your wages. God will take care of the rest."

Other clergymen also found laissez faire to be the proper nostrum for the ills of labor, and they therefore condemned all of labor's weapons: trade unions, strikes, and labor legislation. Trade unions, they alleged, served but to drag down the superior workman to the level of the inferior and to introduce class lines into American society. "The Trades' Unions," charged the *Christian Advocate,* "are despotic and revolutionary in tendency. . . . The worst doctrines of communism are involved in these unions. . . . Legislate Trades' Unions out of existence." . . .

The close alliance between the Protestant church and wealth and the attitude of Protestant clergymen toward the labor struggle were among the factors that contributed to the decline in the church attendance of Protestant workingmen in the decades after the Civil War. The workers, Samuel Gompers declared in response to a query as to why laborers had become alienated from the church, "have come to look upon the church and ministry as the apologists and defenders of the wrongs committed against the interests of the people, simply because the perpetrators are the possessors of wealth." Clergymen, he charged, were using "their exalted positions to discountenance all practical efforts of the toilers to lift themselves out of the slough of despondency and despair." "We believe much in Jesus and in his teachings, but not much in the teachings of his pretended followers," one workingman declared. "A civilization that permits man to be the greatest enemy of man . . . is a cheat and a sham; the political economy that permits it is a falsehood and a fraud; and a religion that allows it without constant, earnest, and persistent protest is a humbug." It was from conditions such as these that the social-gospel movement sought to rescue the Protestant church.

UNREGULATED SPECULATION:
THE GOLD CORNER OF 1869

The reality of Jim Fisk was incredible, for the living man resembled a Thomas Nast caricature more than life itself. Flamboyant Jim aligned himself with a shrewd, secretive little man named Jay Gould. In the late 1860's they stole the Erie Railroad, manufactured stocks on their own printing press, bribed legislators and judges, and even became a scandal to Wall Street itself.

Their greatest attempted coup was the effort to corner the gold supply. In a series of moves as sinister and carefully planned as the steps taken by political revolutionaries, these two men built their offensive, which reached its climax on Friday, September 24, 1869.

The following excerpts from The New York Times consist of a description of the Gold Room during the panic and an editorial. Note the antidote suggested for such events—regulation by Wall Street itself, with no suggestion of government control.

THE NEW YORK TIMES, News Item of September 25, 1869

... Before 9 o'clock the brokers commenced to congregate at the Board, knowing from their experiences of the night before that the price of gold would reach its *ultimatum*. At about 9 o'clock business commenced, and from the first assumed a tone indicative of the day's transactions. Parties who had bought largely on the night before (for the transactions of Wednesday were transferred to the Fifth-avenue Hotel, and prolonged until late in the evening) came to the Board smiling and happy, assured that their ventures would be successful. Most of them held to their gold, anticipating that the "clique" would close on the "shorts," thus compelling a rise, but others, more prudent and less avaricious, sold at the market rate before the opening, and thus secured a handsome profit.

At ten o'clock the market opened amid great excitement, the quotation being 150. Within two minutes a rise of one-eighth was recorded by the faithful indicator, and until 11 o'clock the market held its own at this figure.

The New York Times, September 25, 1869.

New York Gold Room during the great excitement of September 24, 1869—gold 160.

From *Frank Leslie's Illustrated Newspaper*, Vol. 29, No. 732 (October 9, 1869).

"...In order to bring before the reader's mind the scene of this exciting conflict between the Bulls and Bears—namely, the New York Gold Room—let him imagine a hippotheatron, with a little fountain in the centre. The centre of the fountain is a bronze Cupid with a dolphin in its arms. From the head of Cupid arises a tiny silver stream, which falls in jets into the basin below. Fancy an iron railing ninety feet in circumference about this basin, then a space about twenty feet between the walls and the fountain, and you have a rough idea of the Gold Room. On one side there are two galleries—the lower for the errand boys, and the upper for the spectators. Beyond the fountain, with his back toward New Street, stands the Secretary, recording the sales which he catches by his ear. Near him is the telegraph operator. Wires run from his machine to nearly five hundred brokers' offices, who are thus instantly informed of the state of the market, and are enabled to make their bids undisturbed by the furious excitement which rules in the Gold Room on important occasions."

[*Harper's Weekly,* Vol. 13, No. 668 (October 16, 1869), p. 660.]

But it was only a temporary lull. At 11 o'clock there was a jump of nearly five per cent (actually closer to 7.5%—Ed.), the indicator marking 155$^{1}/_{4}$. At about this hour the grand excitement of the day commenced. Newstreet, opposite the Gold Room, was rendered almost impassable by a dense crowd, whose gaze was fixed on the ever-varying indicator, which marked the upward progress of gold. As each change was marked it was greeted by a howl from those inside the Gold Room, while the outsiders, happy perhaps in their exile, hailed it with a murmur of astonishment, but seldom allowing the spirit of the contending factions within to move them from their equanimity. At times, however, when the stride of gold was one per cent without an intermediate stoppage, a cheer would break forth, and for the moment even the clamor of the Gold Room itself would be smothered by the uproar outside. And the outsiders formed an assemblage strange to the scene, at least since the days when men resorted to the Gold Room to hear the "latest" news of the war. Representatives of almost every class were there. The great merchant stood side by side with the *sans culotte*—the gutter snipe of society; the man of law compared notes with the Wallstreet "goat," an individual known only to brokers; and, in fine, everybody, not forgetting the bootblacks and a few City politicians, found standing room opposite the Gold Room, and looked in gaping astonishment at the kaleidoscopic indicator. From 155¼ to 162½ the premium rose with lightning-like rapidity, so that parties who had lost sight of the indicator for only a few moments, turned toward it again only to see that while their backs were turned an advance of over 7 per cent had been made.

Inside the room the scene almost beggars description. While the "bull" party were frantically bidding above the market rates, in one part of the room, the "bears" were offering gold in another at much below them. Around the fountain, which occupies the center of the room, some 200 persons were collected, and he who can imagine the din created by 200 human voices, all hoarse and discordant from over-use, and all exerted to the utmost at the same moment, may perhaps form a slight conception of the Bedlam here presented. Nor did the doughty bulls and bears confine themselves to bellowing and roaring. Their gesticulations, their jostling and crowding, their restless change of position, all indicated the excitement under which they labored. A stranger, viewing them for the first time, would have supposed that their excitement would lead to unpleasant results physically, but further inspection would have convinced him that they were not actuated by anger, but by a passion much more to be deplored—avarice.

Within a few moments of the highest quotations, a rumor reached the Board that Treasurer Boutwell had ordered Assistant Secretary Butterfield to sell a large amount of gold (rumor said $15,000,000) and in an instant the market experienced a reverse. Down from 162½ to 135, the premium fell with one grand rush—the bulls in the meanwhile endeavoring to sustain it by bidding far above the market rates. ...

NEW YORK TIMES EDITORIAL, The Gold Gamblers and Their Work

Seldom has so disastrous a condition of affairs existed in Wall-street as that which the public have witnessed during the last few days. How much longer it will continue scarcely any amount of "information," special or general, would enable us to determine. It is, however, quite certain that the persons who are chiefly responsible for the present crisis will not be the only, or even the principal, sufferers. Innocent men, who never allowed themselves to be drawn into the whirlpool of gold gambling, are now undergoing the penalty which strict justice would inflict on the ringleaders in a

The New York Times, September 29, 1869.

desperate and unscrupulous conspiracy. A few individuals, whose names are on everybody's mouth, have literally sacked the City, and it is no satisfaction to honest people to learn that they have betrayed each other. The mischief does not stop there. A handful of adventurers may combine to produce a panic which would extend to almost every commercial circle, and carry misery to thousands of homes. It is worse than idle to say, as some are doing, that the "gamblers deserve their fate." If general rumor is not entirely groundless, the gamblers who caused the mischief are not likely to smart. By a trick to which it would be difficult to find a parallel in the whole history of dishonest speculation, they have plundered their own friends while attempting to defraud their customary victims. There is an old tradition that even the class which habitually preys upon society have a code of honor for their own guidance. In this case we see the conspirators coolly rifling each other's pockets, while the chiefs in the foray walk off with the spoils. That such men should still be in a position to laugh over the suffering of their victims, and devise fresh intrigues against the fair trading of the country, is one of the mysteries of commercial morality in this City, and we hope business men can explain it to their satisfaction.

There have been commercial misfortunes which scarcely any ordinary foresight or precaution could have provided against. But the present unhappy conjuncture has been produced by no national reverses, and by no unavoidable pressure arising from the exigencies of the trade. A handful of gamblers have been able to bring it about simply by defying all the principles which govern mercantile men when they are dealing fairly with each other. Circumstances, unhappily, conspired to assist them. The chance visit to the city of Mr. Boutwell, at the moment the plot was nearly ripe, was made an occasion for further hoodwinking "outsiders." It was boldly alleged that Mr. Boutwell would not interfere, that gold could consequently be forced up to 200, and that traffickers in the precious metal would be compelled to submit to heavy blackmail from the sole possession of it. Whether Mr. Boutwell has acted the part of a grand financier during the last fortnight, is a question which will have to be discussed some day, but which we may for the present pass by. What is quite clear is, that he has tried the two policies of non-interference and interference and done mischief with both. When he might have frustrated the general scheme of spoliation he was inactive. When he could no longer do injury to the chief tricksters, he interfered. It is impossible that he can suppose his reputation has been enhanced by his double course.

There are those who tell us that the chartered brigandage lately perpetrated would be impossible if we had recurred to specie payments a year ago. This may be very wise, but it does not help the commercial classes out of their present difficulties. It would be as much to the purpose to tell them that the world would not have been drowned four thousand years ago if there had been no deluge. What they want is some practical remedy for their troubles, and we are sorry to say that in the quarters where they had chiefly a right to look for it they have been disappointed. The management of the Gold Exchange Bank during the crisis has been so inefficient that it threatens to become a scandal. At the first pressure it fell to the most miserable confusion. It was yesterday only clearing up Thursday's business [making it six days behind—Ed.], so that it must have been in arrears before the height of the gold panic arrived. If an institution of this kind cannot withstand an occasional heavy strain, of what use is it? It would be far better out of existence altogether. At present it is in the anomalous position of employing policemen to keep out its customers. It has aggravated all the embarrassments under which "the Street" has been laboring. That it facilitates gambling transactions at all times is inevitable, but that it should become an active agent in rendering a panic utterly unmanageable is nothing less than a public disaster. The Bank of New York found itself unable to extricate it from its confusion. If confidence is restored today, business men will have nothing in the welcome change for which to thank official persons.

When the storm has entirely passed over, business men of all kinds will probably stand on a sounder foundation. But what security is there against another deep-laid scheme on the part of men who are willing to sacrifice friends and foes alike so that they may seize the booty? Until these "rings" are broken up, the whole trade of the country is jeopardized. The notorious gamblers of the day prepare an ambuscade, and our loose system of national finance helps them to inveigle all classes into it. The fever infects young and old, as it did in the days of the South Sea bubble, or Law's wild and reckless schemes. The moment this huge cheat is forgotten, another fraud will be concocted in dark corners, the confederates will make another raid, and we shall see all business relations thrown once more into chaos. People will still compete with each other for the honor of doing business for plotters who have succeeded in degrading the morals of footpads. Neither law nor remonstrances can step in to prevent this. No doubt the ruined victims of "colossal speculators" are full of anger now, but other persons are standing ready to be duped. Public opinion fails to inflict retribution on the offenders—they find that they can defy public opinion, and still exist. Where, then, is our safeguard for the future? It must be found in "the Street" itself. It might devise some protection against its own worst enemies. We can only hope that the Government, at least, will not again give any excuse for the reproaches which, justly or unjustly, have been cast upon it during the last few days.

HIGH FINANCE IN THE GILDED AGE: THE GREAT DIAMOND HOAX

"There's a sucker born every minute," P. T. Barnum, the great showman, is supposed to have said, and he was in his prime in the Gilded Age. The age was naive about get-rich-quick schemes, about the most lurid descriptions of bogus gold and silver mines, about investment deals that promised profits up to sixty or seventy percent a year on the original investment. There were just enough fortunate tycoons around—Lucky Baldwin, Frederick Augustus Heinze, William Andrews Clark, and H. A. W. Tabor, for example—to convince the gullible that lightning might strike, and some gold mine in the sky might pay off. With no Securities and Exchange Commission to protect the credulous, and few statutes to enforce against schemers, the mails were full of brochures, and the streets busy with salesmen.

The biggest fraud ever perpetrated in the American West, if not in the United States, was the Great Diamond Hoax of 1872. As with most shady deals, precise details of this one are difficult to define or substantiate. Recent research has reduced the extent of travel said to be done by the hoaxers, Arnold and Slack; has clarified the part played in the exposure by Clarence King and certain members of his Fortieth Parallel Survey; has reduced somewhat the estimates of the sums of money the hoaxers realized; and has revealed what became of the silent rascal, Slack. (See Bruce Woodard, Diamonds in the Salt, or Richard A. Bartlett, Great Surveys of the American West, Chapter 9, for additional information.)

But A. J. Liebling, for many years before his death a crack journalist for The New Yorker, best conveyed the flamboyant, naive, optimistic spirit of the Gilded Age in his description of this greatest, boldest, most barefaced scheme of all. Because of this, his essay, although it contains some minor inaccuracies and lacks documentation, is reprinted here.

A. J. LIEBLING, The American Golconda

The first and, as far as history records, the last American to salt a diamond mine was a man named Philip Arnold, who died of shotgun slugs as a

A. J. Liebling, "The American Golconda," in The New Yorker, Vol. 16 (November 16, 1940), pp. 41–48. Reprinted by permission; copyright © 1940, 1968 by The New Yorker Magazine, Inc.

sequel to a business argument in Elizabethtown, Hardin County, Kentucky, in the year 1873. Arnold was the man who set a limit to American optimism, realistically revising the nation's ideas about its future and its resources, and it is a wonder that historians have not as yet given him his due. Arnold was a banker worth a mere $300,000 when he died, but it was as a creative prospector in the West that he made his impress on his country's imagination. An ordinary prospector merely tries to find deposits of precious minerals; a creative prospector places them in the ground for others to find.

Arnold was born in Hardin County (which gave Abraham Lincoln to the nation) about 1830. When a young man, he inherited a small farm there and married. Shortly before the Civil War he left his wife and a couple of children on the Hardin County place and went out to California to look for gold. Several times, after making small strikes, he returned to Kentucky. In the early sixties, with a partner named John Slack, he developed a claim near Marysville, California, that the two sold for $50,000. Arnold took most of his share of the money home to Kentucky and placed it in a large safe on his farm. By 1869 he was back in California, looking for something to do. Since no new gold fields had recently been reported, he took a job as assistant bookkeeper with the Diamond Drill Company of San Francisco. This firm sold diamond-pointed rock drills to mine-owners. The foundations of the great West mining fortunes had been laid; men like George Hearst, James Fair, Darius Ogden Mills, and William Chapman Ralston, chairman of the board of the Bank of California, controlled the best properties. The haphazard days of Forty-nine were long over, but their tradition lingered in the form of a chronic optimism. An army of disappointed miners was still billeted on the Coast, ready to march at the first report of a new field. In the East and in England, investors, despite a number of unfortunate experiences, were still willing to put money into Western mines. The bonanza business needed only a new stimulus. The first hints of what this stimulus was to be came in the form of newspaper stories about the discovery of the diamond fields in South Africa, the third great source of diamonds in the world's history. The mines of Golconda, in India, had supplied most of the world's diamonds until the eighteenth century, when the Portuguese had discovered deposits in Brazil. South Africa eclipsed both these older fields. American prospectors almost immediately began to look for diamonds in Arizona and New Mexico Territories, where there were said to be geological formations like those in the African diamond lands.

Arnold, still at his job with the drill company, displayed great interest in diamonds. He explained to the head bookkeeper, another ex-miner, named Cooper, that he wanted to learn all about precious stones before he began looking for them. The company kept a considerable stock of diamonds on hand, of the flawed or discolored sort used for pointing drills, so Arnold had a chance to handle a variety of the stones and perhaps secrete a few. He used to question Cooper about tests employed to determine if diamonds were genuine and about the differences in appearance of diamonds from the three known fields. When he had pumped Cooper dry, he bought books about diamonds and studied them. By the spring of 1871 he knew as much about diamonds as anybody on the Coast. Reports from South Africa, ever more glowing, maintained the excitement in America. None of the prospectors in America had found any diamonds, but some of them had come back from Arizona with garnets, which they thought were rubies. To doubt the eventual discovery of diamonds here seemed like selling America short. The public was prepared for a diamond rush.

Arnold took a leave of absence early in 1871. He returned to San Francisco two months later, saying he had been into eastern Arizona with his old mining partner John Slack, and he showed Cooper the result of their prospecting: a handful of desert sapphires and rubylike garnets, with a few small uncut diamonds of the type that the Diamond Drill Company used. Arnold said that they had obtained the diamonds by trading with an Indian, to whom they had promised a gallon of whiskey if he would get them some more stones. The two prospectors had then followed the Indian and thus had found where the field was. The field lay within Apache territory, Arnold said, where it would have been dangerous for two white men to remain, so, after killing the Indian, the partners had marked the site of the field and headed back for California, to get help in developing them. Arnold and Slack took their stones to Asbury Harpending, a flamboyant San Franciscan who had once been a filibuster in Nicaragua and was at the time dividing his energies between land speculation and the promotion of wildcat mines. Harpending had known Arnold for a long time, for which reason, perhaps, he took no stock in the story. If the partners returned to their field and found a really impressive lot of stones, he suggested, they would have no trouble getting financial backing. Arnold and Slack then announced they were going back to the Arizona desert, and left town.

The two men reappeared in San Francisco several months later, worn and weatherbeaten. They called on George D. Roberts, another mining promoter, and asked permission to deposit a sack in his office safe, as it was after banking hours and they couldn't place it in the vaults of the Bank of California. This naturally made Roberts curious. He engaged Arnold in conversation—Slack seldom had anything to say—and learned that the sack contained diamonds, rubies, and emeralds, all from a mysterious region that the partners refused to locate specifically. Roberts was in no position to know that Arnold had just made a trip to London, embarking at Halifax, a port where he had been tolerably sure to meet no other Californians, and returning the same way. Arnold had brought back from this expedition about $12,000 worth of imperfect precious stones, uncut. On his return trip, Arnold had been met at St. Louis by Slack, who had remained in this country. They then had traversed the part of Arizona where the Indians traded garnets and had bought a peck or so of the red stones to give their collection bulk and foster the idea that the diamonds and garnets were found in the same general region. The bad feature of their strike, the partners told Roberts, was that it was situated in a section full of hostile Indians. To work it, they would have to organize an expedition strong enough to fight off the redskins, and they hadn't enough money for that.

Arnold and Slack did not ask Roberts to help them; Roberts insisted. Feeling that it would be too big a proposition for one man to swing, he went to the house of William Ralston, the banker, that night and let him in on the secret. Roberts and Ralston sneaked the stones out of Roberts' safe and submitted samples to San Francisco jewellers for appraisal. This was what Arnold had expected them to do, and he had correctly calculated the jewellers' reactions. He knew that there was no jeweller in San Francisco who had any large experience with uncut stones. All of them were familiar with tests by which to prove a stone was genuine; after the tests they could be counted on to set an arbitrary average price per carat, assuming that some of the stones in any given collection were good and others not so good. If they had known that the stones were all malformed culls, they would have named a much lower figure, but they didn't, of course, have that knowledge. The San Francisco jewellers set a value of $100,000 on the prospectors' $12,000 worth of flawed beauties. The stones looked like excellent samples, especially as Arnold and Slack said the lot represented only a few hours' digging. Under no conditions, the partners said when Roberts approached them, would they part with a controlling interest in their claim, but they would sell a good part of it in order to obtain working capital.

Roberts introduced Ralston, who said that he would put in some money if the partners first convinced him by taking a personal representative to the site of the field. Arnold agreed to take a man there on condition that the man should be blindfolded from the moment the party left the railroad. "Otherwise," Arnold said, "our secret is out and he can lead you back to the claim without us." Ralston took command of the promotion. He sent as his agent a satellite named General David D. Colton, a cool, sensible gold miner, not given to enthusiasm. Colton, however, had never seen a diamond field. Arnold and Slack took the agent by train to Rawlins, a station on the Union Pacific, in Wyoming Territory, where the three alighted.

This rather surprised Colton, as he had assumed the field was in Arizona. Arnold told him that they had purposely given that impression to throw possible claim-jumpers off the track. Rawlins is not far north of the Colorado line, and the diamond field seems to have been in what is now Jackson County, Colorado. Arnold blindfolded Colton and put him on a horse. The three men rode for four days, the partners taking the hoodwink from Colton's eyes only after sundown, when they encamped. On the fourth day, when Arnold whipped the bandage from Colton's face, the agent found himself blinking on a mesa 7,500 feet high, which he supposed to be deep in the wilderness. The men dismounted and began to walk about the mesa, and before long Colton saw a great anthill sparkling in the sun. Approaching the mound, he found that it was powdered with diamond dust. Arnold came up and dug into the anthill with a knife and soon pulled out a small diamond. Colton then began digging and in a few minutes discovered a diamond for himself. During the day he got forty or fifty diamonds and emeralds, most of them in a gulch which intersected the mesa. Next day, Arnold told Colton they would have to move on, as he feared they had been observed by Indians. After another long, hard journey, during which Colton was blindfolded, they got back to the railroad. The gems which Colton brought in his pocket proved real, like the first batch. They were worth only a few hundred dollars, a jeweller told him, but it seemed a fair assumption that if a man digging with a pocketknife could find that many in a day, the deposits were of unexampled richness.

It appeared to Ralston, after he received Colton's report, that he had stumbled upon a big thing, perhaps the greatest promotion of his life. He believed he might need operating funds of several million dollars, and that meant he would have to enlist Eastern capital. Speed was essential, because some trapper or independent prospector might at any moment find what Ralston was already calling in conversation the American Golconda. Since Ralston's own money was pretty well tied up in investments, he admitted a few more of his West Coast friends to the cabal. One was General G. M. Dodge (the country swarmed with generals for twenty years after the Civil War). Another was a promoter named William M. Lent, and a third was the dashing Asbury Harpending. Each, on being approached, expressed skepticism. Each, on learning of Colton's trip and the high valuation set upon the gems, became convinced. General Dodge, who, Harpending said long afterward, "had a low opinion of his fellowmen," talked to Arnold for a while and then said that he would stake his life on the fellow's integrity.

The promoters decided to go to New York, taking with them Slack, Arnold, and a bag of gems from the American Golconda. On the way East the financiers wrangled a bit with the two discoverers. Arnold and Slack now appeared suspicious and said that they wanted some tangible guarantee of the promoters' good faith. Lent gave them $100,000 as earnest money. It was not hard for the Westerners to get a hearing in financial circles here, especially as the head of the Bank of California had retained General Samuel L. M. Barlow, the most distinguished New York corporation lawyer of the day, to act as intermediary and legal adviser. General Barlow had engaged as associate General Benjamin F. Butler, an influential congressman. Barlow had bespoken the interest of a group of New York bankers including August Belmont and Henry Seligman. Before proceeding with the deal, however, the New Yorkers insisted that Charles Tiffany, the founder of the great jewelry house, be permitted to appraise the samples from the diamond field. In the event that Tiffany's appraisal was favorable, Belmont and Seligman wanted a mining expert of national reputation to go out to the site and make a report upon it. Arnold agreed to both tests, but said that his partner and he were not going to lead an expert to the mine until they had some sort of written contract protecting their rights. He signed an agreement with the promoters providing that if Tiffany and the mining expert endorsed the samples and the mine, the promoters would pay to the prospectors $650,000 in cash as the full price of their claim.

It is impossible, in retrospect, not to marvel at Arnold's composure as he went to the meeting with Tiffany, reputed to be America's greatest judge of gems. The rendezvous was at General Barlow's mansion at 1 Madison Avenue. Horace Greeley, the editor of the *Tribune,* soon to be an unsuccessful Presidential candidate, was at the house when the Californian party arrived, as were the Eastern financiers and General George B. McClellan, former Commander in Chief of the Union Armies, who had been an unsuccessful Presidential candidate in 1864. Greeley liked to be in the know even though he had to pledge secrecy. McClellan was slated for a job on the board of directors of the projected mining company. He had a fine mustache and made good window dressing.

Tiffany, as Arnold must have been aware, knew no more about uncut stones than most other American jewellers. He had begun life as a Yankee notion peddler and had never served an apprenticeship on the Continent. He knew that the diamonds before him were real, and that several presumably competent experts on the Coast had made flattering estimates of their value. After a brief glance at the gems, followed by a regal wave of his hand, the whiskery jeweller said, "I cannot fix an exact value until my lapidary has had a chance to inspect each stone, but I can assure you that they are worth at least a hundred and fifty thousand dollars." Arnold, watching him, never blinked.

The meeting, although supposedly secret, was the chief talk of hotel bars and Wall Street offices the next day. That night, Arnold came to the Western promoters and said Slack was fed up with the whole business and would sell his share for $100,000, chargeable against the final purchase price. They got the money for Slack by morning. The two miners now had $200,000 between them. The Easterners who had witnessed the appraisal were feverishly hot on the enterprise and a struggle for the control of the corporation began before it officially came into being. Since it appeared that the financial and technical negotiations, including the selection of a mining expert to examine the property, would take several months, Arnold announced that he and Slack were going back to the West, and that they would leave their precious stones with the promoters as security.

Instead of going West, the prospectors travelled up to Quebec and took ship for London, carrying with them most of their bankroll. They needed more gems with which to resalt the mine. Arnold was not the man to jeopardize a $650,000 deal by skimping on a few quarts of niggerhead diamonds, as the dealers called imperfect South African stones. The pair bought about eleven hundred diamonds in London and then made a business-and-pleasure trip to the Continent, where they bought many of the worst diamonds in Amsterdam and Antwerp. Altogether they spent around $50,000. After their shopping spree in Europe, the partners returned to Colorado and installed the props. The mesa where they had fooled Colton was in fact only about fifteen miles from the Union Pacific railway tracks; they had led him there by a carefully circuitous course. It was near the north end of a pine-clad ridge that ran east and west, to the north of Brown's Hole in Colorado and eight miles below the Wyoming line.

The Eastern and Western promoters in the combination agreed on Henry Janin, the leading mining engineer of his time, to make the inspection. The mine expert's fee was to be $2,500, plus an option on a thousand shares at $10 each. Only a Philip Arnold would have led a Janin to a salted mine. The prospector had the intuition of a great poker player for an opponent's foible. For the fact was that Janin had never in his life seen diamond land, and he was disarmed in advance by the high appraisal of the sample stones. Surely, he must have felt, if a sample from a mine was worth $150,000, the property was bound to be valuable.

Janin went out to the claim in the spring of 1872. Lent, General Dodge, General Colton, and several other Californians who had remained in New York for the winter went out with him. Arnold and Slack met them at Omaha. The party got off the train at a station in Colorado Territory late one night. Horses were waiting; the men mounted and rode off into the unknown. Arnold and Slack, leading their companions by roundabout trails, made the journey long and difficult, as they had done when they had convoyed Colton. Janin and most of the promoters were physically soft, and the prospectors kept them riding for several days. When the money men got to the mesa they were dead tired and the provisions were low.

Within a few minutes after their arrival, Colton found the anthill shining with diamond dust he remembered from his first visit. Almost instantly the men started spading into the ground, shouting with pleasure like children at a picnic as they turned up their shining finds. Many of the stones, it appeared, were near the surface. Arnold and Slack pointed out places for their backers to dig, and whenever a promoter followed their advice he found a diamond. The party remained eight days on the ground. During that time, Janin reported, working with spades and knives, the men turned up 256 carats of large diamonds worth $4,096 at prevailing rates, 568 carats of small ones worth $1,704, and four pounds of rubies worth $2,226. Since the party had dug up what was estimated to be about a ton and a half of rock and dirt, this indicated to Janin that the mesa assayed better than $5,000 to the ton, a figure unparalleled in mining history. He conservatively estimated that the land should yield $5,000,000 an acre. "With a hundred men and proper machinery," he told Lent, "I would guarantee to send out a million dollars in diamonds every thirty days." The mesa contained at least three thousand acres, and Janin said there was no reason the rest of it shouldn't yield as heavily as the spot they had started on. As for the surrounding land, that was of a conspicuously similar geological nature. It might yield billions.

The investigators went on to San Francisco, again led over a circuitous route back to the railroad by Arnold, leaving Slack at the diggings as a guard. Nobody ever reported seeing Slack again. It will never be known whether he lost his nerve and went off with the money he had already made or whether he died by violence. He simply disappeared. Janin sold his thousand-share option to one of the California men at $40 a share, making a profit of $30,000. He said that he did not wish to retain stock in the company, as his report would then be construed as a boost for his own prosperity.

In San Francisco, the promoters organized the San Francisco & New York Mining & Commercial Company, with 100,000 shares of stock. None were offered to the public. The shares were divided among twenty-five leading West Coast mining sharps, men like Ralston, Roberts, Lent, and Harpending. Each of them paid $40,000 into the company's treasury for initial expenses. One of the incorporators, a banker named Gansl, acted as the West Coast representative of Baron Rothschild. Janin released a favorable report and it appeared in the *Mining & Engineering Journal* and in the San Francisco newspapers. It caused a sensation. When Arnold saw the report, he pretended to be very angry. He said he had not realized the property was that good. Roberts and Ralston reminded him of his contract and virtually forced the $450,000 balance of the agreed purchase price upon him. They were glad when he left town. He said he was going back to Kentucky, where he would have a loaded shotgun always ready to welcome any San Francisco mining sharps who came to visit him.

The San Francisco & New York Company opened tremendous offices in the California city, featuring General McClellan and a permanent display of the largest diamonds from the diggings. Would-be investors besieged the place, but the fortunate shareholders would sell no stock. As always on the flanks of a great financial operation, a number of imitations had sprung up. These corporations claimed to have diamond lands of their own, but the public knew that they were only waiting for the big company to reveal the location of its holdings, when they would rush out prospecting gangs and file claims as near the company's diggings as was legally possible. In Paris Baron Rothschild rejoiced that he had a finger in the pie, even though it was not a controlling interest. "America is a rich land," he sententiously told an interviewer. "It has given us many surprises. It reserves many more."

The exposure came in a curious manner. To explain it requires the introduction of a character who had had no direct connection with the affairs of the San Francisco & New York Mining & Commercial Company. He was a thirty-year-old government geologist named Clarence King, a member of the first class to be graduated from the Sheffield Scientific School at Yale. King is credited with being the founder of the United States Geological Survey; readers of the *Education of Henry Adams* will remember him as one of Adams' closest friends. In 1872, King, with a party of assistants, had completed a survey of the fortieth parallel of latitude in the United States, which had led him through the salted-mine territory. It piqued him that in his painstaking inventory of mineral resources he had come across no trace of diamond lands. Feeling that his professional reputation was at stake, King went back over the ground he had covered to find, if possible, where he had slipped up. Any party travelling through that country at that time was conspicuous; King located some sheepherders who had seen the Janin party on the march. Guided by them, he set out with a small expedition and found the mesa. The aspect of the place aided him, for Arnold, well documented in diamond mining, had picked the sort of site where diamonds might well have been found.

"The section of the geological locality is so astonishingly considered," King reported later to the unhappy directors of the company, "that I can feel no surprise that even so trustworthy and cautious an engineer as Mr. Janin should have brought home the belief he did." This was much kinder to Janin than most of King's statements. Making his way to the top of the mesa, the government geologist found "in conjunction four kinds of diamonds, Oriental rubies, garnets, spinels, sapphires, emeralds, and amethysts—an association of minerals impossible of occurrence in nature." "The gems exist in positions where Nature alone could never have placed them," he wrote in his report. "They do not exist where, had the occurrence been genuine, the inevitable laws of Nature must have carried them." It was a polite way of saying that he found stones which had been obviously stamped into the ground by a man's boot and others placed in the crevices of rocks. There was even one in a tree stump. The most absurd discovery of all was made by a German in charge of King's pack animals. "Look, Mr. King," the German said, pulling a bright chip out of the ground near the anthill, "this is the bulliest diamond field as never was! It not only produces diamonds, it cuts them!" He had found a cut diamond, one which must have got in among the rough stones by mistake when a dealer in Antwerp or London was wrapping Arnold's purchases.

King rode to Laramie, Wyoming Territory, where he sent a telegram to Ralston, the most prominent director of the company, and then boarded a train for San Francisco. When he arrived in that city he sent the following note:

To the Board of Directors of the San Francisco & New York Mining & Commercial Company:

I have hastened to San Francisco to lay before you the startling fact that the diamond fields upon which are based such large investment and such brilliant hope are utterly valueless, and yourselves and your engineer, Mr. Henry Janin, the victims of an unparalleled fraud.

Ralston persuaded him to hold off his announcement while the directors of the company considered what to do. King agreed to wait for a fortnight on Ralston's promise to prevent trading in the stock. During this time, King guided a party of the directors back to the site and convinced them that their mine was worthless. Colton was one of the group and so was Janin. The fraud now seemed to them terribly obvious. On November 27, 1872, a long story appeared on the front page of the San Francisco *Bulletin*, embodying the text of King's report to the directors and a statement by Janin admitting he had been deceived. Most of the sharped sharpers felt too foolish to be angry at anybody; Lent was the only one of the crowd who was not ashamed to go after Arnold for his money. He had, it appeared, bought out several of his colleagues, and was hooked for more than $300,000.

Slack had disappeared, but Arnold's whereabouts was no secret. He was home in Kentucky, where, in the short time following his return from

California, he had become one of the local nabobs. He had bought himself an $18,000 house on a plot of thirty-two acres near Elizabethtown, moving into it on the day of the purchase and on the next day spending $4,000 for livestock. In the house he had a great safe, and in the safe, according to Elizabethtown gossip, he had at least $500,000 in cash. The late war was a fresh and rankling memory in Hardin County. Most of Arnold's friends were retired Morgan raiders, and indeed he is said to have ridden on a few raids himself during his holidays from the gold fields. Arnold did not fear whatever prosecution might be instituted by Yankees in Hardin County, nor was there any chance that the governor of Kentucky would allow him to be extradited. The governor had a prejudice in favor of Kentuckian defendants.

When Lent came to Louisville and instituted a civil suit against Arnold to recover $350,000, the Kentuckian played injured innocence. Arnold's attorney issued a statement that his client would fight the case to the bitter end "for the sake of suffering humanity, which has been robbed and swindled by these California mining sharks for the last twenty-five years." The initial difficulty in Lent's suit was that nobody could be hired to serve the attachments on Arnold. The retired prospector continued to live at Elizabethtown, but Hardin County people insisted he wasn't there. It seemed neither polite nor judicious to contradict them.

Lent and some California friends stayed at the Galt House in Louisville, drinking the wine of the country while they waited for the case to get under way, and every day or so the *Courier-Journal* carried a humorous story on the "search" for Arnold. One day, said the newspaper, a process-server announced that he had got to Arnold by disguising himself as a tramp and had pressed the papers on the miner and escaped before Arnold could get to his shotgun. This was immediately denied by Arnold's friends, whose version was that "a suspicious, seedy-looking man" had been seen by workmen to climb "out of the sewer leading to Arnold's privy." Arnold, they said, was ready with the shotgun and would have fired had not the stranger "dashed through a nearby creek and up the Louisville & Nashville tracks for about two miles" without leaving any papers behind him. The discouraged Lent at last went back to California, but his lawyers kept up such a running fire on Arnold that the former prospector agreed to compromise the case. He might have remained safe in Hardin County for the rest of his life without paying a cent, but he would have risked legal trouble any time he crossed the county line. So he settled Lent's claim with a payment of $150,000.

Of the first $200,000 that Arnold and Slack received, they had spent about $50,000 on stones for salting and another $10,000 for expenses. If, as seems probable, they divided the rest, Arnold got $70,000, which, with the final payment of $450,000, brought his net receipts from the hoax to $520,000. After disgorging $150,000 to Lent and paying his lawyer $25,000, he remained a very wealthy man for Elizabethtown.

After the settlement, Arnold acquired about five hundred acres of good farming land. He built the first store in Elizabethtown to be equipped with plate-glass windows. He announced that he had discovered a silver deposit in Kentucky worth $9,000,000 and that he would soon start work on it. He also entered the banking business, and that was a mistake. There was another bank in Elizabethtown, managed by two partners. The banks' interests clashed, and the odds, because of the code of Hardin County, were two to one against Arnold. The retired gold miner shot one of his competitors in the arm, but the fellow's partner sneaked up behind Arnold and let him have a charge of buckshot in the back. This was fatal to Arnold, a man who has left his mark on the American psyche. Arnold had found investors willing to believe absolutely anything. He left them willing to believe not quite everything. Their credulity never rebounded to the pre-Arnold level. The Age of Innocence was over.

GOVERNMENT AND BUSINESS:
THE CREDIT MOBILIER

Four years after the Gold Corner the nation was angered by revelations of corruption in Congress. The Credit Mobilier scandal involved the construction company for the Union Pacific Railroad. The corporation was a product of the U.P. entrepreneurs, and was rightly expected to pay enormous dividends. To reduce the possibility of trouble in Congress, bribes in the form of Credit Mobilier stock were distributed to certain members of that body.

What is notable, but not so often perceived, is the strong surge of morality that was present in the Gilded Age. Men were shocked at the excesses of dishonesty, bribery, and corruption, and Committees of Investigation stated their findings in Reports teeming with moral indignation; certainly most of the wrath they expressed was genuine. If corruption was on the rise, men were nevertheless stunned by it, and determined to crush it if possible.

The following excerpts from The Congressional Globe reveal the strong moral tone that has never been entirely extinguished in American society, as well as the defense by those who justified the chicanery.

*Report of the Select Committee
to Investigate the Alleged Credit Mobilier Bribery*

The select committee appointed under the resolution of the House of January 6, 1873, to make inquiry in relation to the affairs of the Union Pacific Railroad Company, the Credit Mobilier of America, and other matters specified in said resolution and in other resolutions referred to said committee, now submit to the House the following report as to a portion of the matter therein . . .

The purpose of the whole act [creating the corporation known as the Union Pacific Railroad] was expressly declared to be "to promote the

---

"Report of the Select Committee to Investigate the Alleged Credit Mobilier Bribery," *Congressional Globe,* House of Representatives, 42nd Congress, 3rd Session (Washington: Government Printing Office, 1873), Appendix, pp. 106–113.

public interest and welfare by the construction of said railroad and telegraph line, and keeping the same in working order, and to secure to the Government at all times, but particularly in time of war, the use and benefit of the same for postal, military, and other purposes."

Your committee cannot doubt that it was the purpose of Congress in all this to provide for something more than a mere gift of so much land, and a loan of so many bonds on the one side, and the construction and equipment of so many miles of railroad and telegraph on the other.

The United States was not a mere creditor, loaning a sum of money upon mortgage. The railroad corporation was not a mere contractor, bound to furnish a special structure and nothing more. The law created a body politic and corporate, bound, as a trustee, so to manage this great public franchise and endowment that not only the security for the great debt due the United States should not be impaired, but so that there should be ample resources to perform its great public duties in time of commercial disaster and in time of war.

This act was not passed to further the personal interest of the corporators, nor for the advancement of commercial interests, nor for the convenience of the general public alone; but in addition to these the interests, present and future, of the Government as such were to be subserved. A great highway was to be created, the use of which for postal, military and other purposes was to be secured to the Government at "all times," but particularly in time of war. Your committee deem it important to call especial attention to this declared object of this act, to accomplish which object the munificent grant of lands and loan of the Government credit was made. To make such a highway, and to have it ready at "all times," and "particularly in time of war," to meet the demands that might be made upon it; to be able to withstand the loss of business and other casualties incident to war and still to perform for the Government such reasonable service as might under such circumstances be demanded, required a strong solvent corporation, and when Congress expressed the object and granted the corporate powers to carry that object into execution, and aided the enterprise with subsidies of land and bonds, the corporators in whom these powers were vested and under whose control these subsidies were placed were, in the opinion of your committee, under the highest moral, to say nothing of legal or equitable obligations, to use the utmost degree of good faith toward the Government in the exercise of the powers and disposition of the subsidies.

Congress relied for the performance of these great trusts by the corporators upon their sense of public duty; upon the fact that they were to deal with and protect a large capital of their own which they were to pay in money; upon the presence of five directors appointed by the President especially to represent the public interests, who were to own no stock; one of whom should be a member of every committee, standing or special; upon commissioners to be appointed by the President, who should examine and report upon the work as it progressed; in certain cases upon the certificate of the chief engineer, to be made upon his professional honor; and lastly, upon the reserved power to add to, alter, amend, or repeal the act.

Your committee find themselves constrained to report that the moneys borrowed by the corporation, under a power given them, only to meet the necessities of construction and endowment of the road, have been distributed in dividends among the corporators; that the stock was issued, not to the men who paid for it at par in money, but who paid for it at not more than thirty cents on the dollar in roadmaking; that of the Government directors some of them have neglected their duties, and others have been interested in the transactions by which the provisions of the organic law have been evaded; that at least one of the commissioners appointed by the President has been directly bribed to betray his trust by the gift of $25,000; that the chief engineer of the road was largely interested in the contracts for its construction; and that there has been an attempt to prevent the exercise of the reserved power in Congress by inducing influential members of Congress to become interested in the profits of the transaction. So that of the safeguards above enumerated none seems to be left but the sense of public duty of the corporators. . . .

[The committee report then traces the steps by which the Union Pacific authorities created the Credit Mobilier of America, a construction company owned by them and used to build their own railroad.]

It appears then, speaking in round numbers, that the cost of the road was $50,000,000, which cost was wholly reimbursed from the proceeds of the Government bonds and first mortgage bonds; and that from the stock, the income bonds, and land grant bonds, the builders received in cash value at least $23,000,000 in profit, being a percentage of about forty-eight percent on the entire cost. . . .

Instead of securing a solvent, powerful, well-endowed company, able to perform its important public functions without interruption in times of commercial disaster and in times of war, and able to maintain its impartiality and neutrality in dealing with all the connecting lines, it is now weak and poor, kept from bankruptcy only by the voluntary aid of a few capitalists who are interested to maintain it, and liable to fall into the control of shrewd and adroit managers, and to become an appendage to some one of the railroad lines of the East. . . .

Before proceeding to discuss the question of remedy, your committee take occasion to say that, in making this investigation they have labored under great disadvantages. The books containing the records of these transactions are voluminous and complicated. The estimates of engineers made before the letting of the various contracts cannot be found. The presence, as a witness, of General Granville M. Dodge, the chief engineer, under whose supervision the principal part of the work was done, could not be procured, although diligent efforts were made to that end. Telegrams were sent to him, inviting his attendance as a witness, and a deputy sergeant-at-arms was sent for him who has diligently sought him for weeks, but has been unable to find him. Your committee have information from which they feel warranted in stating that they believe that he has been purposely avoiding the service of the summons. . . .

Speech of Representative Ben Butler
in Defense of Representative Oakes Ames

. . . He [Ames] had business capacity, and he forecast the future. He foresaw that some man who might wish to have a rival road, or that some Congressman from some fancied slight or personal pique, might get up here, and if there was nobody to look after the interests of the Union Pacific Railroad Company, which Ames believed to be the interest of the Government as well, by putting through a resolution that nobody knew anything about and nobody cared anything about, nobody looking into it in any form, might thereby ruin him and the great enterprise which was to him as dear as his life, and which he looked upon as a part of the Government itself. What did he do? He agreed with his associates that he would give to certain gentlemen, then in Congress and out of it, who had power and intelligence, by purchase, an interest in this stock. "I," said he, in the truthful, simple language of the old blacksmith, "I find I know enough of Congress to know that it is very difficult to get men to attend to something that they do not know anything about. Now, I will give a man a chance to buy some of this stock, and then he will be watchful to see that no wrong is done to the road, and a wrong done to the road is a wrong to the Government." That is the extent of his offending. . . .

"Speech of Representative Ben Butler in Defense of Representative Oakes Ames, February 26, 1873," *Congressional Globe*, House of Representatives, 42nd Congress, 3rd Session (Washington: Government Printing Office, 1873), Appendix, p. 180.

Speech of Representative Thomas Swann
Favoring Censure or Expulsion of Representatives Ames and Brooks

. . . The growing tendency to corruption which appears to be taking possession of the active business of the country in all its important pursuits
is strongly illustrated by the history of the Union Pacific road. The Government charter under which it was projected, so liberal in its features,
and hedged around by such ample safeguards in its protection, shows to
what extent the avarice and cupidity of designing man, uncontrolled by a
proper moral standard, may thwart the best intentions of a Government
striving to respond to the claims of her citizens and to meet the requirements of a great public necessity. With what emphasis does all this speak
to us here, as the great source and fountain of the law-making power. How
long shall we be able to hold in check the insidious approaches which are
now threatening us if they have not already made a breach into our most
trusted strongholds. The honest men of the country are beginning to
tremble for the safety of their institutions. Let us pause now for a moment,
and see how far we have drifted and what dangers surround us at the
moment.

We have been called to witness the most stupendous frauds in all
sections of the country—municipalities reduced almost to the verge of
ruin by men who have abused the confidence reposed in them. We have
seen the Government robbed of large sums of money by delinquent officers
who have been serving terms in the penitentiary; we have seen our State
Legislatures invaded, and in some instances controlled by enormous bribes
to secure elections in the Senate of the United States; we have witnessed
the lobbies of this House not unfrequently outraged by persons coming
here to influence legislation; and we have seen honorable members of this
House approached by the offers of bribes, ingeniously contrived to prevent
discovery, so barefaced as to excite the shame and indignation of the whole
American people. Public virtue has almost ceased to exist as a controlling
power in our republican system, and corruption is now holding its orgies in
every section of our beloved country. We may treat these untoward in-
dications with indifference and levity; we may mock at and deride the
growing feverishness of the people, who are already struck with alarm at

---

"Speech of Representative Thomas Swann Favoring Censure or Expulsion of Representatives Oakes Ames and James Brooks for Alleged Unlawful Activities Connected
with the Credit Mobilier, March 3, 1873," *Congressional Globe,* House of Representatives, 42nd Congress, 3rd Session (Washington: Government Printing Office, 1873),
Appendix, p. 163.

the dangers impending over them; but the time has arrived when, if something is not done to check the downward tendency of our public morals and to rescue the Government from the maelstrom into which we have unhappily fallen, we may look in vain for the realization of those cherished visions of grandeur and prosperity which inspired the hopes and nerved the arms of the early founders of the Republic.

Mr. Speaker, the existing condition of things canot be permitted to go on with the sanction and countenance of the House. Our Halls of Legislation at least must be kept pure. . . .

Speech of Representative L. P. Poland

. . . As said in our report, the country is filling rapidly with gigantic associations which command great influence and great money power. The people are fast learning that when necessary to secure aims and interests of their own these associations can lay temptations in the way of their public servants too strong for them to resist, and that, unless some check be found, their rights, if not their liberties, will soon be at the mercy of these great and fast-increasing monopolies. . . .

JUSTIFICATION OF THE STATUS QUO

He was a little man with an erect posture and a quick gait. He said that he had enjoyed his life, and few who knew him would have disagreed. For to Andrew Carnegie, son of poor but literate and socially active Scotch artisans, life was an exciting success story that had brought him from humble employment as a bobbin boy in a textile factory to the status of one of the richest men in America.

"Speech of Representative L. P. Poland, February 27, 1873," *Congressional Globe*, House of Representatives, 42nd Congress, 3rd Session (Washington: Government Printing Office, 1873), Appendix, p. 198.

He was also a thinker, something of a philosopher, and a man concerned with the moral questions involved in the acquisition of great wealth. Eventually he evolved his Gospel of Wealth, in which he justified its acquisition on the basis of what could be done with it.
Many of his thoughts are embodied in the following article.

ANDREW CARNEGIE, *Wealth*

The problem of our age is the proper administration of wealth, so that the ties of brotherhood may still bind together the rich and poor in harmonious relationship. The conditions of human life have not only been changed, but revolutionized, within the past few hundred years. In former days there was little difference between the dwelling, dress, food, and environment of the chief and those of his retainers. The Indians are to-day where civilized man then was. When visiting the Sioux, I was led to the wigwam of the chief. It was just like the others in external appearance, and even within the difference was trifling between it and those of the poorest of his braves. The contrast between the palace of the millionaire and the cottage of the laborer with us to-day measures the change which has come with civilization.

This change, however, is not to be deplored, but welcomed as highly beneficial. It is well, nay, essential for the progress of the race, that the houses of some should be homes for all that is highest and best in literature and the arts, and for all the refinements of civilization, rather than that none should be so. Much better this great irregularity than universal squalor. Without wealth there can be no Mæcenas. The "good old times" were not good old times. Neither master nor servant was as well situated then as to-day. A relapse to old conditions would be disastrous to both— not the least so to him who serves—and would sweep away civilization with it. But whether the change be for good or ill, it is upon us, beyond our power to alter, and therefore to be accepted and made the best of. It is a waste of time to criticise the inevitable.

It is easy to see how the change has come. One illustration will serve for almost every phase of the cause. In the manufacture of products we have the whole story. It applies to all combinations of human industry, as stimulated and enlarged by the inventions of this scientific age. Formerly articles were manufactured at the domestic hearth or in small shops

Andrew Carnegie, "Wealth," in *The North American Review*, Vol. 148, No. 391 (June, 1889), pp. 653–664.

which formed part of the household. The master and his apprentices worked side by side, the latter living with the master, and therefore subject to the same conditions. When these apprentices rose to be masters, there was little or no change in their mode of life, and they, in turn, educated in the same routine succeeding apprentices. There was, substantially, social equality, and even political equality, for those engaged in industrial pursuits had then little or no political voice in the State.

But the inevitable result of such a mode of manufacture was crude articles at high prices. To-day the world obtains commodities of excellent quality at prices which even the generation preceding this would have deemed incredible. In the commercial world similar causes have produced similar results, and the race is benefited thereby. The poor enjoy what the rich could not before afford. What were the luxuries have become the necessaries of life. The laborer has now more comforts than the farmer had a few generations ago. The farmer has more luxuries than the landlord had, and is more richly clad and better housed. The landlord has books and pictures rarer, and appointments more artistic, than the King could then obtain.

The price we pay for this salutary change is, no doubt, great. We assemble thousands of operatives in the factory, in the mine, and in the counting-house, of whom the employer can know little or nothing, and to whom the employer is little better than a myth. All intercourse between them is at an end. Rigid Castes are formed, and, as usual, mutual ignorance breeds mutual distrust. Each Caste is without sympathy for the other, and ready to credit anything disparaging in regard to it. Under the law of competition, the employer of thousands is forced into the strictest economies, among which the rates paid to labor figure prominently, and often there is friction between the employer and the employed, between capital and labor, between rich and poor. Human society loses homogeneity.

The price which society pays for the law of competition, like the price it pays for cheap comforts and luxuries, is also great; but the advantages of this law are also greater still, for it is to this law that we owe our wonderful material development, which brings improved conditions in its train. But, whether the law be benign or not, we must say of it, as we say of the change in the conditions of men to which we have referred: It is here; we cannot evade it; no substitutes for it have been found; and while the law may be sometimes hard for the individual, it is best for the race, because it insures the survival of the fittest in every department. We accept and welcome, therefore, as conditions to which we must accommodate ourselves, great inequality of environment, the concentration of business, industrial and commercial, in the hands of a few, and the law of competition between these, as being not only beneficial, but essential for the future progress of the race. Having accepted these, it follows that there must be great scope for the exercise of special ability in the merchant and in the manufacturer who has to conduct affairs upon a great scale. That this talent for organization and management is rare among men is proved by the fact that it invariably secures for its possessor enormous rewards, no matter where or under what laws or conditions. The experienced in affairs always rate the MAN whose services can be obtained as a partner as not only the first consideration, but such as to render the question of his capital scarcely worth considering, for such men soon create capital; while, without the special talent required, capital soon takes wings. Such men become interested in firms or corporations using millions; and estimating only simple interest to be made upon the capital invested, it is inevitable that their income must exceed their expenditures, and that they must accumulate wealth. Nor is there any middle ground which such men can occupy, because the great manufacturing or commercial concern which does not earn at least interest upon its capital soon becomes bankrupt. It must either go forward or fall behind: to stand still is impossible. It is a condition essential for its successful operation that it should be thus far profitable, and even that, in addition to interest on capital, it should make profit. It is a law, as certain as any of the others named, that men possessed of this peculiar talent for affairs, under the free play of economic forces, must, of necessity, soon be in receipt of more revenue than can be judiciously expended upon themselves; and this law is as beneficial for the race as the others.

Objections to the foundations upon which society is based are not in order, because the condition of the race is better with these than it has been with any others which have been tried. Of the effect of any new substitutes proposed we cannot be sure. The Socialist or Anarchist who seeks to overturn present conditions is to be regarded as attacking the foundation upon which civilization itself rests, for civilization took its start from the day that the capable, industrious workman said to his incompetent and lazy fellow, "If thou dost not sow, thou shalt not reap," and thus ended primitive Communism by separating the drones from the bees. One who studies this subject will soon be brought face to face with the conclusion that upon the sacredness of property civilization itself depends—the right of the laborer to his hundred dollars in the savings bank, and equally the legal right of the millionaire to his millions. To those who propose to substitute Communism for this intense Individualism the answer, therefore, is: The race has tried that. All progress from that barbarous day to the present time has resulted from its displacement. Not evil, but good, has come to the race from the accumulation of wealth by those who have the ability and energy that produce it. But even if we admit for a moment that it might be better for the race to discard its present foundation, Individualism,—that it is a nobler ideal that man should labor, not for himself alone, but in and for a brotherhood of his fellows, and share with them all in common, realizing Swedenborg's idea of Heaven, where, as he says, the angels derive their happiness, not from laboring for self, but for each other,—even admit all this, and a sufficient answer is, This is not evolution, but revolution. It necessitates the changing of human nature itself—a work of æons, even if it were good to change it, which we cannot know. It is not practicable in our day or in our age. Even if desirable theoretically, it belongs to another and long-succeeding sociological stratum. Our duty is with what is practicable now; with the next step possible in our day and generation. It is criminal to waste our energies in endeavoring to uproot, when all we can profitably or possibly accomplish is to bend the universal tree of humanity a little in the direction most favorable to the production of good fruit under existing circumstances. We might as well urge the destruction of the highest existing type of man because he failed to reach our ideal as to favor the destruction of Individualism, Private Property, the Law of Accumulation of Wealth, and the Law of Competition; for these are the highest results of human experience, the soil in which society so far has produced the best fruit. Unequally or unjustly, perhaps, as these laws sometimes operate, and imperfect as they appear to the Idealist, they are, nevertheless, like the highest type of man, the best and most valuable of all that humanity has yet accomplished.

We start, then, with a condition of affairs under which the best interests of the race are promoted, but which inevitably gives wealth to the few. Thus far, accepting conditions as they exist, the situation can be surveyed and pronounced good. The question then arises,—and, if the foregoing be correct, it is the only question with which we have to deal,—What is the proper mode of administering wealth after the laws upon which civilization is founded have thrown it into the hands of the few? And it is of this great question that I believe I offer the true solution. It will be understood that *fortunes* are here spoken of, not moderate sums saved by many years of effort, the returns from which are required for the comfortable maintenance and education of families. This is not *wealth,* but only *competence,* which it should be the aim of all to acquire.

There are but three modes in which surplus wealth can be disposed of. It can be left to the families of the decedents; or it can be bequeathed for public purposes; or, finally, it can be administered during their lives by its possessors. Under the first and second modes most of the wealth of the world that has reached the few has hitherto been applied. Let us in turn consider each of these modes. The first is the most injudicious. In monarchical countries, the estates and the greatest portion of the wealth are left to the first son, that the vanity of the parent may be gratified by the thought that his name and title are to descend to succeeding generations unimpaired. The condition of this class in Europe to-day teaches the futility of such hopes or ambitions. The successors have become impoverished through their follies or from the fall in the value of land. Even in Great Britain the strict law of entail has been found inadequate to maintain the status of an hereditary class. Its soil is rapidly passing into the hands of the stranger. Under republican institutions the division of property among the children is much fairer, but the question which forces itself upon thoughtful men in all lands is: Why should men leave great fortunes to their children? If this is done from affection, is it not misguided affection? Observation teaches that, generally speaking, it is not well for the children that they should be so burdened. Neither is it well for the state. Beyond providing for the wife and daughters moderate sources of income, and very moderate allowances indeed, if any, for the sons, men may well hesitate, for it is no longer questionable that great sums bequeathed oftener work more for the injury than for the good of the recipients. Wise men will soon conclude that, for the best interests of the members of their families and of the state, such bequests are an improper use of their means.

It is not suggested that men who have failed to educate their sons to earn a livelihood shall cast them adrift in poverty. If any man has seen fit to rear his sons with a view to their living idle lives, or, what is highly commendable, has instilled in them the sentiment that they are in a position to labor for public ends without reference to pecuniary considerations, then, of course, the duty of the parent is to see that such are provided for *in moderation*. There are instances of millionaires' sons unspoiled by wealth, who, being rich, still perform great services in the community. Such are the very salt of the earth, as valuable as, unfortunately, they are rare; still it is not the exception, but the rule, that men must regard, and, looking at the usual result of enormous sums conferred upon legatees, the thoughtful man must shortly say, "I would as soon leave to my son a curse as the almighty dollar," and admit to himself that it is not the welfare of the children, but family pride, which inspires these enormous legacies.

As to the second mode, that of leaving wealth at death for public uses, it may be said that this is only a means for the disposal of wealth, provided a man is content to wait until he is dead before it becomes of much good in the world. Knowledge of the results of legacies bequeathed is not calculated to inspire the brightest hopes of much posthumous good being accomplished. The cases are not few in which the real object sought by the testator is not attained, nor are they few in which his real wishes are thwarted. In many cases the bequests are so used as to become only monuments of his folly. It is well to remember that it requires the exercise of not less ability than that which acquired the wealth to use it so as to be really beneficial to the community. Besides this, it may fairly be said that no man is to be extolled for doing what he cannot help doing, nor is he to be thanked by the community to which he only leaves wealth at death. Men who leave vast sums in this way may fairly be thought men who would not have left it at all, had they been able to take it with them. The memories of such cannot be held in grateful remembrance, for there is no grace in their gifts. It is not to be wondered at that such bequests seem so generally to lack the blessing.

The growing disposition to tax more and more heavily large estates left at death is a cheering indication of the growth of a salutary change in public opinion. The State of Pennsylvania now takes—subject to some exceptions—one-tenth of the property left by its citizens. The budget presented in the British Parliament the other day proposes to increase the death-duties; and, most significant of all, the new tax is to be a graduated one. Of all forms of taxation, this seems the wisest. Men who continue hoarding great sums all their lives, the proper use of which for public ends would work good to the community, should be made to feel that the community, in the form of the state, cannot thus be deprived of its proper share. By taxing estates heavily at death the state marks its condemnation of the selfish millionaire's unworthy life. ...

There remains, then, only one mode of using great fortunes; but in this we have the true antidote for the temporary unequal distribution of wealth, the reconciliation of the rich and the poor—a reign of harmony—another ideal, differing, indeed, from that of the Communist in requiring only the further evolution of existing conditions, not the total overthrow of our civilization. It is founded upon the present most intense individualism, and the race is prepared to put it in practice by degrees whenever it pleases. Under its sway we shall have an ideal state, in which the surplus wealth of the few will become, in the best sense, the property of the many, because administered for the common good, and this wealth, passing through the hands of the few, can be made a much more potent force for the elevation of our race than if it had been distributed in small sums to the people themselves. Even the poorest can be made to see this, and to agree that great sums gathered by some of their fellow-citizens and spent for public purposes, from which the masses reap the principal benefit, are more valuable to them than if scattered among them through the course of many years in trifling amounts.

If we consider what results flow from the Cooper Institute, for instance, to the best portion of the race in New York not possessed of means, and compare these with those which would have arisen for the good of the masses from an equal sum distributed by Mr. Cooper in his lifetime in the form of wages, which is the highest form of distribution, being for work done and not for charity, we can form some estimate of the possibilities for the improvement of the race which lie embedded in the present law of the accumulation of wealth. Much of this sum, if distributed in small quantities among the people, would have been wasted in the indulgence of appetite, some of it in excess, and it may be doubted whether even the part put to the best use, that of adding to the comforts of the home, would have yielded results for the race, as a race, at all comparable to those which are flowing and are to flow from the Cooper Institute from generation to generation. Let the advocate of violent or radical change ponder well this thought.

We might even go so far as to take another instance, that of Mr. Tilden's bequest of five millions of dollars for a free library in the city of New York, but in referring to this one cannot help saying involuntarily, How much better if Mr. Tilden had devoted the last years of his own life to the proper administration of this immense sum; in which case neither legal contest nor any other cause of delay could have interfered with his aims. But let us assume that Mr. Tilden's millions finally become the means of giving to this city a noble public library, where the treasures of the world contained in books will be open to all forever, without money and without price. Considering the good of that part of the race which congregates in and around Manhattan Island, would its permanent benefit have been better promoted had these millions been allowed to circulate in small sums through the hands of the masses? Even the most strenuous advocate of Communism must entertain a doubt upon this subject. Most of those who think will probably entertain no doubt whatever.

Poor and restricted are our opportunities in this life; narrow our horizon; our best work most imperfect; but rich men should be thankful for one inestimable boon. They have it in their power during their lives to busy themselves in organizing benefactions from which the masses of their fellows will derive lasting advantage, and thus dignify their own lives. The highest life is probably to be reached, not by such imitation of the life of Christ as Count Tolstoï gives us, but, while animated by Christ's spirit, by recognizing the changed conditions of this age, and adopting modes of expressing this spirit suitable to the changed conditions under which we live; still laboring for the good of our fellows, which was the essence of his life and teaching, but laboring in a different manner.

This, then, is held to be the duty of the man of Wealth: First, to set an example of modest unostentatious living, shunning display or extravagance; to provide moderately for the legitimate wants of those dependent upon him; and after doing so to consider all surplus revenues which come to him simply as trust funds, which he is called upon to administer, and strictly bound as a matter of duty to administer in the manner which, in his judgment, is best calculated to produce the most beneficial results for the community—the man of wealth thus becoming the mere agent and trustee for his poorer brethren, bringing to their service his superior wisdom, experience, and ability to administer, doing for them better than they would or could do for themselves.

We are met here with the difficulty of determining what are moderate sums to leave to members of the family; what is modest, unostentatious living; what is the test of extravagance. There must be different standards for different conditions. The answer is that it is as impossible to name exact amounts or actions as it is to define good manners, good taste, or the rules of propriety; but, nevertheless, these are verities, well known although undefinable. Public sentiment is quick to know and to feel what offends these. So in the case of wealth. The rule in regard to good taste in the dress of men or women applies here. Whatever makes one conspicuous offends the canon. If any family be chiefly known for display, for extravagance in home, table, equipage, for enormous sums ostentatiously spent in any form upon itself,—if these be its chief distinctions, we have no difficulty in estimating its nature or culture. So likewise in regard to the use or abuse of its surplus wealth, or to generous, freehanded cooperation in good public uses, or to unabated efforts to accumulate and hoard to the last, whether they administer or bequeath. The verdict rests with the best and most enlightened public sentiment. The community will surely judge, and its judgments will not often be wrong.

The best uses to which surplus wealth can be put have already been indicated. Those who would administer wisely must, indeed, be wise, for one of the serious obstacles to the improvement of our race is indiscriminate charity. It were better for mankind that the millions of the rich were thrown into the sea than so spent as to encourage the slothful, the drunken, the unworthy. Of every thousand dollars spent in so called charity to-day, it is probable that $950 is unwisely spent; so spent, indeed, as to produce the very evils which it proposes to mitigate or cure. A well-known writer of philosophic books admitted the other day that he had given a quarter of a dollar to a man who approached him as he was coming to visit the house of his friend. He knew nothing of the habits of this beggar; knew not the use that would be made of this money, although he had every reason to suspect that it would be spent improperly. This man professed to be a disciple of Herbert Spencer; yet the quarter-dollar given that night will probably work more injury than all the money which its thoughtless donor will ever be able to give in true charity will do good. He only gratified his own feelings, saved himself from annoyance—and this was probably one of the most selfish and very worst actions of his life, for in all respects he is most worthy.

In bestowing charity, the main consideration should be to help those who will help themselves; to provide part of the means by which those who desire to improve may do so; to give those who desire to rise the aids by which they may rise; to assist, but rarely or never to do all. Neither the individual nor the race is improved by alms-giving. Those worthy of assistance, except in rare cases, seldom require assistance. The really valuable men of the race never do, except in cases of accident or sudden change. Every one has, of course, cases of individuals brought to his own knowledge where temporary assistance can do genuine good, and these he will not overlook. But the amount which can be wisely given by the individual for individuals is necessarily limited by his lack of knowledge of the circumstances connected with each. He is the only true reformer who is as careful and as anxious not to aid the unworthy as he is to aid the worthy, and, perhaps, even more so, for in alms-giving more injury is probably done by rewarding vice than by relieving virtue.

The rich man is thus almost restricted to following the examples of Peter Cooper, Enoch Pratt of Baltimore, Mr. Pratt of Brooklyn, Senator Stanford, and others, who know that the best means of benefiting the community is to place within its reach the ladders upon which the aspiring can rise— parks, and means of recreation, by which men are helped in body and mind; works of art, certain to give pleasure and improve the public taste, and public institutions of various kinds, which will improve the general condition of the people;—in this manner returning their surplus wealth to the mass of their fellows in the forms best calculated to do them lasting good.

Thus is the problem of Rich and Poor to be solved. The laws of accumulation will be left free; the laws of distribution free. Individualism will continue, but the millionaire will be but a trustee for the poor; intrusted for a season with a great part of the increased wealth of the community, but administering it for the community far better than it could or would have done for itself. The best minds will thus have reached a stage in the development of the race in which it is clearly seen that there is no mode of disposing of surplus wealth creditable to thoughtful and earnest men into whose hands it flows save by using it year by year for the general good. This day already dawns. But a little while, and although, without incurring the pity of their fellows, men may die sharers in great business enterprises from which their capital cannot be or has not been withdrawn, and is left chiefly at death for public uses, yet the man who dies leaving behind him millions of available wealth, which was his to administer during life, will pass away "unwept, unhonored, and unsung," no matter to what uses he leaves the dross which he cannot take with him. Of such as these the public verdict will then be: "The man who dies thus rich dies disgraced."

Such, in my opinion, is the true Gospel concerning Wealth, obedience to which is destined some day to solve the problem of the Rich and the Poor, and to bring "Peace on earth, among men Good-Will."

THE ECONOMICS OF THE GILDED AGE: AN APPRAISAL

The following selection from Professor Edward C. Kirkland's Industry Comes of Age *presents a perceptive, succinct appraisal of changes that took place in American industry and labor in the Gilded Age. Professor Kirkland, who has had a long and distinguished career as an economic historian, also carries his summation into the philosophical realm: "Was it all wrong?" he asks. His conclusions might well serve as an introduction for additional research, discussion, and speculation.*

EDWARD C. KIRKLAND, *Multiplication, Division, Materialism*

THE TOTALS OF WEALTH

In 1869 David A. Wells felt that the inflation of the time had hit the workers harder than the capitalist and that the rich were becoming richer and the poor poorer. The idea, constantly repeated, endured. In 1895 the Massachusetts Bureau of Labor Statistics gave the concept a full rehearsal. "That the rich are becoming richer and the poor poorer, is frequently asserted to be one of the results of the prevailing industrial system. The belief that the facts support this assertion finds constant expression in speeches, magazines, books, newspapers, and conversation, and while the impatience of a few inspired by this belief leads at times to violent outbreaks against the social order, there are many of a milder nature who are dissatisfied because the idea [a more equal division] of wealth is not more closely attained."

Certainly the industrial years, covered by this volume [1860–1897, Ed.], greatly increased the national wealth, a concept defined as the sum of the values of property within the nation. Figures of this sort, going back to the seventeenth century, originally overemphasized the nation's treasure in the precious metals; by the nineteenth century the concept stretched to cover land, natural resources, plants and railroads: national wealth was a "national inventory or stocktaking." It consisted of things that could be seen,

From Edward C. Kirkland, *Industry Comes of Age: Business, Labor, and Public Policy, 1860–1897.* New York: Holt, Rinehart, and Winston, 1961; Chicago: Quadrangle Books, 1967. Pp. 399–409 in both editions. Reprinted by permission.

counted, and appraised. Perhaps a more informative substitute for the last word was "assessed." For one of the reasons for using the concept of national wealth was the existence of data which tax officials, usually local ones, all over the nation had assembled. By a resort to arithmetic, it was possible to elevate "the appraised value" to "the true value," "the fair selling price cf property." No matter how crude such data were, the period here under scrutiny exhibited a "gratifying" increase in national wealth. Its "estimated true value" in 1860 was $16,159,616,068; in 1900, $88,517,-306,775.

By dividing these dollar totals by the number of inhabitants, enumerators concluded that the "true wealth" per capita had risen between 1860 and 1900 from $514 to $1,165. These figures do not reveal how wealth is really distributed. Per capita wealth is the wealth no capita has. From the few figures available it is clear that there was a very high concentration of wealth. Between 1879 and 1881, approximately 15 per cent of the estates of males probated in Massachusetts were under $500; 65 per cent—this figure includes the former—were under $5,000; roughly a half of one per cent were $50,000 or over. In sum the richest 2 per cent of the population owned two-thirds of the state's wealth. Little wonder that popular opinion tended to focus on the fact of large fortunes. One writer, a corporation lawyer and convert to Henry George, asked, as others have since, "Who owns the United States?" and announced that 40,000 persons owned one-half the national wealth. By extrapolating from individual fortunes and their rate of increase, he concluded at the end of the eighties "the American billionaire might reasonably be looked for within . . . [forty years] . . . and several billionaires might be expected within sixty years." Incidentally, John D. Rockefeller, the closest competitor, never made it. . . .

In the nineteenth century the lack of statistical sophistication and the absence of data prevented anything but a start being made on determining the amount and distribution of the national income, defined as "the net product of or net return on the activity of individuals, business firms, and the social and political institutions that make up a nation." In the twentieth century statisticians have far surpassed the tentative efforts of the Federal censuses and of individuals such as Edward Atkinson, to arrive at conclusions. According to the estimates of one of these experts, the functioning of the economy in the era covered by this volume greatly increased the national income. With adjustments made for changes in the price level, the average per year increased from $9,300,000,000 in the period 1869–1878 to $24,200,000,000 in 1889–1898. Per capita this meant an increase from $215 to $357. Such increases, greater than in other industrialized countries and than in America before 1860, led one informed statistician to conclude in 1915: "Beginning with 1870, there has been an increase in the national dividend so enormous that it cannot logically be ascribed to anything but the tremendous advance in productive power due to the revolution by improvements in industry which have characterized the last half century. It seems improbable that any other great nation has ever experienced such sweeping gains in the average income of the inhabitants."

Not only did national income increase, its division among various economic activities altered. Thus between 1869–1879 and 1889–1899, the percentage distributed to agriculture declined from 20.5 to 17.1. Meanwhile that for manufacturing rose from 13.9 to 18.2, for mining from 1.8 to 2.5. The share of construction, transportation, and service declined slightly. While these figures might partially account for the presence of agricultural discontent, they have little bearing on the division of income between capital and labor, between rentier, manager, and wage earner. Between 1860 and 1900 the percentage of national income going into wages and salaries rose from 37.2 to 47.3; in rent it fell from 8.8 to 7.8; and in interest rose only from 14.7 to 15; the share to profits fell from 39.3 to 30.3. Whereas in 1860 the sum of all the returns paid for wages was approximately the same as for profits, in 1900 the sum for wages was much the larger.

Before 1890 most data on wages are highly speculative. In so far as wages can be stated, they are wage rates without allowance for the degree of unemployment; they are not useful, therefore, for ascertaining a worker's annual income. When all reservations have been made, there is little question that money wages, "nominal wages," rose during the late nineteenth century. The index of money hourly wages for men in all industries practically doubled between 1860 and 1890; it shrank a bit in the mid-nineties. Since the index of commodity prices fell rapidly after 1865, the purchasing power of wages, "real wages," often attained a spectacular improvement. At no time during the depressions of the seventies and nineties did an index of wages in purchasing power sink as low as in 1860 and the preceding fifties; in intervals of prosperity the power of wages over goods was much more favorable than in the good old days. Little wonder, when Mr. Gompers was asked in 1900, "You would not agree to the statement sometimes made that the conditions of the working men are growing worse and worse?" he answered, "Oh, that is perfectly absurd."

THE AMERICAN STANDARD OF LIVING

For rich as for poor, measurements of the resulting standard of living depend upon other factors than prices and the ability to pay them. A standard of living, for instance, also depends upon the overall technical level an economy has attained. The backwardness of the plumbers' art may thus account alike for the noisome toilets of a tenement and the fact that a bath tub costing $7,000 in a tycoon's palace built by McKim, Mead, and White had its outlet sloping toward the tub. A standard of living also depends upon what people think they ought to have and do have in terms of services and commodities. Thus a cotton operative comparing 1848 with 1883 confessed: "We get many things now that we did not have then. ... We have gas to pay for now, and ice, and such things." To those leading the procession, the well-being of those farther down the line seemed fabulous. In 1880 the President of the American Society of Mechanical Engineers informed his hearers that the American cotton industry made and sold cotton goods so cheaply "that the very beggars in our metropolitan cities, and the 'tramps' sleeping in our fields or under the roof that shelters our cattle, wear a finer fabric than kings could boast a century ago." Though this seems a somewhat ambiguous endorsement of the functioning of the economy, he thought the "golden age" and the "millenial period" were at hand.

To most people a millennium implies spiritual overtones. So does the standard of living. Though most intangible items elude the quantifier's grasp, an exception is the length of the working day. Whereas at the beginning of the Civil War, the ten-hour day prevailed in the building trades and in certain skilled occupations, the average day the country over was eleven hours. Gradually the standard day shrank. By century's end the work week was 57.3 hours, and Gompers, president of the A.F. of L., was estimating that the average hours of labor of the American worker were 9 to 9$^1/_2$ a day.

Less measurable satisfactions and benefits were flowing from public education, an advantage of American life increasingly available to children whose earnings parents could forego or whom parents could support. Indeed compulsory education acts made it imperative that parents make this sacrifice or break the truant laws. Though education was a community enterprise and thus not at first hand dependent upon the economy, in the last analysis American productivity and wealth furnished the taxes for the improved curriculum of the grades and the establishment and spread of the public high school.

For a generation which made a gospel of work and which worked hard, it was somewhat paradoxical to estimate the achievements of the economy in terms of fewer hours at labor and more at leisure. The nature of work itself was a more acceptable measure. Certainly the economic development of the nation and the organization of business enterprise had greatly altered the nature of work. Though it placed millions under an industrial discipline to which they had to conform, it freed others from forms of labor which Americans had long felt were characterized by a stultifying dependence and inferiority. No change, for instance, in the labor force was more startling than the failure of the numbers in personal and domestic service to increase as rapidly as those in other industrial divisions. More Americans proportionately than ever before could boast they wore no man's livery, and housewives and others began the long lamentation over the difficulty of getting maids, cooks, and the like.

Meanwhile, within the employment categories reflecting at first hand the industrial transformation, the number of unskilled laboring positions vis-à-vis those in directing or superintending capacities declined. ... Most categories about skilled and unskilled workers, as well as most judgments based upon them, are transistory things; but perhaps it was plausible to distinguish, as the census did, a class of labor "comprising those employments which are, as a rule, the more laborious, and in which the bulk of the work done does not call for a high degree of mechanical skill or ability, such as agricultural laborers, boatmen, fishermen ... sailors, draymen, hostlers ... messengers, packers, porters, miners, quarrymen, servants, and the like." The percentage of the population gainfully employed in this category declined between 1870 and 1890. "The increased proportion of workers is found generally in the higher walks of business life and in those occupations which call for skilled labor principally rather than in the lowest or most laborious forms of employment." Invention sought to replace mere muscular strength with power and to place on a mechanized basis tasks which the day regarded as "brutalizing" or "degrading." This was as true of farm as of factory. As one engineer summarized it in 1899: "We know that in these latter days, it is *intelligent* labor rather than *hard* labor that counts."

In spite of the economic advance of all classes in this period, the statement that the rich were getting richer and the poor poorer persisted in one form or another. Perhaps the fact that journalists just before the Civil War put the number of millionaires in metropolitan Eastern cities at less than a hundred but by the nineties were reporting 4,407 millionaires in the country as a whole provided evidence for this notion. On the other hand Carroll D. Wright, the most social-minded of American statisticians, could hardly contain his impatience with the inaccuracy of the observation: "a wandering phrase, without paternity or date; it is not authority but familiarity that has given it weight. ... To the investigator the real statement should be, The rich are growing richer; many more people than formerly are growing rich; and the poor are better off. If the sum total of wealth were stationary, any increase in the wealth of the rich would be an exploitation of the poor. ... But the sum total of wealth is not stationary; it increases with great rapidity, and while under this increase the capitalistic side secures a greater relative advantage than the wage-earner of the profits of production, the wage-earner secures an advantage which means the improvement of his condition." In 1900 Mr. Gompers' judgment of the rich-richer and the poor-poorer concept was "a catch phrase."

WAS IT ALL WRONG?

To many sensitive observers of the era both the qualitative changes in the way the country's work was performed and the growth in production, wealth, and wages were beside the point. Tests such as these, critics asserted, merely proved the nation's achievement was not ideal or spiritual but material. E. L. Godkin, editor of the *Nation*, scolded the rich for "the worship of wealth, in its coarsest and most undraped form . . . that is, wealth, as a purveyor of meat, drink, clothing, and ornamentation, which . . . 'makes hay' of all noble standards of individual and social conduct." And few can read the literature of business apologetics without realizing it was unpleasantly easy for the well-to-do to identify progress with material things. Such identification was not a class matter. The American standard of living sought by organized labor was no more exalted. Godkin, who liked to censure impartially, concluded, "The poor are less discontented when they consume more of the necessaries and luxuries, because . . . as a rule, physical comfort among the great bulk of mankind tends to produce happiness" and that the masses in a democracy inherently elevate "material luxury into the great end of social progress.". . .

. . . [T]hose operating on a level more mundane than the stratosphere pointed out that the attainment of welfare made possible by the economic order was an essential prelude to shattering the age-old handicaps to a cultural awakening. No doubt a Chicago University professor's conclusion that Rockefeller had done more for the world than Shakespeare was calculated to make the judicious as well as the genteel grieve; it accorded nonetheless with an assertion by Charles Elliott Perkins, president of the Chicago, Burlington, and Quincy Railroad: "Have not great merchants, great manufacturers, great inventors, done more for the world than preachers and philanthropists? . . . Can there be any doubt that cheapening the cost of necessaries and conveniences of life is the most powerful agent of civilization and progress? Does not the fact that well-fed and well-armed men make better citizens, other things being equal, than those who are cold and hungry, answer the question? Poverty is the cause of most of the crime and misery in the world—cheapening the cost of the necessaries and conveniences of life is lessening poverty, and there is no other way to lessen it, absolutely none. History and experience demonstrate that as wealth has accumulated and things have cheapened, men have improved . . . in their habits of thought, their sympathy for others, their ideas of justice, as well as of mercy. . . . Material progress must come first and . . . upon it is founded all other progress."

In terms of economic factors we can ascribe the achievement of the era to a sequence of important inventions which from science and technology flowed swiftly into production. As new goods, made in new ways, came upon the market, they were originally expensive. Experience in production and the quick application of mass methods of manufacture and distribution soon made them cheaper. The structure of the economy was still so competitive that the advantage of the new system flowed into the hands of consumers. The effective organization of labor prevented the sequestration of gains in the hands of lenders and managers.

But the generation which accomplished all this had a distaste for explanations so matter-of-fact. They preferred to ascribe the industrial triumph to "character." Education should teach character, and charity or relief should take care, according to the most prominent social worker of the time, lest it undermine "the character of a poor man—for it is his all." In the cluster of specific qualities upon which the business and industrial discipline placed a premium, a changing economic scene brought about some shift. Whereas in the earlier days of commerce frugality, industry, punctuality, and integrity had been the road to fortune, wealth now came "rapidly" through "lucky strokes" and "bold and ingenious combinations." In spite of the authority and astuteness of this observation (it came from E. L. Godkin of the *Nation*), the generation did not cease to admire or practice the traditional virtues; it simply added to them an appreciation of the ones the new day required—alertness, activity, and audacity. In a period of transition and depression, alive with dangers and uncertainties, the useful qualities were "hustle," ambition, dedication to the job, and above all, the willingness to take risks and strike out along new paths. They called it "gumption," they called it "pluck."

This individualistic industrial ethic of self-reliance was certainly both bleak in terms of social relationships and deficient in the reflective or contemplative qualities. But its positive aspects, carried to the pitch of genius by business leaders and enjoying the approbation of the majority of ordinary Americans, were neither mercenary nor ignoble. Exercised in relative freedom and with a conscious view to national greatness as well as private gain, the talent for business enterprise was the source of that abundance which, in later days, democracy would administer differently. And today many nations seeking industrialization would be fortunate if they had, not so much America's resources, but the national qualities which gave birth to our industrial strength and the institutions under which these qualities flowered to achievement.

II / LABOR IN THE GILDED AGE

INTRODUCTION

Though the Gilded Age was an era of unbridled business development, it was a period of restiveness and frustration for American labor. As American society barely comprehended the strides taken by industry, so did it also fail to understand the emergence of the working class. Men still thought in terms of the employer whom the worker could approach, an employer from whom he could request the day off because, for example, his wife had had a baby the night before. But in reality employment now meant a massive factory employing thousands, with only a hired foreman to whom the worker could go. That official's loyalty was to the company, not to the workers.

While American society still envisioned the laborer, unemployed in time of depression, as raising food in his garden or even moving to a new frontier, the reality was an emaciated man in an urban slum, desperate for food, clothing, and shelter, and filled with a hatred for the system that punished him for striking, deprived him of his job, or worked him long hours at whatever pay the employer chose to give him.

This discrepancy between the old ideal and the new reality was never entirely understood by the American people in the Gilded Age—if it is today. They continued to equate success and steady employment with hard work and sobriety, and placed all the blame for failure on the backs of the unemployed. That a man could be a sober, steady, punctual, responsible worker and still be thrown out of work never crossed their minds. Social Darwinism merely served to bolster and reinforce the old ideas with scientific laws that were considered absolute.

A small percentage of the workers fought back. As early as 1866 there was a National Labor Union, and in 1869 Terence V. Powderly's Knights of Labor began to grow rapidly. Advocating the eight-hour day, arbitration of labor disputes, Chinese exclusion, an end to contract labor, and the abolition of child labor, the movement possessed a viable program, a measure of good leadership, and the widest possible base for its membership— virtually all laborers, regardless of age, sex, or race were welcome.

After the tragic summer of 1877 and the brief flurry of victories in the early 1880's—the strike against the Gould lines is most notable—labor suffered its "Great Upheaval." The year was 1886, when Chicago and the nation became panicky and emotional over the Haymarket Affair. After that the Knights declined rapidly, and more conservative craft unions, led by Samuel Gompers, formed a loosely knit association called The American

Federation of Labor. In the 1890's more defeats were recorded. Eugene V. Debs' American Railway Union lost the Pullman strike, and the steel workers were defeated at Homestead, Pennsylvania.

The intensity of violence is usually proportionate to the intransigency of the opposition. Conservative America reacted to union efforts with a sternness that in turn bred more misunderstanding and resentment. Labor's replies were occasionally marked by "the deed" (as anarchists called acts of violence), such as murders by the Molly Maguires in Pennsylvania's coal fields, the throwing of a bomb at Haymarket Square in Chicago, or the burning of company property, as in the Railroad Strike of 1877. When the Gilded Age ended, and labor looked forward into the Twentieth Century, it still had a long way to go.

INTERPRETATION

In the summer of 1877, in the middle of the Gilded Age, the laboring man struck back. It was the fifth year of depression, and unemployment, wage cuts, long hours, and insecurity finally led to a near-spontaneous eruption. So much of the story of labor in the Gilded Age is embodied in this one year that the readings in this section are concentrated on this one segment of the thirty-five year era.

In 1877: Year of Violence, Robert V. Bruce, Professor of History at Boston University and an authority on economic and recent U.S. history, has written an almost flawless account of the Great Railroad Strike of 1877. The excerpts contained below remind us that mobs are not new to America, that they all contain such ingredients as teenagers, looters, and arsonists, along with a mass psychology which justifies it all and imparts a holiday atmosphere to the days and nights of chaos. And perhaps they grant us some solace, too, in reminding us that the long, hot summers of the 1960's had their counterparts 90 years ago, and the nation survived.

ROBERT V. BRUCE, The Fuse and The Crossing

THE FUSE

No year in the history of American railroading has ever ended more terribly than 1876 or begun more bleakly than 1877.

Darkness and blinding snow filled the night of December 29. Shortly before eight o'clock, the Lake Shore Road's Pacific Express, drawn by two locomotives and carrying 159 human beings, started over an iron truss bridge at Ashtabula, Ohio. As the lead locomotive reached the far abutment, its engineer heard a cracking sound beneath him, felt the bridge sink and instinctively opened the throttle. The locomotive sprang forward, tearing loose from its coupling. He looked back from the cab window in time to see the second locomotive turn turtle and fall into the ravine sixty-nine feet below. The bridge crumpled slowly from one end to the other and crashed down, carrying with it four baggage cars and seven

---

stove-heated passenger cars. After the long drawn-out tumult of the fall came a hush in which only the wind was heard. Then, here and there along the wreck, orange tongues of flame sprang out of darkness and began licking at the broken cars. Perhaps as many as twenty people already lay broken and dead within. At least sixty more were trapped and burned alive in the wreckage.

Since at least half of the dead were consumed utterly, no exact accounting was possible. Nevertheless, the Ashtabula horror stood unchallenged as the worst rail disaster America had ever suffered. The Lake Shore's chief civil engineer shot himself a few days later; the strong-willed financier who had insisted on an unsound bridge design endured five years of reproach before following suit. The impact on the public mind was tremendous. Just as the public had come to believe railroads perfectly safe, observed the *Railway World,* "a new horror occurs to weaken confidence."

On the same stormy night of December 29, 1876, every train in motion west of Montreal on the Grand Trunk Railway of Canada was being stopped and the locomotive fires drawn. Thus the Brotherhood of Locomotive Engineers replied to the Grand Trunk's violation of agreements and dismissal of Brotherhood leaders. Aided by the storm, the strikers completely blocked the single-track road. Next day they turned back strikebreakers, while sympathizers held the roundhouses. On January 3, 1877, the Grand Trunk capitulated, even to reimbursing the Brotherhood's Grand Chief Engineer, Peter M. Arthur, for travel expenses he had incurred during the strike.

Only a similar victory over the Central of New Jersey in the previous October matched this latest triumph of the Brotherhood. A new force confronted railroad management. Before 1876 railroad strikes had almost all been wildcat affairs. The Brotherhood of Locomotive Engineers had concentrated on temperance work and mutual insurance. Now, with its membership passing 10,000 and its treasury well filled, it was brandishing a club which had proved formidable even in the hands of a leaderless, planless few. And management did not like it.

The day after the Grand Trunk's surrender, ragged newsboys yelled, "Extry, extry, death of Commodore Vanderbilt!" The indomitable old man who had hammered together the great New York Central system, whose death had been awaited since May by relays of card-playing reporters across the street, who had outlived two of the doctors attending his last illness, was mastered at last. In his final hours he quavered a favorite hymn, which ran "I am poor, I am needy." This was only a little premature. Of the $105,000,000 which he proved unable in the end to take with him, more than $90,000,000, including absolute control of the New York Central, went to his eldest son, the prudent, plodding William H. Vanderbilt. The

Commodore's death had been discounted for months, the son had been managing the Central for years, and yet the final stilling of the formidable old man seemed to mark the end of an era. The railroad world wondered.

Three blows in one week—and in those days, when the railroads shivered, the nation shook.

Mark Twain had already pinned a label on the times with his novel *The Gilded Age*. He could as well have called it *The Railroad Age*. Wherever you looked in the America of 1877—in politics, industry, agriculture, morals, technology, even in the arts—you saw somewhere, plain or subtle, the mark of the rails.

A locomotive in passage, the new prime mover of the nation, roused Walt Whitman as it did his fellow Americans in those years:

> Thy black cylindric body, golden brass and silvery steel...
> Thy great protruding head-light fix'd in front,
> Thy long, pale, floating vapor-pennants, tinged with delicate purple,
> The dense and murky clouds out-belching from thy smokestack,
> Thy knitted frame, thy springs and valves, the tremulous twinkle of thy wheels...
> Type of the modern—emblem of motion and power—pulse of the continent...
> Fierce-throated beauty!

Whitman voiced the wonder that kept boys of the seventies hanging around depots at traintime, stopped them in fields to watch passing freights, stirred them from sleep at the far-off hallooing of night trains in pursuit of the horizon. They hardly needed Oliver Optic's "Lake Shore" stories about heroic young engineers and firemen. (" 'She is safe!' cried Tom, at the top of his voice, as he leaped from the engine upon the ground, and placed the little girl in the arms of her mother.") They read the stories nevertheless, and others too, and dreamed of more. And now and then, when a fast express thundered through the town, even the grownups felt their pulses beating to its rhythm.

The railroad! On it depended almost all that made the new America different from the old. Where would the new West of the farmer be without it? The railroad took the farmer there in the first place—lured him there sometimes with its high-spirited handbills and easy rates for settlers. The railroad sold him his land, brought in his supplies and, above all, provided his only outlet to the markets of the world. If the railroad were cut off, the buffalo would be saved; but the Great Plains farmer would be a vanishing species.

Industry? Railroads were big customers, as the people of Pittsburgh well knew. But that was only part of it. What made the new industry different from the old was the scope of its market and the scale of its operations. Whole cities took up specialties. Chicago turned hog butcher for the nation, Minneapolis became the nation's miller, Lynn its cobbler, Paterson spun its silk, St. Louis brewed its beer. Railroads made possible that triumph of mass production and marketing.

Railroads drew the map of the new urban age. They turned fields into cities and cities into backwaters. Altoona was a child of the Pennsylvania. The Lackawanna made Scranton out of Slocum's Hollow. Without the Baltimore & Ohio, Baltimore would have been much quieter, greener and smaller than it was. Having helped create the new towns and cities, railroads hauled in the herds of cattle, rivers of milk and mountains of flour that kept their millions fed.

There were highways still, of some use for local horse-drawn traffic. The rivers still ran, and people read about the race of the *Robert E. Lee* with the *Natchez*. Even at Pittsburgh towboats were thick along the forks of the Ohio. Some canals kept up a rearguard fight against weeds and silt; and now and then in the warm season, the larger ones, like the Erie Canal or the Chesapeake and Ohio, roused themselves to a flurry of serious competition with the rails. Nevertheless, those arteries flowed too sluggishly to sustain by themselves the vigor of the world's newest industrial giant. It was the railroads that carried the lifeblood of America in 1877.

All this had come about within the memory of living men. Peter Cooper, whose Tom Thumb of 1830 had been the first locomotive built in America, was alive and busy in 1877, a year after running for President on the Greenback ticket. Men still putting in a long day's work on the railroad could remember when Cooper's contraption had eaten the dust of a horse-drawn rail car. Starting from nothing, railroads had grown faster and farther than had the United States itself in those expansive years. Now they spanned the nation and accounted for a tenth of all its property.

Much of that growth was the work of a half-dozen years. In 1865, after marking time through nearly a decade of turmoil and civil war, American railroads had leaped forward, sped by huge Federal and state grants of land and credit. The Great Plains lay open for development, the newly industrialized East needed connecting and feeder lines, great systems awaited only the shaping hands of organizers like Vanderbilt, railroad builders moved at last to link the oceans. The railroads themselves pumped in streams of immigrants, who swelled the pent-up demand for housing, spread out over the plains and spilled into the labor market. Railroad consolidations and technical advances lowered freight rates, and industry quickened in turn. Business was good, money was easy and confidence was boundless. The railroads had no trouble selling their stocks and bonds. Indians and buffalo might be the only commuters present along some of the projected Western lines, but investors considered high interest rates, government benevolence and, above all, the glowing future; and they bought. Over 1,000 miles of new road were laid down in 1865. By 1867 the annual new mileage was topping 2,000. It hit 3,000 in 1868, 6,000 in 1870, and more than 7,000 in 1871.

With that year the country's current needs were nearly satisfied. In 1872 new mileage dropped under 6,000 and in 1873 barely reached 4,000. After the Credit Mobilier scandal broke, subsidy bills were political poison; and so in 1872 every party included an anti-land grant plank in its platform. Meanwhile, crop production went up 50 per cent, farm prices fell accordingly and the hard-pressed Western farmer began kicking at the floor of railroad rates. Members of a farmers' social organization known as the Grange moved into state politics and put through rate-regulating "Granger laws" to curb the railroad "robber barons."

Back east, on September 18, 1873, came a sudden crash that froze bankers and businessmen in their tracks: Jay Cooke and Company had closed its doors, bankrupt! Cooke, the leading banker of his day, had tried to finance the building of the Northern Pacific Railroad by selling $100,000,000 worth of its bonds. But railroad investors were growing wary. With a 1,000-mile gap still unclosed, Northern Pacific bond sales fell off. To keep the road going Cooke borrowed heavily at short-term, counting on a revival of confidence among long-term investors before the loans came due. He soared out over the tanbark with a nonchalance surprising in a man of such solid repute, only to find no one on the other trapeze. And when he looked down, lo! there was no net.

The fall of Cooke caused a brief banking panic, which in turn forced a short but deadly slackening of trade. No more was needed. The nation slid down a spiral of depression which was to last longer than any other in its history. And the railroads suffered like the rest.

To be sure, total net earnings were a shade higher in 1876 than in 1873. But they had to be spread over 6,540 more miles of road. And they had been shored up only by ruthless economizing in the face of sagging revenues. Between 1873 and 1876, operating expenses per mile, including wages, were cut 18 per cent. Furthermore, the burden of capital stock and bonded debt had grown by 16 per cent. Perhaps as telling as any statistic was the fact that road after road went crashing down into foreclosure or receivership—seventy-six in the Centennial Year alone.

With it all, 1876 brought rate wars of unprecedented ferocity among the five main lines linking the Northeast to the West—the Grand Trunk, the New York Central, the Erie, the Pennsylvania and the Baltimore & Ohio. Railroad competition in hard times was a deadly game. Bankrupt roads were run by their receivers not so much for profit as for business—at any price. Their competitors had to match their rate cutting in order to pay interest on bonds, maintain equipment and keep a minimum corps of employees. The Grand Trunk happened to be bankrupt. So in 1876 rates fell like Lucifer from Heaven. Along the Baltimore & Ohio they were cut in two. One could ride the New York Central from Chicago to New York City for thirteen dollars. A hundred pounds of farm products could be shipped from Chicago to New York for eighteen cents instead of the usual fifty, and to Boston via the Grand Trunk for twenty cents instead of seventy-five. Among its other effects, the trunk-line war of 1876 finished off the Atlantic & Great Western Railroad.

This, as 1877 began, was the climax now capped by the Ashtabula horror, the Grand Trunk strike and the death of Commodore Vanderbilt. No wonder the *Railway World* omitted allusions to a "Happy New Year." "Railway management has been more than one-half failure," it noted. "The stockholder is alarmed, and not without cause; the bond-holder sees his security weakened...Anarchy prevails in the conflict of roads."

Talk as one might about "long lanes" and "darkness before dawn," the sunrise could warm only those who lived through the night. And as the first weeks of 1877 wore by, no rosy glow lighted the horizon. On the contrary, darkness deepened on March 1 when the Supreme Court upheld the Granger laws. The *Railway World* threw up its hands at what it called "the most important, and, in some respects, the most unfortunate decision ever made by an American court of last resort."

Reported receipts of seventeen western lines during January and February fell a half million dollars short of the same period in 1876. Bad spring floods cut down business and raised expenses on the Atchison, Topeka & Santa Fe. The breaking up of a hard winter made tributary wagon roads almost impassable in the Kansas Pacific's territory, and railroad business fell off in consequence. Later in the year the Chicago & Alton lost through failure of the corn crop in its area, the Central Pacific through a drought in California. Rocky Mountain locusts, which had lately devastated vast areas of the Great Plains, sowed the ground thickly with eggs in the fall of 1876. Fearing fresh onslaughts in 1877, farmers husbanded their money and merchants kept their stocks low. Railroads felt the effects.

"The distress in railways is greater than ever before," wrote the board chairman of the Illinois Central in April. "It is important," he warned the road's president, "that we should have every dollar that we can possibly command before August 1st for the quarterly dividend of 2 per cent." The receiver of the Kansas Pacific ordered all expenses cut "to the very lowest points"; and his general superintendent began filling every vacancy at lower wages, taking off trains, laying off construction gangs and reducing the number of section men.

On the stock exchange, rails sank lower and lower. Baltimore & Ohio stock dropped from 191 at the start of 1876 to 79 in the early summer of 1877. Lake Shore fell from 96 to 50, Pennsylvania from 56 to 32. Even the rock-solid New York Central slipped from 117 to 90. In London, a vital source of railroad capital, American railroad bonds, good and bad, inspired an "intense feeling of anxiety and distrust." That winter and spring, 7,225 more miles of railroad went into receivership or under foreclosure.

And then, in one sector after another, the tide of battle seemed to turn.

The first break came on the labor front. Early in 1876 the Boston & Maine had cut wages 10 per cent for all employees. After its usual 6 per cent dividend, the road ended 1876 with a surplus. In January 1877 it raised the salaries of its president and superintendent. Self-confident after drubbing the Jersey Central and the Grand Trunk, the Brotherhood of Locomotive Engineers demanded a raise of ten cents per day for the road's sixty-seven engineers. President White contemptuously refused to spend an additional $6.70 a day. On the afternoon of February 12, after a four-hour ultimatum, the Brotherhood engineers stopped trains wherever they happened to be. "The result," commented the *Railway World,* "is awaited with much interest, because the failure of the strike will probably lead to the avoidance of future conspiracies against railway companies and the traveling public."

The company having put non-union standbys aboard every train, a sketchy and haphazard service was resumed within hours. And the hard times brought in crowds of job seekers. Most were unqualified, but some usable men turned up. The Brotherhood tried to buy off the strikebreakers. Other roads serving Boston offered aid and men to the Boston & Maine, a development which goaded Grand Chief Arthur into a vague threat of a general rail stoppage at Boston.

Despite Arthur's ill-judged threat, the public cheered for the Brotherhood. Commuters said they would rather walk than see the men beaten down. One prominent stockholder asserted publicly "that he didn't care if he missed his dividends for years to come, but he wanted the engineers to gain their point, for he believed they ought to be paid well." Another element showed its temper in a preview of things to come: Boston police were called in to clear the Boston & Maine station "of the crowd of loafers which has infested it since the beginning of the strike."

But public sympathy counted for nothing in a contest of treasuries. The road's officers ignored sentimental stockholders and stood on principle.

Gradually the Brotherhood ran out of money. Train service improved steadily, though the road was not back to normal until midsummer. The striking engineers were replaced and, in most cases, were still looking for work a year later.

During the strike, Boston heard from a son of the Adams family, a family long noted (with an exception named Samuel) for its impatience with both crowds and loafers. In 1866 Charles Francis Adams II, a firm-jawed ex-colonel of thirty-one, had deliberately mapped out the campaign of his life. "I fixed on the railroad system," he recalled later, "as the most developing force and largest field of the day, and determined to attach myself to it." First he wrote a stream of magazine articles on railroad problems. Then he proposed a State Board of Railroad Commissioners and in 1869, after three years of lobbying, saw it created—the first effective body of its kind in the nation. At once Adams became one of the three members and, as he frankly admitted, "by common consent the controlling mind."

The Boston & Maine strike was, in the opinion of himself and his friends, Commissioner Adams' finest hour. On the evening after his board's hearings on the strike, he wrote a report which was adopted and published without the change of a word. "A good, square blow well got in," he labeled it in his private diary. Condemning the strikers, it suggested impartial public investigation as the cure-all for labor disputes. As a supplement Adams offered the draft of a law imposing a heavy fine or a year or more in jail on any railroader who refused to handle the rolling stock of his own or another struck road, or abandoned a train between stations or intimidated strikebreakers. Even peaceful dissuasion of strikebreakers on company property would incur a $300 fine or three months in prison.

Adams' proposed strike law encountered some angry dissents. The *Railroad Gazette* warned against abridging the liberties of one class "in order to secure to another complete immunity from loss." Mutterings of discontent are heard all over the land," said the *Engineers' Journal*, "and unless this policy is abandoned, we shall hear the dread cry in our own land of 'bread or blood.'" And Adams' own state refused to enact his strike bill. But somewhat milder measures, punishing the obstruction or abandonment of trains but not the mere quitting of work, were passed that spring by Pennsylvania, Delaware, Michigan, New Jersey and Illinois.

Adams was not yet done. Early in March 1877, needing the money to buy himself a new bookcase, he dashed off a two-part article on "The Brotherhood of Locomotive Engineers" for the *Nation,* the country's most influential weekly. In light-hearted anonymity, he spoke his mind: "the Brotherhood of Locomotive Engineers has got to be broken up . . . it has become a mere common nuisance . . . a standing public menace. The only question is how to proceed so as to break it up most quietly and most effectually." He offered an answer: the corporations must create a regular graded service, with its promotions, its life insurance and its pensions. "The men would [not] . . . sacrifice, by joining in strikes, what represented the accumulation of years of service." In short, railroaders would serve under a sort of peace bond.

A week before Adams' *Nation* article appeared, a committee of engineers and firemen on the Philadelphia & Reading Railroad had petitioned the Reading management for a 20 per cent raise. Their petition set no time limit, it threatened no strike and it had nothing to do with the Engineers' Brotherhood. Five days after the *Nation* article, with the wildcat petition as a pretext, Reading engineers suddenly were told by the management to quit either the Brotherhood or the Reading. Those who stayed with the road might, if they chose, enjoy the benefits of a proposed company-run substitute for Brotherhood insurance. All the money an employee paid in, however, would be forfeited, if he quit his job or went on strike. "The Reading Railroad seems to agree with the *Nation*," commented the *Railroad Gazette*.

Denouncing the "scurrilous sheet" which he considered to have been the Reading's inspiration, Grand Chief Arthur hurried off to Philadelphia. Arthur must have grasped the meaning of the struggle. As the *Railroad Gazette* put it, "in this case, really, it is the company and not the Brotherhood which strikes." Evidently the forces of management were on the move not just to tame the Brotherhood but to "break it up." And in this crucial fight, the Brotherhood was up against a man who had already proved himself to be organized labor's most brilliant and remorseless enemy: the Reading's president, Franklin B. Gowen.

In 1877 Franklin Gowen was forty-one and at the height of his fame. In an age of business giants few matched his command over the public's emotions. Finance was his field; but his soul, like his magnificent voice and his solidly handsome face, belonged to an actor. In his heyday he could deliver a stockholders' report from the stage of the Philadelphia Academy of Music and hold a large audience spellbound. His wit, eloquence and stage presence seemed to administer a local anesthetic to the seat of logic. Even in cold print, and in this age of understatement, his speeches tend to unsettle the judgment.

Gowen's talent for melodrama had served him well as a young Pottsville lawyer. In his adventurous career as president of the Philadelphia & Reading Railroad—a height he scaled in his early thirties—that talent was indispensable. His life was a cavalcade of thrillers, written, produced and directed by their star. Most grandiose of all, perhaps, was his move to make the coal-carrying Reading its own principal customer by purchasing a lion's share of the Schuylkill County coal fields it served. This massive gulp gave the Reading a case of financial indigestion which in 1877 was already acute. But Gowen's gift of corporate faith healing staved off the collapse for years.

Gowen never set up company stores through which to gouge his employees. He insisted on investigation of every injustice charged against bosses. In 1870 he arranged for the first written contract between American miners and operators, and in 1875 set up the first company-supported benefit system in the anthracite industry. The public knew Franklin Gowen best, however, by his crusade for (as he put it) "the right of the individual laboring man against the tyranny of trades unions."

Gowen's reputation as a union buster was solidly established in 1875 with the destruction of the Workingmen's Benevolent Association, an organization of anthracite miners which had been the first notable industrial union in the United States. It seems to have been the individual mine operators, rather than Gowen, who polished off the W. B. A. But Gowen helped rally and inspirit the operators. And he himself later bragged to the Reading stockholders that he had done the deed, though it cost the company $4,000,000.

In 1877 Gowen was fresh from his greatest dramatic success: the overthrow of the "Molly Maguires." Under the spell of his romantic oratory, the entire country came to believe that a secret band of labor terrorists who called themselves "Molly Maguires" had held the Schuylkill mining region in their grip for twenty years past, murdering mine foremen, superintendents and strikebreakers in vague but enormous numbers. After diligent research some historians remain unconvinced that any such secret organization ever existed. Two brief spells of violence had indeed troubled the Schuylkill region like many another community in those brawling times, one outbreak in the mid-sixties, the other in the summer of 1875. Six murders were committed by members of the Ancient Order of Hibernians in the latter period; but the murderers seem to have acted in a purely private capacity, and only three of the victims could have been involved in labor troubles.

Nevertheless, Gowen's forensic fireworks cast such quibbles into the shade. As one of the counsel for the prosecution, Gowen dominated the trial of six alleged "Mollies" in the spring of 1876. The climax came when a Pinkerton detective took the stand with a thrilling story of counterespionage in behalf of Gowen and the Reading. Perhaps the world believed it all because it was just too good to be false. Certainly the story, scarcely altered or embellished, did well as a play, *Secret Service,* and provided Conan Doyle with a full-length Sherlock Holmes novel, *The Valley of Fear.*

By March 1877, when Gowen struck at the Engineers' Brotherhood, ten "Mollies" lay under sentence of death; and before the long hysteria ended, the gallows would claim ten more. The Reading's "Coal and Iron Police" was meanwhile being transformed from a group of mine guards into an efficient police force. Violence and crime were to continue in Schuylkill County, but no one thereafter would dare lift a hand against the Reading.

Peter Arthur and his Brotherhood met the Reading's attack squarely. The grand chief, himself a fluent and persuasive orator, spoke to large and sympathetic audiences throughout the region. When the Reading's superintendent turned down a request for arbitration, the Brotherhood called a strike for midnight on Saturday, April 14, 1877. Half of the Reading's engineers quit, carefully taking all trains to their destinations first, so as to keep clear of the new Pennsylvania law.

Surprised in his turn, Gowen recovered quickly. Loyal men were given raises. Dispatchers and superintendents were called out of Sunday services and put to work, some still wearing silk hats. On Monday Gowen began hiring new men. Unlike the Boston & Maine, he took on many greenhorns, to the heavy cost of the road in burned-out engines and wrecked cars. The Brotherhood made the most of these mishaps, ringing changes on the Ashtabula theme; Gowen counterattacked with charges of Brotherhood sabotage. But trains were running regularly even if hazardously within a week. And Gowen was able to announce "with pardonable pride" that not one of the Reading's 22,000 men "will hereafter be obliged to submit to the degradation of asking his fellowman for leave to earn his daily bread."

With head high, but treasury low and prestige trailing, the Brotherhood of Locomotive Engineers was now in full retreat.

Meanwhile, peace impended on another front. The trunk-line rate wars had scarcely started in 1874 when the combatants began seeking a durable settlement. Time after time agreements were negotiated only to collapse. Sometimes the fault lay with ambitious underlings, anxious only to make a good showing for their own divisions. Sometimes the top men turned marplots. The death of Commodore Vanderbilt changed the picture. The father had loved a good fight for its own sake. The son, William H. Vanderbilt, preferred a compromise, so long as there was profit in it.

On March 9, 1877, therefore, President John W. Garrett of the Baltimore & Ohio wrote jubilantly to his London banker: "I have recently spent a week in New York, engaged in what will prove, I hope, the most important conference ever held between the Trunk Lines." The other conferees were Vanderbilt, Hugh J. Jewett of the Erie and Thomas A. Scott of the Pennsylvania. Conversations, reported Garrett, were "full and free." For the first time in trunk-line history, all troubles and difficulties were reviewed minutely, "in a spirit of candor and justice, without the slightest interference or influence on the part of subordinates." Garrett used all his "personal influence" to bring Vanderbilt and Jewett into harmony, and Scott of the Pennsylvania "joined cordially and heartily in this work... Mr. Vanderbilt, for the first time in my knowledge at such a meeting fully representing his entire lines, showed . . . a sincere . . . cooperative spirit." Rates on westbound freight were hiked 50 per cent immediately as a sort of aperitif. "The great principle upon which we all joined to act was," Garrett, "to earn more and to spend less."

After this heartwarming agreement in principle came a series of conferences, lasting through the spring, for the working out of details. In mid-May the four leaders developed a traffic pooling scheme like one already successful among southern roads. It applied only to freight westbound from New York, the Erie and the New York Central each to get 33 per cent of the tonnage, the Pennsylvania 25 per cent and the Baltimore & Ohio 9 per cent. Eastbound freight could not be pooled so well, because many independent feeder lines were involved. Later, however, similar pools might be made for freight westbound from other cities. Though the Grand Trunk still held aloof, circumstances had toned down its former intransigence. On June 8, after "a very harmonious meeting," the heads of the four major American lines formally signed the pooling treaty. The war was over.

It seemed that railroad luck was finally turning. The grasshopper scare in the West proved to be a false alarm; by late spring, a bumper crop seemed in prospect, with consequent fat freight earnings at harvesttime. The disputed Presidency of the United States was awarded to Rutherford B. Hayes just in time to avert anarchy and possible bloodshed. Under pressure from public opinion and his Southern Democrat allies, the new President pulled Federal troops out of the last three occupied states of the South. Reconstruction was over. The new tranquillity of both North and South encouraged business planning. Even the outbreak of the Russo-Turkish War in late April brought a certain ghoulish satisfaction. Grain prices rose immediately.

Yet this was not enough. The trunk lines were determined not only to "earn more," but also to "spend less." How to do this? They could drop unprofitable services formerly maintained for competition's sake. Higher rates for grain tended to reduce volume and hence operating expenses. Above all, the recent routing of the Engineers' Brotherhood invited a cut in wages.

The Boston & Maine strike in February had led to numerous proposals that employers combine against organized labor. In April it was noted that a recent traffic pool among the anthracite carriers had helped the Reading to weather its shutdown. Guaranteed its share of the season's coal business anyway, that road could hold out all summer without actually losing a ton of coal freight, the major source of its income. Naturally enough, in view of all this, people now suspected a similar strike insurance plan among the four trunk lines. One of the four would reduce wages. The other three would hold off, and the pooling arrangement would make up to the fourth for any strike losses. Then the remaining roads would take their turns.

The Pennsylvania made its cut a month before the pool took effect, but a secret agreement could have taken care of this. The trunk-line pool as published did not include eastbound traffic to New York or any at all to Philadelphia. But later testimony by Scott implied the existence of an unpublicized eastbound pool, beginning a month before the wage cut and lasting into the summer. Scott denied under oath that the trunk lines had agreed among themselves to cut wages. But in weighing this, we might remember that a prominent Baptist layman named John D. Rockefeller stated not long afterward—also under oath—that he had no interest in the Standard Oil Trust. And Scott was less noted for piety than was Rockefeller. The best that history can do is to bring in a Scottish verdict of "not proven."

In any case, financial desperation, plus the notion that labor had been tamed, made the pay cuts logical enough. "The Brotherhood is destroyed as a dictatorial body," said the New York Times in April; "neither railroad nor engineer will fear it henceforth or regard its ukases. ... Both steps in the action of the Reading Company—the stand against the union and the plan of substitution as to its benefits—are an example which should be imitated by employers generally." A few days later, the president of the Illinois Central wrote the board chairman: "If Mr. Gowen is successful ... all the companies in the west could combine and offer the engineers the same or even better advantages than they now obtain in their own association." And he sent to Gowen for a half-dozen copies of the Reading's insurance plan. Other roads did likewise, and included in their letters best wishes for Gowen's success. On May 15 the Missouri Pacific cut engineers' pay by 12 per cent. The men took it quietly.

But the real test would come only when the eastern trunk lines made the experiment. And the railroad world therefore braced itself expectantly on May 24 when the Pennsylvania announced a 10 per cent reduction, to take effect June 1 for all employees earning more than a dollar a day. On the Pennsylvania, this would be the second such cut since the Panic.

Would the men submit? Or would the "mutterings of discontent" heard by the Engineers' Journal indeed harden into "the dread cry of 'bread or blood' "?

THE CROSSING

[There were troubles at Martinsburg, West Virginia, and at Baltimore, but when the rioting began at Pittsburgh, it exceeded in violence and destruction, in arson and looting, anything short of actual warfare. In the following selection, from the same book, note the elements present in the trouble at Pittsburgh: the mob, the teenagers, the leaders, the arson, the looting, and the mob psychosis.

References to Adjutant General Latta and General Brinton allude to Pennsylvania state officials who were trying to maintain law and order at Pittsburgh. "The Crossing" refers to the 28th Street crossing, mentioned in the first sentence, near where the "great barbecue" began.]

... The great barbecue began at about quarter to eleven with the firing of a freight car two or three blocks beyond the Twenty-eighth Street crossing. Some said that small boys began it; but whoever struck the match, strong backs must have given the burning car the impetus with which it careered down the grade, trailing smoke and sparks through the darkness. Perhaps deliberately, a misplaced switch sent the car tumbling off the track near the "upper roundhouse" at Twenty-eighth Street. Then a half dozen coke cars rumbled down and fetched up against the derailed car with a crash heard plainly by the thousands of spectators on the hillside opposite. Oil cars were touched off and shoved along. Great clouds of smoke boiled up from the flaming mass. Whenever cars slowed up on their descent into the inferno, a gang of twenty or so would give them a fresh start. According to one spectator, these expediters were "nearly all boys, fourteen to sixteen or seventeen years of age." The prime movers in all this, however, were grown men who went at it systematically, passing orders back and forth like a gang of efficient workmen. One of these, a machinist from the city of Allegheny across the river, was recognized as he crouched in a coke car setting fire to a pile of shavings; as a result, he later drew a six-year term in the penitentiary.

The sand house caught fire first. Then, very slowly, the flames worked to the upper roundhouse. Long before the buildings got going, however, the light from strings of burning cars had reddened the night sky. Before the huge crowd on the hillside a spectacle unfolded to be remembered for a lifetime. Reflected fire glittered from the eyes of thousands. General Brinton, at bay in the lower roundhouse, first saw the glare in the sky about eleven. Latta and his frightened colleagues watched the spreading colors from their hotel window a mile away. Before the night was out, farmers a dozen or so miles out in the country began to wonder about the strange glow on the horizon over Pittsburgh way.

The same financial pinch that cut off half the Pittsburgh police force in July had also nipped twenty-two men from the fire department, leaving

From *Harper's Weekly*, Vol. 21, No. 1076 (August 11, 1877).

"The Great Strike—Pittsburgh in the hands of the mob."

a working force of ninety-four. These did their best. At about eleven o'clock the crowd on the hillside clearly heard Number Seven's steam engine start up at Twenty-third and Penn, heard the clatter of hoofs, the noise of the gong and the rumble of wheels, and then a significant lull, peppered by the sound of distant oaths: at pistol point in a Penn Avenue gutter Number Seven's crew were drawing their engine's fire. Other engines rocked along the streets, horses at a gallop, until the cursing crowd grabbed the halters. Number Three ran a gauntlet of musket and pistol fire for several blocks, but all in vain. When hose was laid the crowd cut it. A fireman knocked down one elegant gentleman whom he found strolling alongside the hose, punching holes in it with a sword cane. One gang of rioters hauled a cannon along Penn Avenue, paused at Twenty-third, aimed the gun at some hose carriages and yelled: "If you don't get out of that, we'll blow you to hell!" Four men with pistols menaced a hose-laying crew until the firemen explained that the hose would only be used to safeguard nonrailroad property. At last the firemen reeled in their hose to save it from the knives of the crowd. All that night the flames fed without stint.

A large part of Pittsburgh's population stayed up to see the show. Thousands made the hillside their grandstand, notwithstanding its recent unhealthiness for onlookers. Thousands more filled Liberty Street down to the Union Depot and beyond. The spectator element watched quietly, almost raptly. The shouts of individual actors in the drama therefore could be heard for a considerable distance. These active participants were comparatively few. Before the lower roundhouse several hundred took the part of besiegers, stupidly collecting on the Liberty Street side, though the yard side was far more vulnerable. A much smaller group, perhaps less than a score, cast themselves as incendiaries and went to work with quiet absorption. Much burning was done at the top of the grade, near Thirty-first and Thirty-second streets. All along the car-packed yards, however, new fires broke forth from time to time at one isolated point after another. In the Pan Handle's yard near Eleventh Street, a city fireman begged: "Don't do it, or you'll set the city on fire!" "We don't care a damn if we do," shouted the arsonists and lit their fires. Still other participants confined themselves to pillaging—or "salvaging," they might have called it. Looting began as a by-product of the burning, then became an end in itself. At midnight, most of the pilferers were teen-age boys and girls, perhaps obeying parental directions, perhaps working on their own hook (for this was, after all, the age of enterprise, and a good Alger hero seized his every chance to acquire goods). Adults soon joined in. By one in the morning, the streets teemed like ant runs with files of citizens bearing burdens. The pillagers, like the firebrands, proceeded almost sedately. At the stationhouse near Penn and Twenty-sixth, the police arrested evident looters as they passed, and the culprits submitted with remarkable passivity. Elsewhere vagrant rumors occasionally scattered the looters in brief panic, but always they returned to the job.

The derailment of the first few cars near Twenty-eighth Street had frustrated the besieging mob's initial attempt to burn out the Philadelphia troops at Twenty-sixth; accessions to the blaze merely piled up at the higher point. At about two o'clock Sunday morning General Brinton's attention was called to a dark object at Liberty and Twenty-seventh. Presently a cloud passed away, and moonlight glinted from a brass field-piece—captured, it later transpired, from the Pittsburgh militia. The gun was aimed at the machine shop, where a number of troops were ensconced. Brinton had fifty men cover the gun with their rifles. As a rioter took the lanyard in his hand, Brinton gave the command to fire. When the smoke cleared away, eleven men lay dead or wounded in the street. Dogged volunteers took their places. Brinton's men shouted a warning, then drove them off with renewed rifle fire. For several hours the shout was heard at intervals, "Go back, go back, one, two, three," followed by the cracking of rifles. Not once did the besiegers manage to fire their little cannon.

As the pale light of Sunday morning dawned, the besiegers gave up the effort and resorted once again to the torch. A track of the Allegheny Valley Railroad ran unobstructed along the Liberty Street wall and passed near the lower roundhouse. Defying the Philadelphians' bullets, a gang of rioters leaped up on the wall and began shoving burning freight cars toward the roundhouse and its adjacent buildings. The troops threw car wheels on the tracks and blocked the fire cars, but not at a very comfortable distance. Fire extinguishers and a hose were discovered inside the roundhouse and put to work. For a couple of hours the fire was held at bay. At last the rioters found some cars loaded with whisky and "high wines," pushed them as close as possible and set them ablaze. Somehow the burning liquor found its way into the cellar of the machine shop, which was presently bathed in flame. Thence the fire spread to other buildings. The roundhouse held out longest, though burning cinders big as a man's hand filled the air around it. Coughing in dense smoke, General Brinton and his staff decided that the time had come to march. At ten minutes past eight Sunday morning the troops made their exit in perfect order. The roundhouse roof was burning. Across Liberty Street lumberyards and shanties were aflame for an entire block, ignited not by the crowd but by heat and sparks from burning railroad property.

ATTITUDE OF THE CHURCHES

The Protestant clergy wielded great influence over American thought in the Gilded Age. Dwight Moody was the precursor of Billy Sunday in the 1920's and of Billy Graham in the 1950's and 1960's. Russell Conwell, a spellbinder who composed a single sermon that seemed to say all that needed to be said, helped cement in men's minds the theory that a man who was poor had only himself to blame. "Acres of Diamonds" was delivered to more than 13,000,000 people, and the title and Conwell's name became indissoluble. But the most controversial man of the cloth was Henry Ward Beecher. An orator who occasionally was accused of falling from the morality expected of the Elect, he at least knew on which side his bread was buttered, as is exemplified in his two sermons delivered during the Great Strike. They are given here as they were reported in The New York Times. In all fairness to Beecher, however, there is a possibility that the reporter misquoted him or slanted the story. Yet the general philosophy is emphatically characteristic of Henry Ward Beecher's approach to society.

HENRY WARD BEECHER, Two Sermons

THE PULPIT ON THE SITUATION
REV. HENRY WARD BEECHER CONDEMNS THE STRIKES
AND DECLARES THAT A FAMILY CAN LIVE ON A DOLLAR A DAY

Plymouth Church was crowded last evening by a large audience, and Mr. Beecher in the course of his discourse alluded to the great railroad strike. He said that disorder had broken out all along the great roads of several portions of the country, and riots of an unusual magnitude had taken place.

The Sabbath day was not, he said, one of stillness, for there were military movements throughout the land, and from their city soldiers were being dispatched to quell the riots. In a few days peace would be restored. Such outbreaks were but transient bubbles, which burst almost as soon as they were formed. They sprang from ignorance and passion. Such riots arose because their promoters and those who abetted them were ignorant of political economy. The question of labor and capital was a

From *The New York Times*, July 22, 1877 and July 30, 1877.

question of citizenship and corporate life. He proceeded to eulogize the working classes, and dwelt particularly on the industry, sobriety and heroism of the railroad employees, and pointed out the necessity for harmonious working together of the laborer and the capitalist. He explained at great length the elementary principles of political economy, and dwelt particularly on the causes which give rise to the long depression of trade in this country. This portion of his discourse was a reproduction of his lecture on "Hard Times," and was frequently applauded. He then said, what right had the working men, the members of those great organizations, to say to anyone, "You shall not work for wages which we refuse." They had a perfect right to say to the employers, "We shall not work for you," but they had no right to tyrannize over their fellowmen. They had put themselves in an attitude of tyrannical opposition to all law and order and they could not be defended. The necessities of the great railroad companies demanded that there should be a reduction in wages. There must be continual shrinkage until things come back to the gold standard, and wages, as well as greenbacks, provisions, and property, must share in it. It was true that $1 a day was not enough to support a man and five children, if a man insisted on smoking and drinking beer. Was not a dollar a day enough to buy bread? Water costs nothing. [Laughter] Man cannot live by bread, it is true; but the man who cannot live on bread and water is not fit to live. [Laughter] When a man is educated away from the power of self-denial, he is falsely educated. A family may live on good water and bread at night. [Continued laughter] Such may be called the bread of affliction. Thousands would be very glad of a dollar a day, and it added to the sin of the men on strike for them to turn round and say to those men, "You can do so, but you shall not." There might be special cases of hardship, but the great laws of political economy could not be set at defiance. He concluded that, in the end, the men on strike would be defeated, trade resumed, and prosperity once more reign throughout the world. [Applause]

[This was too much for honest working people to take, and Beecher was roundly denounced for his stand, so much so that he replied to his adversaries the very next Sunday, the first time he had had to explain himself, he said, in his 30 years in the pulpit. Ed.]

COMMUNISM DENOUNCED

So much discussion has been had, and so much ill will disseminated against Rev. Henry Ward Beecher at communistic meetings of his sermon on the 22nd inst., that it was shrewdly guessed that Mr. Beecher would take an early opportunity of more clearly defining his position on the question of the rights of laboring men. The expectation of such a discussion may, and probably did, have some effect in filling the interior of Plymouth Church last evening. The church was in fact overcrowded. On the pulpit were a number of vases of flowers, which rather relieved the sombre look of the stand below the organ loft. The Police authorities, in anticipation of any trouble which might have arisen, sent about 30 policemen in citizen's clothes, who were distributed among the congregation, and a squad of detectives were placed in the immediate neighborhood of the church. Mr. Beecher seemed in good health and spirits, and entered into his discussion of the questions of labor and capital, which formed the theme of his sermon, with apparent earnestness and great feeling. In the prayer preceding the discourse Mr. Beecher invoked the Deity to have a blessing rest on all the land, and to bless those who have taken part in the recent disturbances by giving them a knowledge of better ways. ... A collection in behalf of the poor was then taken up, and was apparently not grudgingly given, for the baskets of the ushers were full when deposited on the pulpit-stand.

Mr. Beecher then said that before beginning his sermon he desired to make a few remarks upon the events which have occurred since Sunday last. He said he had been grossly misrepresented—not willfully or intentionally, but by careless reporting—as saying what he did not say and does not believe. The reports had had the effect of bringing to him a score of letters, some of them obscene, others expressing indignation, some threatening, many from cowardly men ashamed of their own names, besides others pleading for the cause of humanity and for the working man. He had received some letters with great pleasure and pain; pleasure, because he liked to be addressed in a manly way from a friend, though he were chided; pain, because his life had been devoted to the cause of the working man and the oppressed, both here and abroad, and he felt the wrong which was done him by such reports as those referred to. So he would step aside for the first time in 30 years to explain his position. He had said nothing which would indicate even the odious meaning which had been given to his remarks. His own services, he thought, should have saved him from the unjust imputation put upon his remarks. Mr. Beecher was here applauded, but the applause was mingled with the hissing of one or two persons, who afterward restrained themselves and were silent.

Mr. Beecher then began his sermon taking his text from Acts xxii, 28: "And Paul said, But I was free-born." Freedom, said Mr. Beecher, has been the aspiration of the human race from the beginning, and men have always longed for liberty. This prerogative was anciently conferred by Kings on privileged classes. The history of the human race has been the history of men who sought to obtain large personal power and influence. To bring about the liberty of the whole mass of society and the happiness of all men because they are men, of all citizens because they are citizens —this is the study which should more deeply than any other interest every thoughtful, Christian man. Is the great working class oppressed? asked the speaker. Yes, undoubtedly it is, he answered, both by the Governments and the rich men, and by the educated classes. This is not because the Governments, the rich men, or the educated forces desire to oppress them, but because it must be so. It is only in the household that it is possible for intelligence, strength, and power not to oppress ignorance, weakness, and helplessness. When men are ignorant and poor and weak, they can't help being oppressed. That is so by a great natural law. It is the cause of being against no being or very little being. It is to say that intelligence gets ahead of ignorance. It is to say that a ton outweighs a half-ton. It can't be said this is so by reason of selfishness or ignorance. The populations of Europe are largely ignorant—that's the matter—and therefore they are largely kept under. They are lacking in personal development; they are lacking in self-government; they are lacking in civil control; they are small in the waist and smaller in the head. They reap the misfortunes of inferiority, not because men desire to oppress them, but because it must be so.

. . . We look upon the importation of the communistic and like European notions as abominations. Their notions and theories that the Government should be paternal and take care of the welfare of its subjects and provide them with labor, is un-American. . . . The American doctrine is that it is the duty of the Government merely to protect the people while they are taking care of themselves—nothing more than that. "Hands off," we say to the Government: "See to it that we are protected in our rights and our individuality. No more than that." The theories of Europe in regard to the community of property we reject because they are against natural law and will never be practicable. God has intended the great to be great, and the little to be little. . . . Persons have the right to work when and where they please, as long as they please, and for what they please, and any attempt to infringe upon this right and to put good workmen on a level with poor workmen—any such attempt to regiment labor is preposterous. . . .

Mr. Beecher made an allusion to the old New Englanders who worked from before sunrise until long after sunset, as persons who did not shun work, who kept the bodily nature subservient to the higher nature, and who advanced by reason of such conduct. He said the workers should call upon God and stop using tobacco and beer, subdue their passions, and try by self-denial to make homes for themselves and families. . . .

ATTITUDE OF THE INTELLECTUALS

Eric Goldman in his excellent book Rendezvous With Destiny *refers to the "Steel Chain of Ideas" which had to be broken before labor could achieve rights which today are accepted without question by most Americans. The vehemence with which most of the nation looked upon the strikers is well exemplified in the following impassioned editorial from* The Nation, *considered in that day an enlightened magazine.*

EDITORIAL FROM *THE NATION*, The Late Riots

... We have had what appears a widespread rising, not against political oppression or unpopular government, but against society itself. What is most curious about it is that it has probably taken people here nearly as much by surprise as people in Europe. The optimism in which most Americans are carefully trained, and which the experience of life justifies to the industrious, energetic, and provident, combined with the long-settled political habit of considering riotous poor as the products of a monarchy and aristocracy, and impossible in the absence of "down-trodden masses," has concealed from most of the well-to-do and intelligent classes of the population the profound changes which have during the last thirty years been wrought in the composition and character of the population, especially in the great cities. Vast additions have been made to it within that period, to whom American political and social ideals appeal but faintly, if at all, and who carry in their very blood traditions which give universal suffrage an air of menace to many of the things which civilized men hold most dear. So complete has this illusion been that up to the day of the outbreak at Martinsburg thousands, even of the most reflective class, were gradually ridding themselves of the belief that force would be much longer necessary, or, indeed, was now necessary in the work of government. It is not many weeks since we sought in these columns to combat this hallucination, apropos of the woman-suffrage question and the South Carolina imbroglio; but since our article appeared, one of the most thoughtful poli-

Editorial, "The Late Riots," from *The Nation*, Vol. 25, No. 631 (August 2, 1877), pp. 68–69.

ticians in the country, Senator Bayard, of Delaware, delivered an address before the Phi Beta Kappa Society at Cambridge, in which, with an eye, however, to the Southern States, rather than to discontented laborers, he preached the possibility of government by moral suasion solely, with great energy and pathos, and he has probably had tens of thousands of readers who rolled the doctrine under their tongues as a sweet morsel.

Another illusion which the riots have dispelled is that the means provided by the several States for the protection of life and property, in the shape of police and militia, are at all adequate. Riots on the scale on which they have taken place during the past fortnight put almost as much strain on the nerves and on the discipline of the force called on to suppress them as the operations of regular warfare. A lawful enemy forms an organization which keeps to itself in a defined position, and its attacks are controlled by rules with which men are more or less familiar, and dictated by motives which can be guessed, and the force of which can be weighed. A mob, on the other hand, is essentially irrational, and its conduct has all the fitfulness and incomprehensibleness of that of a wild beast, and is just as merciless and destructive. It requires, therefore, to be met by a coolness and cohesiveness, and a presence of mind, which are not often called for in actual campaigning. Nothing can supply these things but the *habit* of obedience—not simply intellectual readiness to obey, as part of a contract, but the habitual readiness to obey a particular man, produced by obeying him every day on all sorts of small matters, and the familiarity with his person and character which results from living under his orders. This regular troops have; this even the best militia has not and cannot have. The consequence is that a militia regiment, no matter how well drilled, when it finds itself acting against a mob, and the temper of the men begins to be tried by missiles and insults, loses very rapidly its sense of organization. The company and the regiment and the officers fade from the private's view, and he becomes in his own eyes an individual man, at whom a fellow on the sidewalk is throwing brickbats, so he gratifies his rage and provides for his personal safety by taking a shot at him. The mob, on its side, takes more or less the same view of the force; that is, it believes it has got before it a body very much like itself, although armed and uniformed, and does not believe in its discipline and cohesiveness, and does believe it can dissolve it by vigorous pelting, or a series of single combats, or by appeals to the sympathies of the men. Regulars, on the other hand, it knows to be a machine—the most terrible of all the machines invented by man, by which the wills of a thousand are wielded, even unto death, by the will of one, and which knows nothing of single shots, which feels every blow through its whole mass, and, when it strikes, strikes like the flail of destiny, without remorse, or pity, or misgiving. The consequence is that many of the horrors and aggravations of mob-risings come from the unsteadiness of militia. Killing by militia is apt to rouse a thirst for vengeance, like the killing in a street-fight, while a volley from regulars has the terrors of legal execution. Of course there are militia regiments which are exceptions to this rule, and several during the late troubles have rendered inestimable service; but they are not to be relied on for serious emergencies, such as we trust every sensible man now sees are among the contingencies of American life.

The kindest thing which can be done for the great multitudes of untaught men who have been received on these shores, and are daily arriving, and who are torn perhaps even more here than in Europe by wild desires and wilder dreams, is to show them promptly that society as here organized, on individual freedom of thought and action, is impregnable, and can be no more shaken than the order of nature. The most cruel thing is to let them suppose, even for one week, that if they had only chosen their time better, or had been better led or better armed, they would have succeeded in forcing it to capitulate. In what way better provision, in the shape of public force, should be made for its defence we have no space left to discuss, but that it will not do to be caught again as the rising at Martinsburg caught us; that it would be fatal to private and public credit and security to allow a state of things to subsist in which 8,000 or 9,000 day-laborers of the lowest class can suspend, even for a whole day, the traffic and industry of a great nation, merely as a means of extorting ten or twenty cents a day more wages from their employers, we presume everybody now sees. Means of prompt and effectual prevention—so plainly effectual that it will never need to be resorted to—must be provided, either by an increase of the standing army or some change in the organization of the militia which will improve its discipline and increase its mobility. There are, of course, other means of protection against labor-risings than physical ones, which ought not to be neglected, though we doubt if they can be made to produce much effect on the present generation. The exercise of greater watchfulness over their tongues by philanthropists, in devising schemes of social improvement, and in affecting to treat all things as open to discussion, and every question as having two sides, for purposes of legislation as well as for purposes of speculation, is one of them. Some of the talk about the laborer and his rights that we have listened to on the platform and in literature during the last fifteen years, and of the capacity even of the most grossly ignorant, such as the South Carolina field-hand, to reason upon and even manage the interests of a great community, has been enough, considering the sort of ears on which it now falls, to reduce our great manufacturing districts to the condition of the Pennsylvania mining regions, and put our very civilization in peril. Persons of humane tendencies ought to remember that we live in a world of stern realities, and that the blessings we enjoy have not been showered upon us like the rain from heaven. Our superiority to the Ashantees or the Kurds is not due to right thinking or right feeling only, but to the determined fight which the more enlightened part of the community has waged from generation to generation against the ignorance and brutality, now of one class and now of another. In trying to carry on the race to better things nobody is wholly right or wise. In all controversies there are wrongs on both sides, but most certainly the presumptions in the labor controversy have always been in favor of the sober, orderly, industrious, and prudent, who work and accumulate and bequeath. It is they who brought mankind out of the woods and caves, and keep them out; and all discussion which places them in a position of either moral or mental inferiority to those who contrive not only to own nothing, but to separate themselves from property-holders in feeling or interest, is mischievous as well as foolish, for it strikes a blow at the features of human character which raise man above the beasts.

ATTITUDE OF POLITICAL PARTIES

The political repercussions from the Great Strike were not slow in appearing. In the week following the worst of the disorders the Ohio Republican Party met in convention. It "viewed with alarm," as all political parties are expected to do, but in advocating remedies for the plight of the workers, the Ohio segment of the Grand Old Party demonstrated that there was some concern on the part of the politically active segments of the population. During the Gilded Age there was indeed some progress toward solving the nation's problems, though the solutions—or attempts at solutions—came years after the problems appeared. Democracy, in other words, did meet the challenge of the new age, slowly, cumbersomely, and not always satisfactorily, yet irrepressibly and positively.

Resolution of the Ohio Republican Party, August, 1877

Resolved, That we view with alarm the present disturbed condition of the country, as evinced by the extensive strikes of workingmen, and followed by the destruction of life and property in different parts of the country; and while we deprecate each and every resort to violence or disorders, and cordially approve the action of our national and state authorities in their efforts to enforce the supremacy of the law, yet we do most heartily sympathize with the condition of the honest and industrious laborers who are willing to work, but remain unemployed, or are employed at wages inadequate to comfort and independence; and, as an earnest of our desire to find a remedy for their condition, we recommend, first, that Congress establish a National Bureau of Industry; second, that Congress exert its authority over all national highways of trade by prescribing and enforcing such reasonable regulations as will tend to promote safety of travel, secure fair returns for capital invested and fair wages to employees, preventing mismanagement, improper discriminations, and the aggrandizement of officials at the expense of stockholders and shippers and employees; third, that provisions be made for statutory arbitrations between employers and employees to adjust controversies, reconcile interests, and establish justice and equity between them.

THE STRIKER'S CAUSE

In the Gilded Age it was always difficult to defend a strike per se, but when destructive rioting took place along with it, the denunciation was so great that the voice of honest labor was stifled. Yet occasionally a literate and clear-thinking man would take pen and paper and defend the

---

"Resolution of the Ohio Republican Party, August, 1877," quoted in *The Nation,* Vol. 25, No. 632 (August 9, 1877), p. 84.

laborer and his actions. Sometimes he found a strong vehicle to disseminate these arguments. The influential North American Review dared publish a laborer's position in its September, 1877 issue. But notice that the editors attempted to protect themselves from criticism by adding a significant "Note" at the end of the Striker's article.

"A STRIKER," *Fair Wages*

The newspapers have fallen into line to defend the railway companies, who thus have brought all the great guns of public opinion to bear on one side of the fight so that the strikers have got the worst of it before the community. We have been so handled that if a workingman stands out to speak his mind, the public have theirs so full of pictures of him and his doings in the illustrated papers, that he is listened to as if he was a convicted rough pleading in mitigation of penalty, instead of an honest and sincere man asking for a fair show. I would not have anyone mistake what my principles are and have been. I don't envy any man his wealth, whether it is ill-gotten or not. I am a workingman, therefore an honest one, and would refuse a dollar I did not earn, for I am neither a beggar to accept charity nor a thief to take what belongs to another, however he came by it. If it be his according to law, I, for one, am ready to protect him in his legal rights, and in return I want to be protected in what I believe to be mine.

Forty years ago my father came over to this country from Sweden. He had a small business and a large family. In Europe business does not grow as fast as children come, and poverty over there is an inheritance. He heard that North America was peopled and governed by working men, and the care of the States was mainly engaged in the welfare and prosperity of labor. That moved him, and so I came to be born here. He, and millions like him, made this country their home, and their homes have mainly made this country what it is. Until lately the States kept their faith and promise to the people, and we, the people, showed ours when trouble came; an assessment of blood was made on our shares of liberty, and we paid it. That is our record. We did not fight for this party or that party, but for the country and against all that were against the United States.

I am no politician, caring little whether one party or another holds the fort at Washington. My father, who, like me, was a workingman, used to

---

"Fair Wages," by "A Striker," in *The North American Review*, Vol. 125, No. 258 (September–October, 1877), pp. 322–326.

say a country fared best where a strong and sound opposition party kept justice awake and made power behave.

So it was before the war, but since then, it seems to me, the power has got fixed so long in one set of hands that things are settling down into a condition like what my father left behind him in Europe forty years ago, and what stands there still. I mean the slavery of labor. The landed aristocracy over there made the feudal system, just as the moneyed men of this continent are now making a ruling class. As the aristocracy used to make war on each other, so in our time the millionaires live on each other's ruin. As the feudal lords hired mercenary soldiers to garrison their strongholds and to prey on the common people, so the railway lords and stock-exchange barons hire a mercenary press to defend their power, the object of both being the same: the spoils of labor. It looks very like as though this country was settling down into the form and system we fled from in Europe.

The rights and value of labor were acknowledged here forty years ago because the country wanted hands. Now we have made it rich, it turns our own earnings against us, and its prosperity becomes our disaster. We are told to look at Europe and perceive that this condition of affairs is the inevitable result of growth, of population, of wealth; but we look over there, and find that discontent, rebellion, and war are also the inevitable results, and it was to avoid such results these States declared themselves free, that Americans should have a government that was not a conspiracy.

That government has been regarded by the laboring classes of Europe and by our people as the stronghold of the workingman, and in this our present difficulty we are referred to its Constitution which should afford us a remedy for our grievances, and the ballot-box is the panacea for all and every complaint. It is not so; and those who point to the remedy know it to be a sham—they know they can buy idlers and vagabonds enough to swell the ranks of wealth and run up a majority whenever a show of hands is required. They recruit the very men that wrecked Pittsburgh, and would pillage New York if they dared to face us, the workingmen, that fill the ranks of the militia.

We are sick of this game, we are soul-weary of looking around for some sympathy or spirit of justice, and finding none, we turn to each other and form brotherhoods and unions, depots of the army of labor, officered by the skilled mechanic.

This organized force is now in process of formation, and prepared to meet the great questions of the age: Has labor any rights? If so, what are they? Our claim is simple. We demand *fair wages*.

We say that the man able and willing to work, and for whom there is work to do, is entitled to wages sufficient to provide him with enough food, shelter, and clothing to sustain and preserve his health and strength.

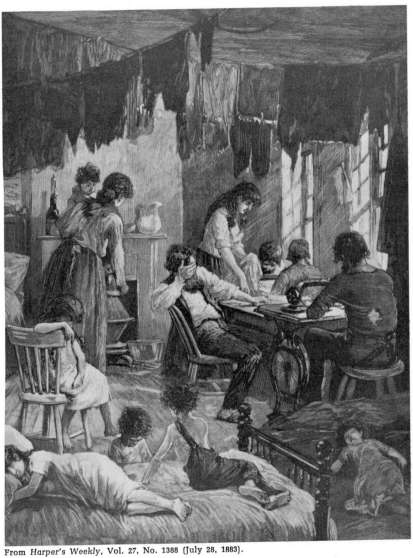

Homes of the poor.

We contend that the employer has no right to speculate on starvation when he reduces wages below a living figure, saying, if we refuse that remuneration, there are plenty of starving men out of work that will gladly accept half a loaf instead of no bread.

We contend that to regard the laboring class in this manner is to consider them as the captain of a slave-ship regards his cargo, who throws overboard those unable to stand their sufferings. Let those who knew the South before the war go now amongst the mining districts of Pennsylvania, and compare the home of the white laborer with the quarters of the slave; let them compare the fruits of freedom with the produce of slavery.

But we know the question is a difficult one to settle—we do not want to force it on with threats. The late strike was not intended to break out as it did; things broke loose and took a direction we regretted. We find ourselves answerable for results we had no share in or control over. Nevertheless we accept the event as a symptom of the disorder that is consuming our body and pray the country to look to it—it is not a passing complaint. Let me put this matter in a plain way, as we understand it, and use round numbers instead of fractions, as we have to deal with hundreds of millions—dividing the subject into sections.

1. In the United States the amount of capital invested in railway property last year was $4,470,000,000, made up of $2,250,000,000 capital stock and $2,220,000,000 bonded debt. The gross earnings were $500,000,000, or about eight and a half per cent [11 per cent—Ed.] on the capital. The running expenses (of which the bulk was for labor) were $310,000,000, leaving $185,000,000 as interest to the capitalist, or barely four per cent on his investment.

Labor is admitted into this enterprise as a preferential creditor, to be paid out of gross earnings before the most preferred mortgage or bond holder receives a dollar. For as capital could not build the roads nor equip them without labor, so the enterprise, when complete, cannot be run without labor.

Capital, therefore, takes a back seat when it comes to the push, and acknowledges not only that labor has the largest interest in the concern, but takes the first fruits.

I take the railroad as a sample out of all enterprises, and if we could get at figures, there is no doubt it is a fair sample of the crowd. If, then, labor is the more important and essential factor in the result, when it comes to the question which of the two shall suffer in moments of general distress, the capitalist in his pocket or the laborer in his belly, we think the answer has been already settled by the rights assumed by one and acknowledged by the other.

2. It is manifestly unjust that the workingman should be subject to under wages in bad times, if he has not the equivalent of over wages in good times. If railroad companies in concert with the laboring class had established a tariff of labor, and paid a bonus on wages at every distribution of dividends, that bonus being in proportion to the profits of the road, so that each man becomes a shareholder in his very small way, then he would have submitted to bear his share of distress when all were called on to share trouble, but to share it equally and alike.

3. When folks say that labor and capital must find, by the laws of demand and supply, their natural relations to each other in all commercial enterprises, and neither one has any rights it can enforce on the other, they take for granted that the labor "market" is, like the produce market, liable to natural fluctuations. If that were so we should not complain. But it is not. The labor market has got to be like the stock and share market; a few large capitalists control it and make what prices they please. This sort of game may ruin the gamblers in stocks, and injure those who invest, but the trouble is confined mostly to those who deserve to lose or those who can afford it.

But not so when the same practice operates in the labor market. The capitalist must not gamble with the bread of the workingman, or if he does, let him regard where that speculation led France one hundred years ago, when the financiers made a corner in flour, and the people broke the ring with the axe of the guillotine.

4. When the railway companies obtained privileges and rights over property, and became by force of law the great landowners of the state, holding its movable property as well, and controlling every avenue and department of business, public and private, they became powerful monopolies. The state endowed them with powers to frame laws of their own and deprived citizens of their property, means, facilities of transport, to vest it all in these corporations. Thus endowed, they cannot pretend they are no more than ordinary commercial enterprises. They are responsible to the state for the result of their operations, if they disturb fatally the order of our concerns. They are not independent. The state has claims upon them it has not on private concerns. They may not accept liabilities and then decline responsibility. It behooves the state to decide what the people are entitled to in return for all they have conceded to these companies, and to enforce such claims.

5. The English Parliament legislated on the question of the number of hours a workingman should labor. It limits them to so many. It legislates for his health and supply of light and water. In all these matters the capitalist has an interest. (He does as much for his horse.) But when it comes to a question of a proper amount of food and clothing, of warmth and shelter, the government declines to interfere. It leaves the question of fair wages to be adjusted between employer and employed.

And so I leave it, fearing I have put the matter in rough language, but not intentionally rude, having a deep and loyal faith in the humanity and justice that abide in the hearts of all this community, and wishing that God has given me the power to touch them.

Note: In this case, as in all others, the Editor disclaims responsibility for the opinion of contributors, whether their articles are signed or anonymous.

CONCERN FOR THE YOUNG

Teen-agers were conspicuously present in the mob actions of 1877, and William Graham Sumner, the great Social Darwinist, focused his attention upon them. He concluded that one of the reasons for teen-age rebelliousness lay in the kind of stories the boys were reading. Generally his criticism was aimed, not at Horatio Alger's success stories, or even at Beadle and Smith's dime novels, but at a third kind, popular with the boys in the streets. These stories emphasized trickery and shrewdness, and contempt for authority. They were heavily sprinkled with contemporary slang. Indeed, the stories Sumner complained of contained an adolescent variety of the adult standards and values in the Gilded Age, when getting ahead, by hook or by crook, was the one great aim, and monetary wealth the sole criterion of success.

WILLIAM GRAHAM SUMNER, *What Our Boys Are Reading*

Few gentlemen who have occasion to visit news offices can have failed to notice the periodical literature for boys, which has been growing up during

William Graham Sumner, "What Our Boys Are Reading," in *Earth-Hunger and Other Essays*, ed. by Albert Galloway Keller (New Haven: Yale University Press, 1913), pp. 367–377.

the last few years. The increase in the number of these papers and magazines, and the appearance from time to time of new ones which, to judge by the pictures, are always worse than the old, seem to indicate that they find a wide market. Moreover, they appear not only among the idle and vicious boys in great cities, but also among schoolboys whose parents are careful about the influences brought to bear on their children. No student of social phenomena can pass with neglect facts of this kind—so practical and so important in their possible effects on society.

These periodicals contain stories, songs, mock speeches, and negro minstrel dialogues—and nothing else. The literary material is either intensely stupid, or spiced to the highest degree with sensation. The stories are about hunting, Indian warfare, California desperado life, pirates, wild sea adventure, highwaymen, crime and horrible accidents, horrors (tortures and snake stories), gamblers, practical jokes, the life of vagabond boys, and the wild behavior of dissipated youths in great cities. This catalogue is exhaustive—there are no other stories. The dialogue is short, sharp, and continuous. It is broken by the minimum of description and by no preaching. It is almost entirely in slang of the most exaggerated kind, and of every variety—that of the sea, of California, and of the Bowery; of negroes, "Dutchmen," Yankees, Chinese, and Indians, to say nothing of that of a score of the most irregular and questionable occupations ever followed by men. When the stories even nominally treat of school-life they say nothing of *school*-life. There is simply a succession of practical jokes, mischief, outrages, heroic but impossible feats, fighting and horrors, but nothing about the business of school, any more than if the house in which the boys live were a summer boarding-house. The sensational incidents in these stories are introduced by force, apparently for the mere purpose of producing a highly spiced mixture.

One type of hero who figures largely in these stories is the vagabond boy in the streets of a great city, in the Rocky Mountains, or at sea. Sometimes he has some cleverness in singing, or dancing, or ventriloquism, or negro acting, and he gains a precarious living while roving about. This vagabond life of adventure is represented as interesting and enticing, and when the hero rises from vagabond life to flash life, that is represented as success. Respectable home life, on the other hand, is not depicted at all and is only referred to as stupid and below the ambition of a clever youth. Industry and economy in some regular pursuit, or in study, are never mentioned at all. Generosity does not consist in even luxurious expenditure, but in wasting money. The type seems to be that of the gambler, one day "flush" and wasteful, another day ruined and in misery.

There is another type of boy who sometimes furnishes the hero of a story, but who also figures more or less in all of them. That is the imp of mischief—the sort of boy who is an intolerable nuisance to the neighborhood. The stories are told from the standpoint of the boy, so that he seems to be a fine fellow, and all the world, which is against him, is unjust and overbearing. His father, the immediate representative of society, executes its judgments with the rod, which again is an insult to the high-spirited youth and produces on his side either open war or a dignified retreat to some distant region.

These stories are not markedly profane, and they are not obscene. They are indescribably vulgar. They represent boys as engaging all the time in the rowdy type of drinking. The heroes are either swaggering, vulgar swells of the rowdy style, or they are in the vagabond mass below the rowdy swell. They are continually associating with criminals, gamblers, and low people who live by their wits. The theater of the stories is always disreputable. The proceedings and methods of persons of the criminal and disreputable classes who appear in the stories, are all described in detail, so that the boy reader obtains a theoretical and literary acquaintance with methods of fraud and crime. Sometimes drunkenness is represented in its disgrace and misery but generally drinking is represented as jolly and entertaining, and there is no suggestion that boys who act as the boys in these stories do ever have to pay any penalty for it in after life. The persons who are held up to admiration are the heroes and heroines of bar rooms, concert saloons, variety theaters, and negro minstrel troupes.

A few illustrations may serve to bring out some of the foregoing statements. One of the school stories before us has a "local color" which is purely English, although the names are Americanized. The mixture is ridiculous in the extreme. The hero is the son of a "country gentleman" of Ohio, and comes to school with an old drunkard, "ex-butler" of the Ohio country gentleman, whom he allows to join him at the Grand Central Depot. This scandalous old rascal is kept in the story apparently because an old drunkard is either a good instrument or a good victim for practical jokes. The hero goes to dine with a gentleman whose place, near the school, is called the "Priory." While waiting for dinner he goes out for a stroll in the "Park." He rescues a girl from drowning, sends back to school for another suit of clothes, goes out again and takes a ride on a bison, is thrown off, strikes, in falling, a professor, who is fortunately fat enough to break his fall, goes to the "snake house" with the professor, is fascinated by the rattlesnake which gets loose, seizes the reptile and throws it away after it has bitten through the professor's trousers—all before dinner. All the teachers, of course, are sneaks and blackguards. In this same story, one of the assistant teachers (usher, he is called) gets drunk and insults the principal, whereupon the latter, while he directs some of the boys to work a garden pump, holds the nozzle and throws water on the assistant, who lies helplessly drunk on the grass—all of which is enforced by a picture. There is not a decent good boy in the story; there is not even the old type of sneaking good boy. The sneaks and bullies are all despicable in the extreme. The heroes are continually devising mischief which is mean and cruel, but which is here represented as smart and funny. They all have a daredevil character, and brave the principal's rod as one of the smallest dangers of life. There is a great deal of the traditional English brutality in exaggerated forms. The nearest approach to anything respectable is that *after* another boy has been whipped for mischief done by the hero, the latter tells an accomplice that they ought to have confessed, whereat the friend replies with the crushing rejoinder that then there would only have been three flogged instead of one.

A character very common in these stories is the city youth, son of a rich father who does not give his son as much pocket-money as the latter considers suitable. This constitutes stinginess on the father's part, although it might be considered pardonable, seeing that these young men drink champagne every day, treat the crowd generally when they drink, and play billiards for one hundred dollars a game. The father, in this class of stories, is represented as secretly vicious and hypocritically pious. In the specimen of this class before us the young man is "discovered" in the police court as a prisoner, whence he is remanded to the Tombs. He has been arrested for collaring a big policeman, to prevent him from overtaking a girl charged with pocket-picking. He interfered because he judged from the girl's face that she was innocent, and it is suggested, for future development in the story, that she was running away from insult and that the cry of "stop thief" was to get help from the police and others to seize her. The hero, who is in prison under an assumed name, now sends for his father's clerk and demands one thousand dollars, saying that otherwise he will declare his real name and disgrace his family. He gets the money. He then sends for a notorious Tombs lawyer, to whom he gives five hundred dollars, and with this sum his release is easily procured. He then starts with his cousin to initiate the latter into life in New York. They go to a thieves' college, where they see a young fellow graduated—his part consists in taking things from the pockets of a hanging figure, to the garments of which bells are attached, without causing the bells to ring. Of this a full-page illustration is given. The two young men then go up the Bowery to a beer saloon, where the hero sustains his character by his vulgar familiarity with the girl waiters. Next they hear a row in a side street; they find a crowd collected watching a woman who hangs from a third-story window, while her drunken husband beats and cuts her hands to make her fall. The hero solves this situation by drawing his revolver and shooting the man. As he and his companion withdraw unobserved, the former wards off the compliments of the latter by saying modestly that he could not bear to stand there and see such a crowd looking on and not knowing what to do, so he just did the proper thing. Next day the hero, meeting the thieves' college graduate in the corridor of the Fifth Avenue Hotel, agrees to receive and hold for him any booty he may seize in the bar room, which he does. At night he and his friend go to a disreputable masked ball, where the hero recognizes his father in disguise amongst the dancers. Securing a place in the same set, during a pause in the dance he snatches the mask from his own face and his father's at the same moment. This edifying incident is enforced by a full-page illustration. A friend suggests the question: what demon of truthfulness makes the artist put such brutal and vulgar faces on the men? In this class of stories, fathers and sons are represented as natural enemies, and the true position for the son is that of suspicion and armed peace.

Here, again, is a story of a boy who was left in charge of a country grocery store. To amuse his leisure he takes a lump of butter from the stock and greases the platform in front of the store. Several village characters, among them an old maid, the parson, and the squire, come to perform on this arena for the amusement of the youth and one or two of his friends. While the squire is trying to get up or get off the platform, the owner of the grocery returns and he and the squire have a fight on the grass-plot over the question whether the grocer greased his own platform or not. Next comes Nemesis in the shape of the boy's father. The conversation between these two, and the dénouement, may be worth quoting. In the soliloquy at the end there seems to be a reminiscence of Fisk.

"James," said he, " you are breaking my heart with your incorrigible conduct."

"Is dat a chowder-gag?" calmly inquired Jimmy.

"Slang—slang, always slang!" groaned his father. "James, will you never reform?"

"Don't wanter; I'm good enough now."

"Think of what you might be, a pattern boy, a—"

"Brass-bound angel, silver-plated cherub, little tin missionary on rollers," put in Jimmy, apparently in confidence to a fly on the ceiling.

"Actually sassing his protector," the deacon said. "Oh, James, you wicked son of Belial."

"Pop's name was Dennis, and he was a short-haired Cincinnati ham," indignantly corrected Jimmy. "I don't know anybody named Belial."

The deacon made a horrified mouth.

"Will you never hearken in quietude and meekness of spirit to words of reproval and advice?" said he.

"Darned sight ruther listen to funny stories," muttered Jimmy.

"You are hopeless," sighed the deacon, "and I shall have to chastise you."

"Dat means a week's soreness," Jimmy reflected; then he changed his tune. "Let me off this time, dad, and I'll be the best boy you ever saw after dis. Stay in nights, stop chewing tobacco, clean my teeth every morning, and welt the life out of anybody dat won't say their prayers regular and go to church every day in the week."

The deacon nodded his head the wrong way.

"You can't play that on the old man again," he said; "it's lost its varnish, it's played out. Step up, my son."

Unwillingly Jimmy stepped up.

In a moment he was stepping up more than ever, for the deacon was pelting him all over with a stout switch, which felt the reverse of agreeable.

But finally he was released and crawled dolefully up to bed.

There are things nicer than going to bed at four o'clock on a bright, breezy, fall day, and Jimmy knew so.

"This here is getting awful stale," he meditated, rolling and tossing in his cot, "and you can smother me with fish-cakes if I stand it. I'm going to run away, and come back to dis old one-hoss town when I'm a man, in a gold-band wagon with silver wheels and six Maltese mules a-drawing it. Probably the old man will be in the poorhouse then, swallerin' shadow soup with an iron spoon, and it will make him cranky to think dat he didn't used ter let me have my own way and boss things. Yes, by golly, I'll give him the sublime skip."

The songs and dialogues are almost all utterly stupid. The dialogues depend for any interest they have on the most vapid kind of negro minstrel buffoonery. The songs, without having any distinct character, seem often to be calculated to win applause from tramps and rioters. The verse, of all before us, which has the most point to it, is the following. What the point is requires no elucidation:

Boss Tweed is a man most talked about now,
His departure last winter caused a great row;
Of course we all knew it was not a square game,
But show me the man who would not do the same.

When Sweeney, Genet and Dick Connolly took flight,
He stood here alone and made a good fight;
He did wrong, but when poor men were greatly in need,
The first to assist them was William M. Tweed.

From the specimens which we have examined we may generalize the following in regard to the views of life which these stories inculcate and the code of morals and manners which they teach.

The first thing which a boy ought to acquire is physical strength for fighting purposes. The feats of strength performed by these youngsters in combat with men and animals are ridiculous in the extreme. In regard to details the supposed code of English brutality prevails, especially in the stories which have English local color, but it is always mixed with the code of the revolver, and in many of the stories the latter is taught in its fulness. These youngsters generally carry revolvers and use them at their good discretion; every youth who aspires to manliness ought to get and carry a revolver.

A boy ought to cheat the penurious father who does not give him as much money as he finds necessary, and ought to compel him to pay. A good way to force him to pay liberally, and at the same time to stop criticizing his son's habits, is to find out his own vices (he always has some) and then to levy blackmail on him. Every boy who does not want to be "green" and "soft," ought to "see the elephant." All fine manly young fellows are familiar with the actors and singers at variety theaters and the girl waiters at concert saloons. As to drinking, the bar room code is taught. The boys stop in at bar rooms all along the street, swallow drinks standing or leaning with rowdy grace on the bar, treat and are treated, and consider it insulting to refuse or to be refused. The good fellows meet every one on a footing of equality—above all in a bar room.

Quiet home life is stupid and unmanly; boys brought up in it never know the world or life. They have to work hard and bow down to false doctrines which parsons and teachers in league with parents have invented against boys. To become a true man, a boy must break with respectability and join the vagabonds and the swell mob. No fine young fellow who knows life need mind the law, still less the police—the latter are all stupid louts. If a boy's father is rich and has money, he can easily find smart lawyers (advertisement gratis) who can get the boy out of prison and will dine with him at Delmonico's afterward. The sympathies of a manly young fellow are with criminals against the law, and he conceals crime when he can. Whatever good or ill happens to a young man he should always be gay;—the only ills in question are physical pain or lack of money and these should be borne with gaiety and indifference, but should not alter the philosophy of life.

As to the rod, it is not so easy to generalize. Teachers and parents in these stories act faithfully up to Solomon's precept. When a father flogs his son, the true doctrine seems to be that the son should run away and seek a life of adventure. When he does this he has no difficulty in finding friends, or in living by his wits, so that he makes money and comes back rich and glorious, to find his father in the poorhouse.

These periodicals seem to be intended for boys from twelve to sixteen years of age, although they often treat of older persons. Probably many boys outgrow them and come to see the folly and falsehood of them. It is impossible, however, that so much corruption should be afloat and not exert some influence. We say nothing of the great harm which is done to boys of that age, by the nervous excitement of reading harrowing and sensational stories, because the literature before us only participates in that harm with other literature of far higher pretensions. But what we have said suffices to show that these papers poison boys' minds with views of life which are so base and false as to destroy all manliness and all chances of true success. How far they are read by boys of good home influences we are, of course, unable to say. They certainly are within the reach of all; they can be easily obtained, and easily concealed, and it is a question for parents and teachers how far this is done. Persons under those responsibilities ought certainly to know what the character of this literature is.

III / THE WEST:
THE LAST FRONTIER YEARS

INTRODUCTION

When the Civil War ended there was still a great gap between the 100th meridian and the Pacific slope. There were cells of population at mining camps and at a few strategically located military posts, but most of the vast heartland was still desolate, dotted with enormous herds of buffalo, peopled by a few nomadic Indian tribes, and traversed only by men on foot, mounted on horses, or riding in vehicles drawn by beasts of burden.

It was during the Gilded Age that this heartland was settled, the bison nearly exterminated, the remnants of once powerful Indian tribes driven onto reservations, and five transcontinental railroads constructed. Miners made new strikes at Cripple Creek, Leadville, Deadwood, and dozens of lesser places. The tough plains sod was broken to the plough; forests were destroyed. Mines extracted metals from the earth and, when the veins petered out, left sterile dumps and mill tailings, and denuded hillsides.

The Far West was, then, the main recipient of the Gilded Age's optimistic construction. The settlers, speculators, and exploiters committed every crime that was possible against the land, and compounded the crimes with errors and ignorance. And they suffered. The railroads fell into bankruptcy during the recurring depressions, the declining price of silver made mining for that metal unprofitable, and the valiant home-steaders—"nesters" or "honyockers"—met drought, blizzards, grasshopper hordes, mortgages, and outrageous railroad and grain elevator charges, until these pioneers, reeling from blows inflicted by nature and man, became Populists, and struck back politically.

In spite of all, the settlers prevailed, sometimes by the mere act of remaining at their homesteads until times grew better. When the new century dawned, and Americans paused to take stock of their condition, they found that the frontier was already a decade past, and they were surprised at what had been accomplished Out West during the Gilded Age: five sets of rails across the continent, total security from the Indians, great ranches and lowing herds of fine beef cattle where the shaggy bison once roamed, and tens of thousands of farms.

The map of the West was dotted with "tank towns"—half a dozen streets laid out at right angles, forming a few blocks of settlement which huddled in the shade of planted trees and found comfort in the civilizing reality of geometrically-planned blocks. The "downtown" included the water tank, grain elevator, railroad station, general store, public school, and church. On the outskirts was the cemetery, with its weed-covered vacant space for anticipated expansion.

And all of this, shimmering beneath the prairie sky, had arisen since the Civil War, built by the gnarled hands of hard-working men. A single generation had built it—the energetic people of the Gilded Age. They were proud of their accomplishments, yet nostalgic. As frontier's end became a reality, Americans were already busy creating a mythology about the Far Western frontier years, making of them a golden age, to linger deep in the nation's memory.

INTERPRETATION

Montana-born, western-raised and educated, Professor Robert G. Athearn of the University of Colorado has devoted his career to the history of the American West. There is a refreshing breeziness in his writing that identifies his western heritage, and promotes a feeling in the mind of the reader that here is a man with a grass-roots knowledge of his subject. The following essay is from his book High Country Empire: The High Plains and Rockies.

ROBERT G. ATHEARN, Dissension in the Desert

... The nation looked on with approval as atlas publishers busily altered their maps, spreading newly made territories and, finally, states, across what once had been labeled the Great American Desert. The task of building America, at least from the political standpoint, appeared to be nearing accomplishment.

Plains residents also were proud. In a few short years after the Civil War they had built an empire in a land their fathers once called useless and fit only for savages. They congratulated each other, and talked of man's ability to combat nature, of the miracles of modern agriculture, of the realization of the American dream. When statehood was bestowed upon the Westerners, they regarded it as a recognition of their achievements and as a kind of valedictory to the days of pioneering. Now they belonged, in every sense, and the feeling was doubly satisfactory, for they had gone out where others feared to go, had laughed at the doubters, and had won a great economic victory. What a country! they said. It was indeed a nation where there were opportunities for all, and undeniable rewards for those who persevered. Even a desert could not stop Americans!

But for the desert, the battle was young. It conceded round one to the onrush of those who would subdue it and patiently bided its time. The day of reckoning for the challengers came early. While the invasion was

Robert G. Athearn, "Dissension in the Desert," from *High Country Empire: The High Plains and Rockies* (New York: McGraw-Hill, 1960; Lincoln: University of Nebraska Press, 1965). Pp. 207–221 in both editions. Copyright 1960 by the author; reprinted by permission of the author.

at its crest, the tide began to turn, and almost overnight the jubilant empire builders saw their ramparts of civilization crumble at the edges. The agrarian storm troopers had swept through the desert's defenses with ease and had penetrated its deepest recesses. When the counterattack commenced the advance guard of farmers wondered if the assault had not been too easy and nervously they looked behind them for support. But there was none. The promoters and land-boomers who had sent them forward with a pat on the back were nowhere to be seen.

During the Eighties the momentum of the westward rush carried thousands of farmers to the new country. For nearly a decade before 1887 rainfall in the desert, particularly its western part, was far above average. The wet years seemed to substantiate all the claims made by the railroad propagandists, and, convinced that such moisture was normal, countless farmers took the plunge. The belt of land from North Dakota southward to Kansas produced a crop of mortgages that stood near the top in national rankings. In some of these states there was one mortgage for every two people; in others, the ratio was one to three. This meant that there were more mortgages than families and it indicates that the title of more than one farm was graced by multiple encumbrances. With interest rates maintaining their earlier high levels, there seemed to be a never-ending supply of eastern money. Despite warnings of overexpansion, loans remained easy.

Then came the Nineties, which some Americans were to remember as gay, but for hundreds upon hundreds of prairie farm families it was a decade of disaster. The trouble began in the late Eighties and mounted in intensity during the remaining years of the century. With the exception of a few bursts of prosperity, the decline that set in during this period has been continuous. The basic ills are still present.

The first signs of impending trouble came in 1886–1887 when white disaster brought an end to the day of the open range and froze out many a cattle king. The farmers were next. Crops failed in 1887, and a wave of mortgage foreclosures followed. With the Panic of 1893 the problem was nationwide. During these years, about half the population of western Kansas moved out and whole sections of the country, clear to the Canadian line, were virtually depopulated. Even cities well back from the desert were struck down in the collapse. Years later, houses in Wichita, Kansas, built or partly completed during boom years, rotted away, uninhabited. In a two-year period that city lost thirteen thousand people and Leavenworth suffered a decline of fifteen thousand. As both urban and rural populations fell off alarmingly in the newborn states, talk of the great agricultural bonanza died upon the lips of the enthusiasts. They were too busy scratching for a living to dream.

Desperately the beleaguered farmers fought for their very existence. When the celestial waterworks went dry, they looked back more than thirty years and remembered the parched days in Kansas during the early sixties. Drought years had come and gone; maybe it would happen again. Frightened men assured each other that the country was basically sound. The cycle would break, the rain would come again. As they waited nervously, eyeing each lonely cloud that drifted by, they made wry jokes about the Garden of Eden the railroad promoters had found for them. Those who lived in Nebraska did not recognize the Platte Valley as a "flowery meadow of great fertility clothed in nutritious grasses, and watered by numerous streams," as the Union Pacific had described it. Dakotans found it hard to laugh over the appellation given their land: "Jay Cooke's Banana Belt." They had come West, listening to Northern Pacific talk of a "Mediterranean climate." The arctic blasts that rocketed in from Canada made them wonder what had happened to the promised Neapolitan zephyrs. But the icy drafts could be tolerated if they would just leave the land some moisture. Instead, subzero temperatures in the winter were quickly exchanged for intolerably hot, dry summers. It was, indeed, a land of extremes.

Climatic problems were hard to solve. As Mark Twain told Americans of his day, everybody talked about the weather but nobody did anything about it. There wasn't much to be done, aside from some experiments in rainmaking. This slight tampering with the elements produced little satisfaction and less rainfall. Besides, it availed a man nothing to cuss the climate or, for that matter, to fight back at such tangible things as grasshoppers. Another villain had to be found, and without much searching around the western farmer fixed the railroads in his political gunsights. Here was a completely satisfactory villain, for not only were the roads guilty of raising their rates, charging more for short hauls than for long hauls, and acting with general arbitrariness, but they had also, said the farmer, engaged in the worst kind of duplicity by enticing emigrants into this economic vacuum to begin with. It was they who had advertised, promoted, wheedled, and propagandized. Like a suitor promising his bride-to-be the moon, the railroads had painted the western picture in rosy hues, and then—said the bitter newcomers—the honeymoon suddenly had ended. Now the railroads were harsh and demanding. Angrily, the victims resolved to punish the perpetrators of this fraud.

What made the railroads a common target was their proximity. In the back of the farmers' minds there was a greater criminal called "the money trust," which was said to be part of an international conspiracy. But it was intangible, faraway, and hard to attack. Closely allied with these invisible forces were the speculators who used their wealth to engulf large tracts of land by means of unrestricted "entry," keeping away what Westerners regarded as the honest tillers of the soil. Land-law provisions, which allowed such unrestricted entry and temporary monopolization of land, were not corrected until 1888. The result was that the small homesteaders frequently were driven beyond the region of arable lands into marginal areas whose promise of productivity was entirely unreliable except in unusually wet years. Unfortunately, like the money trust, the speculators were also frequently hard to lay hands on.

Some of the disgruntled Westerners blamed fate and circumstance for their dilemma. They believed that the closing of the frontier, and the consequent absence of more rich soil, was to blame. It was not, however, their inability to continue westward toward new lands that caused the trouble. On the contrary, many of them already had moved too far west, beyond a point of adequate rainfall, and traditionally wasteful frontier agricultural methods were now catching up with them. They did not understand the diversity of American soils or the fact that old, humid-area methods would not always work. But to admit this would have been to put blame upon themselves. It was far easier to accuse someone else. The railroads, close at hand, were naturally the first objects of their retaliation.

In little gatherings western farmers began to discuss their common predicament. They recalled that in addition to inducing them to settle upon marginal lands that would produce a living only under the most favorable circumstances, the railroads had persuaded them to finance rail facilities through the sale of bonds. More than one farmer had mortgaged his farm in order to make what appeared to be a necessary investment. Then through some kind of financial legerdemain, performed in eastern offices, road reorganizations took place which mysteriously melted away the value of the stocks and bonds. In addition to declining values in rail investments, as well as in agricultural prices, the farmer-investor found himself faced with higher shipping rates and higher taxes. The latter situation arose because many a town and county had also bought stock and it had somehow to be paid for. It is small wonder that the plowman talked darkly about the captains of industry and the intricacies of high finance. It reminded him of the shell game he had tried at the county fair, an expensive experience.

Before the nineteenth century came to a close, prairie farmers had worked themselves into a mass anger that historians have called an "agrarian revolt." It might better have been termed a dissent, for by and large the farmers did not regard their attitude as revolutionary, at least not in the subversive sense. They were not out to overturn the established system; what they wanted was a major overhaul and a reorientation that would adjust what they regarded as a growing economic inequity. They did not see themselves as any more revolutionary than the Jeffersonians who sought equality of opportunity and showed a hostility to special privilege, concentrated economic power, and vested interests. The Populists' Omaha Platform of 1892 expressed this view when it asked that government be freed from corporate control so that there might be equal rights and equal privileges for all.

The fact that western farmers organized the better to voice their demands caused surprise and concern among urban elements. Traditionally the American farmer has been the most independent, individualistic, and hard-to-organize member of society. When it was revealed that he was prepared to ride twenty or thirty rough miles in a springless wagon to meet with his fellows in some lonely prairie schoolhouse and there to pledge his support to an agrarian cause, Easterners became uneasy. In an era when the courts were solidly antilabor and society in general approved of the suppression of the workingman's demands, it was not hard to frown upon the complaints of the farmer.

America's material prosperity was greater than ever before and the average home was supplied with more of life's necessities, and even luxuries, than at any previous time in the nation's history. It was true, admitted the smaller-town storekeeper or newspaper editor, that industrial America might have some small maladjustments in its magnificent growth, but these were necessary evils attendant on such expansion. Things would even out. People must be patient. These western farmers were a strident lot. They ought to remember that they were but a part of the national family and they could well hold their tongues. So the small-town businessman went on, attending his Monday noon knife-and-fork club, listening to the gospel of "boost, don't knock," and felt a lurking resentment for the wild-eyed plowmen of the plains who seemed dissatisfied with their place in the world's greatest economic system.

Leaders of the agrarians were not apologetic about their position. They were radicals and they admitted it. There was nothing inconsistent between radicalism and the American tradition. The two ideologies had enjoyed a measure of compatibility since the days of Thomas Paine and the Democratic Republican Clubs a century earlier. For decades farmers had railed against the monopolies of money, transportation, and land. When the Populists of the Nineties powered their political drive with the element of antimonopolism they were using a traditional fuel. Through some refinements the propellant had a little higher octane rating, and it was injected into a hotter combustion chamber, giving it a more revolutionary appearance than it really had. In other words, Westerners felt that because of their widespread complaint, now rising to fever pitch, the time and the place were right for an all-out battle. They saw nothing un-American about fighting for what they regarded as their rights.

That the aggrieved chose the railroads as their chief adversary is not surprising. The roads represented but one enemy, it is true, but they were in the West, tangible and subject to punishment. They were not only villains because they held hostage the farmer's crops until he was ready to pay the necessary ransom to get them to market, but they also represented monopoly at large. An Omaha paper stated the case in 1890 when, praising the growth of the Farmers' Alliance, it said that the development was "a gratifying evidence of an awakening among the producers. ... Organization among the farmers has become an urgent necessity. Confronted on every side by combines and trusts, they are forced to unite to protect themselves from the grasping greed of corporations. It is hoped that strong, conservative men will be placed at the helm of the alliance—men who know the right of the producers and who will demand and secure just treatment from the transportation companies of the state." Radicals, not conservatives, grasped the helm; Nebraska farmers and their brothers in other plains states applauded as the helmsmen steered straight into the storm of eastern disapproval. As the movement gathered momentum, western railroads quailed before the coming onslaught.

The roads had a right to be apprehensive. When "Sockless" Jerry Simpson, the Populist congressman, told his listeners that eight thousand miles of Kansas railroads cost a hundred million dollars to construct but were capitalized at three times that figure in stocks, and a like amount in bonds, road-owners were hard put for an explanation. Nor did they have a satisfactory answer to the charge made by farmer-orators that it took a bushel of wheat or corn to pay freight on the same amount of produce to get it to the market. They also had to admit it was true that western rates were often two to three times higher than those charged for similar distances between places like Minneapolis and Chicago or Chicago and New York, where competition was keen.

Nor was this all. Dakota and Montana farmers angrily trumpeted the fact that Jim Hill not only took them into camp with high freight rates, but he also refused to haul grain from elevators of less than thirty-thousand-bushel capacity. The "Hill system" both milked the shippers for haulage and held them up for elevator-storage and service charges by obliging them to sell their grain at places the railroad operators selected. The elevator operator was king. He could determine the grade, hence the price; could assess the amount of smut and dirt in the grain and dock the price proportionately; or he might charge excessive storage rates if a farmer chose to wait for a better price before selling. It was the redress of grievances like these that farmers sought in their state legislatures.

The determination of the agrarians to enter the political arena to right some wrongs came at an interesting time for some of the farming communities. Four prairie territories—Montana, Wyoming, and the Dakotas—were elevated to statehood with the entrance of the six omnibus states. When Dakota Territory was divided in two, in 1889, and each part given statehood, the farmers did not have to revolt against any established state administration to gain control. It is true that there were territorial political bosses, but the change in political status gave the agrarians a chance to enter the picture with a better opportunity to gain their share of the spoils. The prize was more than mere office-holding. If government could smile upon industry, as it unquestionably was doing elsewhere, it could be made to favor agriculture. And agriculture needed favor, for already there were clouds of doubt in men's minds about their ability to conquer the desert as individuals.

The struggle in North Dakota commenced at the constitutional convention when a delegate submitted a constitution favored by the president of the Northern Pacific Railroad. There was an immediate outcry against it, and the other delegates showed their temper by drawing up a document of their own choosing, including in it a board of railroad commissioners to be elected by the people. The first state legislature followed this lead by enacting additional grain-trade legislation, only to see it thrown out by the attorney general upon motion from the Elevator Association.

After several years of such frustrated attempts to work within the framework of regular parties, the North Dakota Populists entered the field in 1892 with their own ticket and won. This victory was short-lived; within two years they lost political control. In their brief reign they set maximum freight rates on coal mined within the state, established public scales that did not have the peculiar balance of those owned by the private elevator companies, outlawed usury, and made railroads responsible for prairie and crop fires started by their locomotives. Then the forces of Alexander McKenzie, longtime Dakota political boss, resumed control and held it for another twenty years. Patiently the farmers came back. Once, when a delegation of them waited upon the legislators with a request, one of the lawmakers asked what business they had trying to browbeat the legislature. Then, as legend has it, he flatly advised them to "Go home and slop the hogs." It was stories like this one, circulated in western rural areas, that goaded the farmers into fury and deepened their resolve to take over the reins of government as soon as possible.

Railroad owners had to admit that they were in a quandary. They had sent forth their respective lines on a wave of optimism and boom spirit, encouraged by the federal government and cheered by the populace at large. Eager farmers had willingly accepted the attractive low fares and had gobbled up lands offered at reasonable prices. A number of the roads asserted, and probably fairly, that they had profited little from the sale of their land grants. Some of them, like the Santa Fe, offered prospective farmers half fare just to go out and have a look, no strings attached, and many an agricultural prospector finally had chosen to take up government land. The low rates offered emigrants on the haulage of their household goods, machinery, stock, and seeds often resulted in a loss for the railroads. But they wanted traffic that settlement would bring and were willing to take a chance. When the gamble failed, farmers accusingly pointed their fingers at the railroads.

Railroaders were in no better position than the settlers to predict the weather. They prayed just as fervently for rain as anyone; their stake in the game was as important to them as the farmer's was to him. The management's extensive advertising, land promotion, and emigrant travel rates were based upon the premise of agricultural prosperity; when it failed to materialize the vendors of transportation were in serious trouble. With a large initial investment, admittedly overextended, the trap in which they were caught was the same as that of the farmer. Plunging grain prices did not take fixed costs downward with them at the same rate of descent, nor did they lessen the weight or bulk of the bushel. There were still payrolls to meet, equipment to replace, and roadbeds to repair if grain—regardless of its price—was to be moved. There were certain fixed charges, such as interest, that did not follow closely the trend of agricultural income. Furthermore, said the railroads, western farmers who were so bitterly critical did not always remember that in their region freight haulage was frequently a one-way proposition. In order to get cars to haul grain out, many of them had to be deadheaded to the West, completely empty, which doubled the cost of movement.

The railroads, like the farmer, were caught in the bind. Besieged by agrarian legislators in the West and engaged in a bitter competitive fight with other roads to the East, the lines fought with their backs to the wall, grasping in desperation at any means of succor. If they charged three or four times as much for prairie transportation as they did in more humid and populated areas, the roads rationalized it as a necessity arising from the present exigency. Many an official knew that it was wrong to make the farmer pay all the traffic would bear in order to have financial resources with which to fight competing roads elsewhere, but in a life-or-death fight principles had to take a back seat. It was as simple as that. From the standpoint of immediate battle tactics the position may have had a practical aspect, but in terms of long-range strategy it was costly. Many years later, after World War II, when the roads were surrendering their passenger traffic to the airlines, a railroad president sadly remarked:

"People think of the airplane in terms of heroes like Lindbergh. But when they think of railroads, they think of robber barons. We're cursed with that reputation." The reputation, which spread from coast to coast, was born largely in the remote and semiarid states of the high plains.

By the Nineties, battle lines were clearly drawn. Western farmers turned their attention from the Indian menace, which was no more, to a new threat—big business in general. After two and a half decades of attempted organization to combat their economic troubles by cooperation within their ranks, the farmers tried politics. Many of them had joined the Grange movement, organized soon after the Civil War, but it was more social than political in purpose. Membership in the organization offered the farmer instruction and encouragement but he was by now more interested in higher prices than in camaraderie. During the Eighties an organization known as the Farmers' Alliance, whose purposes were admittedly political, attracted the distressed Westerners. Here was an opportunity to gain political control and combat the money of the corporate world with agricultural legislation.

Resolutely the western farmers set about the task of capturing the machinery of government. So successful were they in Kansas that the state came to be regarded as representative of the Populist movement. In 1890, Kansas farmers thoroughly frightened the established parties by electing ninety members to the lower house of their legislature while the Republicans captured only twenty-seven seats and the Democrats eight. Meanwhile, in Nebraska the defection caused the Republicans to lose the governorship and in Colorado to win only by a significantly reduced majority.

While Alliance members in the South showed a greater inclination to work within established party framework, plainsmen of the Northwest chose an independent course. In 1891, encouraged by local successes, the People's Party was organized at Cincinnati and in the summer of 1892 its first national convention met at Omaha, deep in the land of agrarian unrest. Taking a leaf from the Republican book, the Populists sought the magic of a military name by nominating General James B. Weaver of Iowa. Mary Elizabeth Lease, the Kansas crusader who once advised farmers to "raise less corn and more hell," seconded the nomination. Burning western issues such as land, transportation, and finance comprised the major planks in the party's platform. These were problems long in the forefront of the farmers' minds. When a strong free-silver plank was inserted, the plains region was politically welded together, for the mountain states—particularly Colorado—were suffering from the falling price of the white metal.

Although the election of 1892 did not bring national victory to the Populist cause, it gave the country pause. By capturing twenty-two of the available four hundred forty-four electoral votes, the young organization accomplished what no other third party had been able to do since 1860. All the votes came from western states: Colorado, Idaho, Kansas, Nevada, North Dakota, and Oregon. Since Weaver's more than a million popular votes came from states in which Republican strength was great, and because Cleveland defeated Harrison by less than four hundred thousand votes, the Populists determined the election's outcome. The canvass was significant, too, in that the Senate was almost evenly divided between Democrats and Republicans and the Populist senators held the balance of power. The fact that the free-silver issue crossed major party lines also contributed to this control.

The shock of 1892 left a deep impression upon the entire country. The *New York Tribune,* explaining the election, perhaps expressed the East's opinion of the militant Westerners when it said: "The chief cause of Republican defeat and Democratic victory is the modern tendency toward socialism." Readers might have agreed with the editorial when they heard the sentiments of the newly elected Populist governor of Colorado, Davis Waite. Speaking in behalf of the downtrodden poor, he announced: "It is infinitely better that blood should flow to our horses' bridles than our national liberties should be destroyed." The public got the impression that a general repudiation of debts, if not outright revolution, threatened Colorado. Pronouncements like those of "Bloody Bridles" Waite caused a shudder of horror among some of the more conservative elements of the country, and there was nervous speculation about the outcome of this spreading rural radicalism.

General gloom developed as the nation staggered from the effects of financial panic in 1893 and appeared to be slumping into a general depression. The mountain states were near desperation over the drastic plunge of silver prices. Conditions in the farm belt worsened as agricultural products went begging for buyers. A leading national magazine bitterly denounced the Populists as "fanatical in the extreme," and possessed of doctrines of advanced socialism. The principal aim of the party, it was said, was "the virtual repudiation of public and private indebtedness, the confiscation of the property of railway and other corporations, and the plunging of the country into a cheap-money debauch," while its elected representatives at Washington were "either fanatics or cranks of limited intelligence and exceedingly pernicious ideas. ..." Even some of the Westerners were frightened by what they had done in 1892. When they went to the polls in 1894 they turned out most of the Populists up for re-election. The party took the governorship of Nebraska, but it was small consolation for the general reverse in the West.

Undaunted by their setbacks and rationalizing that defeats in the western states arose more out of local complications than a general disapproval, the Populists continued to beat the political drums in anticipation of the next general election. Despite their surrender of some of the western strongholds gained in 1892, they were powerful in other parts of the country, particularly the South, increasing their popular vote in 1894 by forty-two per cent. Aside from such statistical encouragement, the party looked with pleasure upon the silver issue that threatened to divide the major parties and at the same time to become the prime catalyst for bonding together under the Populist banner all the nation's silverites. The demonetization of silver in 1873, accomplished without much uproar, suddenly became the "Crime of '73" when the market price of silver sagged badly. The Populists, whose followers generally favored cheap money, quickly unfurled their "free and unlimited coinage of silver" banner and the crusade was on.

The election of 1896, often referred to as "the battle of the standards," saw a Westerner, William Jennings Bryan of Nebraska, pitted against William McKinley, author of the protectionist tariff. Bryan, in his mid-thirties and known as the "boy orator of the platte," used his forensic powers to gain the Democratic presidential nomination, and the Populists—who felt that the Democrats' acceptance of their free-silver crusade would offer a better chance to win than as a third party—decided to throw in with that organization. Led by one of their own, Westerners launched themselves into the grand attack upon the "goldbugs" of the East. While Bryan took the electoral vote of every state west of the Mississippi except five, and the South remained generally true to the Democrats, the bid failed. McKinley squeaked by with a mere six hundred thousand popular vote majority, as the eastern states turned back the agrarian hordes led by that political cossack from the steppes of Nebraska. For the Populists it was all or nothing at all. They had surrendered their very existence on one throw of the dice, giving up their political organization for a chance to win with another party. And they had lost. It was the end of Populism and defeat for the farmers until the New Deal came along in the next century to give them much of what they had sought for more than half a century.

The political battle of the century marked the end of an era. While most of the participants did not recognize it, the climactic campaign was another indication that the frontier was gone. For over two hundred years the settlers had edged ever westward, taking up land, exploiting the bounty of resources laid out before them, operating all the while in an atmosphere of individual enterprise. Then the largess of nature ran out. By the Nineties the nation, already near the end of its westward population expansion, had entered a period of adjustment to more stabilized conditions. While the supply of free land was not exhausted, the best had been claimed and henceforth the pickings would be relatively slim. As this period of development came to a close, another already had begun to overlap it. Industrial America was assuming that position of dominance that soon would characterize the nation in the eyes of the world.

Even in the deepest recesses of the Populist stronghold there were Westerners whose innate conservatism made them embarrassed by the flamboyance of the agrarian radicalism. Although they were by no means disciples of the high priests of the industrial cult, they harbored a hidden desire to conform and to assume a more moderate political stand. The best known of them was a twenty-nine-year-old Emporia, Kansas, editor, William Allen White, who soared to national fame by his bitter editorial attack upon the Populists, "What's the Matter With Kansas?" In it he expressed the view that the hell-raising tendencies of the Populists had brought shame and ridicule upon his state and bitterly he twitted them for their leveling tendencies. The acerbity of the attack so appealed to the rest of the country that it was widely reprinted throughout the nation's press and circulated by the Republican campaign committee in the election of 1896. In thousands of middle-class homes the editorial was accepted as a simple explanation that the political renegades of the prairies were fanatics and demagogues.

White, and millions of his fellow Americans, missed the point of the great political crusade. What to them were the ravings of a lot of wild-eyed farmers, were actually warning flags that revealed growing inequities in our system, rumblings at the foundation of the whole economic structure that indicated the need for serious readjustment and predicted the coming of the progressives. In the new order of things, a segment of the population was getting pinched. When the western farmers endured and suffered, and then fought back at the polls—quite within the American tradition—their actions were termed a "revolt." Other third parties had been and would be established, for economic or sectional reasons or both, but no one called it political revolution. ...

THE 1890 CENSUS TRACES SETTLEMENT
AND NOTES THE END OF THE FRONTIER

The single most important essay in American history is Frederick Jackson Turner's Significance of the Frontier in American History, first read to the American Historical Association in 1893. In it he suggested that "the existence of an area of free land, its continuous recession, and the advance of American settlement westward, explain American development."

Turner's essay provided nearly two generations of American scholars with a thesis which could orient their approach to American history. Hardly a history textbook at high school or college level was published that did not assume the validity of the thesis, and millions of Americans were taught the Turnerian ideas, though most of them had never heard his name.

He began his essay by quoting the very last sentence in the informative Introduction to the Census Bureau Report for 1890. Some of this Introduction appears in the following excerpts, which trace the development of the West from 1870 to 1890.

Excerpts from the Eleventh Decennial Census

1870

... Settlement has spread westward to the boundary of the state in southern Minnesota, and up the Big Sioux river in southeastern Dakota. Iowa is entirely reclaimed, excepting a small area of perhaps 1,000 square miles in its northwestern corner. Through Kansas and Nebraska the frontier line has moved steadily westward, following in general the courses of the larger streams and of the newly constructed railroads. The frontier in Texas has changed but little, that little consisting of a general westward movement. In the Cordilleran region settlements have extended but slowly. Those upon the Pacific coast show little change, either in extent or density. In short, we see everywhere the effects of the war in the partial arrest of the progress of development.

Eleventh Decennial Census (Washington: Government Printing Office, 1893), pp. xxv–xxxiv. The essay contains statistics from the 10th and 9th Censuses of 1880 and 1870, as well.

The settlements in the west, beyond the frontier line, have arranged themselves mainly in three belts. The most eastern of these is located in central Colorado, New Mexico, and Wyoming, along the eastern base of and among the Rocky mountains. To this region settlement was first attracted in 1859 and 1860 by the discovery of mineral deposits, and has been retained by the richness of the soil and by the abundance of water for irrigation, which have prompted the agricultural industry.

The second belt of settlement is that of Utah, settled in 1847 by the Mormons fleeing from Illinois. ... The settlements of this group ... extend from southern Idaho southward through central Utah, and along the eastern base of the Wasatch range to the Arizona line. They consist mainly of scattered hamlets and small towns, about which are grouped the farms of the communities.

The third strip is that in the Pacific states and territories, extending from Washington territory southward to southern California and eastward to the system of "sinks," in western Nevada. This group of population owes its existence to the mining industry. Originated in 1849 by a great immigration movement, it has grown by successive impulses as new fields for rapid money getting have been developed. Latterly, however, the value of this region to the agriculturalist has been recognized, and the character of the occupations of the people is undergoing a marked change.

These three great western groups comprise nine-tenths of the population west of the frontier line. The remainder is scattered about in the valleys and the mountains of Montana, Idaho, and Arizona, at military posts, isolated mining camps, and on cattle ranches.

The frontier line in 1870 embraces 1,178,068 square miles, all between 27°15' and 47°30' north latitude, and between 67° and 99°45' west longitude. From this, however, deduction is to be made of 37,739 square miles on account of interior spaces containing no population. To what remains we must add 11,810 square miles on account of settled tracts east of the one hundredth meridian, lying outside of the frontier line, and 120,100 square miles on account of settlements in the Cordilleran region and on the Pacific coast, making the total area of settlement for 1870 not less than 1,272,239 square miles, the aggregate population being 38,558,371, and the average density of settlement 30.31 to the square mile.

1880

... The settlements in Kansas and Nebraska have made great strides over the plains, reaching at several points the boundary of the humid region, so that their westward extension beyond this point is to be governed hereafter by the supply of water in the streams. As a natural result, we see settlements following these streams in long ribbons of population. In Nebraska these narrow belts have reached the western boundary of the state at two points: one upon the South Platte and the other upon the Republican river. In Kansas, too, the settlements have followed the Kansas river and its branches and the Arkansas nearly to the western boundary of the state. Texas also has made great strides, both in the extension of the frontier line of settlement and in the increase in the density of population, due both to the building of railroads and to the development of the cattle, sheep, and agricultural interests. The heavy population in the prairie portions of the state is explained by the railroads which now traverse them. In Dakota, beside the agricultural region, in the eastern part of the territory, we note the formation of a body of settlement in the Black Hills, in the southwest corner, which, in 1870, was a part of the reservation of the Sioux Indians. This settlement is the result of the discovery of valuable gold deposits. In Montana there appears a great extension of the settled area, which, as it is mainly due to agricultural interests, is found chiefly along the courses of the streams. Mining has, however, played not a small part in this increase in settlement. Idaho, too, shows a decided growth from the same causes. The small settlements which, in 1870, were located about Boise city, and near the mouth of the Clearwater, have now extended their areas to many hundreds of square miles. The settlement in the southeastern corner of the territory is almost purely Mormon, and has not made a marked increase.

Of all the states and territories of the Cordilleran region Colorado has made the greatest stride during the decade. From a narrow strip of settlement, extending along the immediate base of the Rocky mountains, the belt has increased so that it comprises the whole mountain region, beside a great extension outward upon the plains. This increase is the result of the discovery of very extensive and very rich mineral deposits about Leadville, producing a "stampede" second only to that of 1849 and 1850 to California. Miners have spread over the whole mountain region, till every range and ridge swarms with them. ...

The length of the frontier line in 1880 is 3,337 miles. The area included between the frontier line, the Atlantic and the Gulf coast, and the northern boundary is 1,398,940 square miles, lying between 26° and 49° north latitude and 67° and 102° west longitude. From this must be deducted, for unsettled areas ... 89,400 square miles, leaving 1,309,540 square miles.

To this must be added the isolated areas of settlement in the Cordilleran region and the extent of settlement on the Pacific coast, which amount, in the aggregate, to 260,025 square miles, making a total settled area of 1,569,565 square miles. The population is 50,155,783, and the average density of settlement 31.96 to the square mile.

Main street of Gunnison, Colorado.

1890

This census completes the history of a century; a century of progress and achievement unequaled in the world's history. ... [It] has witnessed ... the spread of settlement across the continent until not less than 1,947,280 square miles have been redeemed from the wilderness and brought into the service of man, while the population has increased and multiplied by its own increase and by additions from abroad until it numbers 62,622,250.

During the decade just past a trifling change has been made in the boundary between Nebraska and Dakota by which the area of Nebraska has been slightly increased. Dakota territory has been cut in two and the states of North Dakota and South Dakota admitted. Montana, Wyoming, Idaho, and Washington have also been added to the sisterhood of states. The territory of Oklahoma has been created out of the western half of the Indian territory, and to it has been added the strip of public land lying north of the panhandle of Texas.

The most striking fact connected with the extension of settlement during the past decade is the numerous additions which have been made to the settled area within the Cordilleran region. Settlements have spread westward up the slope of the plains until they have joined the bodies formerly isolated in Colorado, forming a continuous body of settlement from the east to the Rocky mountains. Practically the whole of Kansas has become a settled region, and the unsettled area of Nebraska has been reduced in dimensions to a third of what it was ten years ago. What was a sparsely settled region in Texas in 1880 is now the most populous part of the state, while settlements have spread westward to the escarpment of the Staked Plains. The unsettled regions of North Dakota and South Dakota have been reduced to half their former dimensions. Settlements in Montana have spread until they now occupy one-third of the state. In New Mexico, Idaho, and Wyoming considerable extensions of area are to be noted. In Colorado, in spite of the decline of the mining industry and the depopulation of its mining regions, settlement has spread, and two-thirds of the state are now under the dominion of man. Oregon and Washington show equally rapid progress, and California, although its mining regions have suffered, has made great inroads upon its unsettled regions, especially in the south. Of all the western states and territories Nevada alone is at a standstill in this respect, its settled area remaining practically the same as in 1880. When it is remembered that the state has lost one-third of its population during the past ten years, the fact that it has held its own in settled area is surprising until it is understood that the state has undergone a material change in occupations during the decade, and that the inhabitants, instead of being closely grouped and engaged in mining pursuits, have become scattered along its streams and have engaged in agriculture. ...

During the decade from 1880 to 1890 the inroads upon the unsettled region have been unprecedented in amount, not less than 377,715 square miles having been redeemed, exceeding by 80,389 square miles the area settled between 1870 and 1880. ...

Up to and including 1880 the country had a frontier of settlement, but at present the unsettled area has been so broken into by isolated bodies of settlement that there can hardly be said to be a frontier line. In the discussion of its extent and its westward movement it can not, therefore, any longer have a place in the census reports. ...

WESTERN SOCIETY

It has been said that the reason there is no truly great work of fiction about the American West is that it is a success story, and only tragic subjects make great novels. The statement may or may not be correct about great fiction, but there can be no doubt about the West's being successful. Optimism and faith in the future were the hallmarks of the American West from the days of the Ohio Valley frontier to those of modern Alaska.

In the Gilded Age the American West of cowboys, Indians, mines, ranches, and railroads was emerging from the status of wild frontier and approaching civilized stability. What was the "flavor" of the West? James Bryce, an English lawyer, historian, statesman, and diplomat, analyzed the West of the Gilded Age in one chapter of his perceptive and momentous work, The American Commonwealth, *first published in 1888.*

JAMES BRYCE, The Temper of the West

... In Western America the presence of the Indians has done no more than give a touch of romance or a spice of danger to the exploration of

From James Bryce, "The Temper of the West," in The American Commonwealth (New York: The Macmillan Co., 1897), Vol. II, pp. 829–834, 836–839.

some regions, such as Western Dakota and Arizona, while over the rest of the country the unhappy aborigines have slunk silently away, scarcely even complaining of the robbery of lands and the violations of plighted faith. Nature and time seem to have conspired to make the development of the Mississippi basin and the Pacific slope the swiftest, easiest, completest achievement in the whole record of the civilizing progress of mankind since the founder of the Egyptian monarchy gathered the tribes of the Nile under one government.

The details of this development and the statistics that illustrate it have been too often set forth to need re-statement here. It is of the character and temper of the men who have conducted it that I wish to speak, a matter which has received less attention, but is essential to a just conception of the Americans of to-day. For the West is the most American part of America; that is to say, the part where those features which distinguish America from Europe come out in the strongest relief. What Europe is to Asia, what England is to the rest of Europe, what America is to England, that the Western States and Territories are to the Atlantic States, the heat and pressure and hurry of life always growing as we follow the path of the sun. In Eastern America there are still quiet spots, in the valleys of the Alleghanies, for instance, in nooks of old New England, in university towns like Ithaca or Ann Arbor. In the West there are none. All is bustle, motion, and struggle, most so of course among the native Americans, yet even the immigrant from the secluded valleys of Thuringia, or the shores of some Norwegian fjord, learns the ways almost as readily as the tongue of the country, and is soon swept into the whirlpool.

It is the most enterprising and unsettled Americans that come West; and when they have left their old haunts, broken their old ties, resigned the comforts and pleasures of their former homes, they are resolved to obtain the wealth and success for which they have come. They throw themselves into work with a feverish yet sustained intensity. They rise early, they work all day, they have few pleasures, few opportunities for relaxation.* I remember in the young city of Seattle on Puget Sound to have found business in full swing at seven o'clock a.m.: the shops open, the streets full of people. Everything is speculative, land (or, as it is usually called, "real estate") most so, the value of lots of ground rising or falling perhaps two or three hundred per cent in the year. No one has any fixed occupation; he is a storekeeper to-day, a ranchman to-morrow, a

---

* In the newer towns, which are often nothing more than groups of shanties with a large hotel, a bank, a church, and inn, some drinking-saloons and gambling-houses, there are few women and no homes. Everybody, except recent immigrants, Chinese, and the very poorest native Americans, lives in the hotel.

miner next week. I found the waiters in the chief hotel at Denver, in Colorado, saving their autumn and winter wages to start off in the spring "prospecting" for silver "claims" in the mountains. Few men stay in one of the newer cities more than a few weeks or months; to have been there a whole year is to be an old inhabitant, an oracle if you have succeeded, a by-word if you have not, for to prosper in the West you must be able to turn your hand to anything, and seize the chance to-day which every one else will have seen to-morrow. This venturesome and shifting life strengthens the reckless and heedless habits of the people. Every one thinks so much of gaining that he thinks little of spending, and in the general dearness of commodities, food (in the agricultural districts) excepted, it seems not worth while to care about small sums. In California for many years no coin lower than a ten-cent piece (5d.) was in circulation; and even in 1881, though most articles of food were abundant, nothing was sold at a lower price than five cents. The most striking alternations of fortune, the great *coups* which fascinate men and make them play for all or nothing, are of course commoner in mining regions than elsewhere.*

But money is everywhere so valuable for the purpose of speculative investment, whether in land, live stock, or trade, as to fetch very high interest. At Walla Walla (in what was then the Territory of Washington) I found in 1881 that the interest on debts secured on good safe mortgages was at the rate of fourteen per cent per annum, of course payable monthly.

The carelessness is public as well as private. Tree stumps are left standing in the streets of a large and flourishing town like Leadville, because the municipal authorities cannot be at the trouble of cutting or burning them. Swamps are left undrained in the suburbs of a populous city like Portland, which every autumn breed malarious fevers; and the risk of accidents to be followed by actions does not prevent the railways from pushing on their lines along loosely heaped embankments, and over curved trestle bridges which seem as if they could not stand a high wind or the passage of a heavy train.

This mixture of science and rudeness is one of a series of singular contrasts which runs through the West, not less conspicuous in the minds of the people than in their surroundings. They value good government, and have a remarkable faculty for organizing some kind of government, but they are tolerant of lawlessness which does not directly attack their own interest. Horse-stealing and insults to women are the two unpardonable offences; all others are often suffered to go unpunished. I was in a considerable Western city, with a population of 70,000 people, some years

---

* In California in 1881 I was shown an estate of 600,000 acres which was said to have been lately bought for $225,000 (£45,000) by a man who had made his fortune in two years' mining, having come out without a penny.

ago, when the leading newspaper of the place, commenting on one of the train robberies that had been frequent in the State, observed that so long as the brigands had confined themselves to robbing the railway companies and the express companies of property for whose loss the companies must answer, no one had greatly cared, seeing that these companies themselves robbed the public; but now that private citizens seemed in danger of losing their personal baggage and money, the prosperity of the city might be compromised, and something ought to be done—a sentiment delivered with all gravity, as the rest of the article showed.* Brigandage tends to disappear when the country becomes populous, though there are places in comparatively old States like Illinois and Missouri where the railways are still unsafe. But the same heedlessness suffers other evils to take root, evils likely to prove permanent, including some refinements of political roguery which it is strange to find amid the simple life of forests and prairies.

Another such contrast is presented by the tendency of this shrewd and educated people to relapse into the oldest and most childish forms of superstition. Fortune-telling, clairvoyance, attempts to pry by the help of "mediums" into the book of fate, are so common in parts of the West that the newspapers devote a special column, headed "astrologers," to the advertisements of these wizards and pythonesses.† I have counted in one issue of a San Francisco newspaper as many as eighteen such advertisements, six of which were of simple fortune-tellers, like those who used to beguile the peasant girls of Devonshire. In fact, the profession of a soothsayer or astrologer is a recognized one in California now, as it was in the Greece of Homer. Possibly the prevalence of mining speculation, possibly the existence of a large mass of ignorant immigrants from Europe, may help to account for the phenomenon, which, as California is deemed an exceptionally unreligious State, illustrates the famous saying that the less faith the more superstition.

All the passionate eagerness, all the strenuous effort of the Westerns is directed towards the material development of the country. To open the greatest number of mines and extract the greatest quantity of ore, to scatter cattle over a thousand hills, to turn the flower-spangled prairies of the North-west into wheat-fields, to cover the sunny slopes of the Southwest with vines and olives: this is the end and aim of their lives, this is their daily and nightly thought . . . .

---

* This makes plausible the story of the Texas judge who allowed murderers to escape on points of law till he found the value of real estate declining, when he saw to it that the next few offenders were hanged.

† Ohio in 1883 imposed a license tax of $300 a year on "astrologers, fortune-tellers, clairvoyants, palmisters, and seers."

The passion is so absorbing, and so covers the horizon of public as well as private life that it almost ceases to be selfish—it takes from its very vastness a tinge of ideality. To have an immense production of exchangeable commodities, to force from nature the most she can be made to yield, and send it east and west by the cheapest routes to the dearest markets, making one's city a centre of trade, and raising the price of its real estate —this, which might not have seemed a glorious consummation to Isaiah or Plato, is preached by Western newspapers as a kind of religion. It is not really, or at least it is not wholly, sordid. These people are intoxicated by the majestic scale of the nature in which their lot is cast, enormous mineral deposits, boundless prairies, forests which, even squandered— wickedly squandered—as they now are, will supply timber to the United States for centuries; a soil which, with the rudest cultivation, yields the most abundant crops, a populous continent for their market. They see all round them railways being built, telegraph wires laid, steamboat lines across the Pacific projected, cities springing up in the solitudes, and settlers making the wilderness to blossom like the rose. Their imagination revels in these sights and signs of progress, and they gild their own struggles for fortune with the belief that they are the missionaries of civilization and the instruments of Providence in the greatest work the world has seen. ...

Confidence goes a long way towards success. And the confidence of these Westerns is superb. I happened in 1883 to be at the city of Bismarck in Dakota when this young settlement was laying the corner-stone of its Capitol, intended to contain the halls of the legislature and other State offices of Dakota when that flourishing Territory should have become a State, or perhaps, for they spoke even then of dividing it, two States. The town was then only some five years old, and may have had six or seven thousand inhabitants. It was gaily decorated for the occasion, and had collected many distinguished guests—General U. S. Grant, several governors of neighbouring States and Territories, railroad potentates, and others. By far the most remarkable figure was that of Sitting Bull, the famous Sioux chief, who had surprised and slain a detachment of the American army some years before. Among the speeches made, in one of which it was proved that as Bismarck was the centre of Dakota, Dakota the centre of the United States, and the United States the centre of the world, Bismarck was destined to "be the metropolitan hearth of the world's civilization," there came a short but pithy discourse from this grim old warrior, in which he told us, through an interpreter, that the Great Spirit moved him to shake hands with everybody. However, the feature of the ceremonial which struck us Europeans most was the spot chosen for the Capitol. It was not in the city, nor even on the skirts of the city; it was nearly a mile off, on the top of a hill in the brown and dusty prairie. "Why here?" we asked. "Is it because you mean to enclose the building

in a public park?" "By no means; the Capitol is intended to be in the
centre of the city; it is in this direction that the city is to grow." It is the
same everywhere from the Mississippi to the Pacific. Men seem to live in
the future rather than in the present: not that they fail to work while it is
called to-day, but that they see the country not merely as it is, but as it will
be, twenty, fifty, a hundred years hence, when the seedlings shall have
grown to forest trees.

This constant reaching forward to and grasping at the future does not
so much express itself in words, for they are not a loquacious people, as
in the air of ceaseless haste and stress which pervades the West.* ... Time
seems too short for what they have to do, and result always to come
short of their desire. One feels as if caught and whirled along in a foaming
stream, chafing against its banks, such is the passion of these men to accomplish in their own life-times what in the past it took centuries to effect.
Sometimes in a moment of pause, for even the visitor finds himself in-
fected by the all-pervading eagerness, one is inclined to ask them: "Gentlemen, why in heaven's name this haste? ... Ages and ages lie before you.
Why sacrifice the present to the future, fancying that you will be happier
when your fields teem with wealth and your cities with people? In Europe
we have cities wealthier and more populous than yours, and we are not
happy. You dream of your posterity; but your posterity will look back to
yours as the golden age, and envy those who first burst into this silent
splendid nature, who first lifted up their axes upon these tall trees and
lined these waters with busy wharves. Why, then, seek to complete in a
few decades what the other nations of the world took thousands of years
over in the older continents? Why do things rudely and ill which need to
be done well, seeing that the welfare of your descendants may turn upon
them? Why, in your hurry to subdue and utilize nature, squander her
splendid gifts? Why allow the noxious weeds of Eastern politics to take
root in your new soil, when by a little effort you might keep it pure? ..."

Being once suddenly called upon to "offer a few remarks" to a Western
legislature, and having on the spur of the moment nothing better to offer,
I tendered some such observations as these, seasoned, of course, with the
compliments to the soil, climate, and "location" reasonably expected from
a visitor. They were received in good part, as indeed no people can be
more kindly than the Western Americans; but it was surprising to hear
several members who afterwards conversed with me remark that the
political point of view—the fact that they were the founders of new
commonwealths, and responsible to posterity for the foundations they

---

* In the West men usually drop off the cars before they have stopped, and do not
enter them again till they are already in motion, hanging on like bees to the end of
the tail car as it quits the depot.

laid, a point of view so trite and obvious to a European visitor that he pauses before expressing it—had not crossed their minds. If they spoke truly—as no doubt they did—there was in their words a further evidence of the predominance of material efforts and interests over all others, even over those political instincts which are deemed so essential a part of the American character. The arrangements of his government lie in the dim background of the picture which fills the Western eye. In the foreground he sees ploughs and sawmills, ore-crushers and railway locomotives. These so absorb his thoughts as to leave little time for constitutions and legislation; and when constitutions and legislation are thought of, it is as means for better securing the benefits of the earth and of trade to the producer, and preventing the greedy corporation from intercepting their fruits.

Politically, and perhaps socially also, this haste and excitement, this absorption in the development of the material resources of the country, are unfortunate. As a town built in a hurry is seldom well built, so a society will be the sounder in health for not having grown too swiftly. Doubtless much of the scum will be cleared away from the surface when the liquid settles and cools down. Lawlessness and lynch law will disappear; saloons and gambling-houses will not prosper in a well-conducted population; schools will improve and universities grow out of the raw colleges which one already finds even in the newer Territories. Nevertheless the bad habits of professional politics, as one sees them on the Atlantic coast, are not unknown in these communities; and the unrestfulness, the passion for speculation, the feverish eagerness for quick and showy results, may so soak into the texture of the popular mind as to colour it for centuries to come. These are the shadows which to the eye of the traveller seem to fall across the glowing landscape of the Great West.

THE COWBOY ERA

The cattleman's frontier is the most common locale for the Western novel, motion picture, or television program. Literary critics, historians, and psychologists all have their theories concerning the continuing interest in the cowboy Western. Whatever its mystique may be, we can be pretty

sure that the "horse opera" will still be with us when professional football
has become as passé as bare-knuckle boxing.

This is all the more remarkable when we realize that historically the
open range lasted just twenty years—from 1866 until 1886, by which time
the range was dangerously overstocked. Shrewd ranchers knew that if
nature acted up, the industry would never be the same again. And nature
did get cantankerous, first offering a drought, then a winter straight out
of the North Pole. These severities of nature, combined with Cleveland's
governmental policies favoring the homesteader and insisting upon honest
land entry, forced the open range to give way to modern ranching methods.
These included the fenced range and blooded livestock. Ranching, in other
words, submitted to restrictions and made adjustments, just as railroads
and industry were shortly to do with the creation of the Interstate Commerce Commission and the passage of the Sherman Act. A new day was
a-dawning.

The cowboy era was, then, completely a product of the Gilded Age. In
its wide-swinging ways, its boisterousness, its heavy investment and big
profits or tragic losses, its easy-going on-again, off-again respect for the
law, and its emphasis on the free individual, it is peculiarly symbolic of
the age in which it flourished.

The late Joseph Kinsey Howard, Iowa-born but Montana-raised, knew
and loved Montana and was critical of its exploiters. From his most notable book, Montana: High, Wide, and Handsome, comes the following
description of the winter that ended the already-declining open range
cattle industry.

JOSEPH KINSEY HOWARD, Kissineyooway'o

... The summer of 1885 was dry; that of 1886 was parching. Great fires
swept the range; those cattlemen who could find new grass began the
move through a haze of smoke which hung over Montana for months.
"There has hardly been an evening in the last week," said the Rocky
Mountain Husbandman in August, "that the red glare of the fire demon

has not lit up our mountain ridges, while our exchanges bring news of disastrous fires in all parts of the Territory."

The grass began to die in July and all but the largest streams and water holes dried up. Water in the creeks became so alkaline that cattle refused to drink it. Cinders, ashes, and hot alkali dust covered the range and even the furniture in the ranch houses.

That fall wild game moved early from its favored shelters in the Missouri badlands and hurried south and west. Birds which customarily remained all winter fled, too. The horses' winter coats appeared earlier than usual; "even the range cattle," said Stuart, "seemed to take on a heavier, shaggier coat of hair."

Nature had set her stage for the last act.

Kissin-ey-oo-way'-o, the Crees said; "it blows cold." The Crees were the northern people, from the Height of Land; they had many words for cold, degrees of coldness, the effects of cold—but none more literally translating into speech the condition it described: in *kissineyooway'o* the north wind sang, softly at first, then rising to a wail and a howl. ... It blows cold.

It began November 16, though Montana seldom has severe cold or heavy snow until after Christmas. The gale was icy, and it had substance: it was filled with glassy particles of snow, like flakes of mica; it roared and rumbled. After the first day the tonal pitch rose: from a roar it became a moan, then a scream. The snow rode the wind, it thrust forward fiercely and slashed like a knife; no garment or hide could withstand it. The gale piled it into glacial drifts; when cow or horse stumbled into them the flesh on its legs was sheared to the bone.

Now suddenly there appeared white owls of the Arctic. The cattlemen had never seen them before; but the Indians and the métis knew them—and like the beasts and birds, they fled south.

Slowly the temperature moderated. The stockmen prayed for what the Indians called "the black wind" from the arch of black cloud on the western horizon from which it emerged; but it was too early in the season for the chinook. The drifts dwindled but did not disappear; they spread, crusting the range.

In December there were two more blizzards.

January is the Moon of Cold-Exploding-Trees. On the ninth day of that month it snowed without an instant's interruption for sixteen hours—an inch an hour; and the temperature fell to 22 below zero. Intermittent snow continued for another ten days, with temperatures ranging from 22 to 46 below in central Montana; in some other sections it was 40 below day in and day out for more than two weeks.

There was a respite of a little more than a week; then, on January 28, the great blizzard struck. For three days and three nights it was impossible to see fifty feet in any direction and ranch thermometers read 63 below zero. A sudden break in the cold and a wind shift gave promise of a chinook, but the storm set in again and lasted through February 3. A rider who dismounted dropped into snow to his waist on level ground.

Cattle which had been pushed over the Missouri in the fall to the better grass on the northern range drifted back, for there was little shelter on the steppes north of the river. Half dead from cold and hunger, their bodies covered with sores and frozen blood, bewildered and blind in a world of impenetrable white, they blundered into the barbed-wire fences, crumpled against them, and perished. They were trapped in drifts above their bellies and stood erect until their bodies froze. They slid into air holes in the rivers.

Cowboys donned two suits of heavy underwear, two pairs of wool socks, wool pants, two woolen shirts, overalls, leather chaps, wool gloves under leather mittens, blanket-lined overcoats, and fur caps. Before putting on the socks they walked in the snow in their bare feet, then rubbed them dry vigorously. After pulling on their riding boots they stood in water, then stood outdoors until an airtight sheath of ice had formed on the boots. Sometimes instead of the riding boots they wore moccasins and overshoes or sheepskin-lined "packs."

Thus prepared, they mounted and fought their way through the snow to extricate cattle stuck in drifts, tried to herd the dying beasts into sheltered ravines and head them off from treacherous rivers. They blacked their faces and eye sockets with lampblack or burnt matches to forestall snow blindness, or they cut holes in their black neckerchiefs and masked their faces, bandit-fashion. They strained and gasped as the icy air stabbed into their lungs and stomachs; they froze hands and feet, and many of them died. Their bodies, frozen stiff, were lashed on the backs of their horses and borne back to the ranch houses, to be thrust into a snowbank until a chinook came because the ground could not be broken for graves.

For all this they got no medals, nor expected any. A cowboy's job was to look after the herd; he was being paid for it—$40 a month. But hundreds of ranchers and riders underwent such hardships in that dreadful winter that they forsook the range forever, crippled in body and spirit.

As the storms and cold continued through February, the tragedy of the range was brought into the towns. Starving cattle staggered through village streets, collapsed and died in dooryards. Five thousand head invaded the outskirts of the newborn city of Great Falls, bawling for food. They snatched up the saplings the proud city had just planted, gorged themselves upon garbage.

Courtesy of the Denver Public Library Western Collection. Photo by Charles Graham.

Cattle in a blizzard on the plains.

Kaufman and Stadler, Helena cattleman, wrote to their foreman in the Judith Basin to inquire about their herd. When the delayed stage delivered the letter, the foreman tossed it with a derisive grin to one of his riders, a young Missourian who had attained some bunkhouse fame for his pencil and water color sketches.

"Got a postcard?" asked the young artist, whose name was Charley Russell. On it he swiftly sketched in water color a gaunt steer, legs bowed and head down, standing in a drift with a coyote waiting nearby. Below he printed a terse legend: "Last of Five Thousand." The card was mailed back to the Helena men without other comment. It was the first Russell work to attain wide circulation; under the title he had originally given it or the later one, "Waiting for a Chinook," it made the artist famous throughout the cow country. It is now owned by the Montana Stockgrowers' Association and hangs in its Helena office. Russell died in Great Falls in 1926; his last painting sold for $30,000. ...

VIOLENCE

Traditionally, the West is thought of as a violent land. Just how accurate is this common view? Probably the violence has been grossly exaggerated. Many thousands of quiet, law-abiding people went about their daily tasks for years at a time, never raising a rifle but for a shot at a jackrabbit or a slinking coyote, and never owning one of the heavy Colt six-shooters. On the other hand, there certainly was some violence. Cattle towns could be pretty rough; it was a rare Saturday afternoon in any border community that did not have at least one good fight, and it was a rare Sunday morning when the sheriff did not release half a dozen drunks who had been sleeping off a binge. There were some organized gangs of train robbers, bank bandits, and rustlers. Those boys meant business, but so did the side of law and order. One day in the ordinarily quiet Kansas town of Coffeyville, the chips were down, and the Dalton gang lost.

That brief episode is described with rare literary skill by the writer-historian Thomas Beer. The reading is from a strangely different history of the 1890's—sort of an impressionist's view of the people and the times; the characters move now busily, now hesitantly, now grotesquely through page after page of Beer's writing. For most people the total effect is enlightening as well as enjoyable, and after reading The Mauve Decade *they have a sense of understanding of the 1890's that they did not possess before.*

THOMAS BEER, *The Last of the Dalton Gang*

... At half past nine on the bright morning of October 5, 1892, a lad named John Sibert was helping his aunt to wash dishes in a house of Coffeyville, Kansas. He had arrived in the little city two days before and was leaving Coffeyville on the train at noon. Coffeyville had two topics, that week; the main street was torn up for new drains and somebody had told somebody else from saddle to saddle on the prairie that Bob Dalton had bragged he would raid his own town in broad daylight. At half past nine, then, John Sibert was helping to wash dishes diligently. Between that moment and the second of twenty-five minutes to ten, rifles crashed. John leaped down his aunt's steps and slid against a post, stopping his watch. Some lad ran past him yelling: "The Daltons are in!" and the word reached a clerk at the station. In a few minutes men in Omaha and Kansas City were shouting the news as the one word, "Dalton, Dalton, Dalton, Dalton..." clicked from the keys all through the midlands. John Sibert loped around a corner and suddenly faced two long, grave young men with rifles in their hands. He didn't know Bob and Emmett Dalton from any other strangers and he started to ask something. Bob drawled: "Keep away from here, bud, or you'll get hurt," and shoved the boy aside placidly, then placidly strolled along with Emmett, snapping his fingers and whistling through his teeth. At once a lad named Luke Baldwin hurried into sight and didn't pause when one of the brothers shouted to him. Bob Dalton killed him forthwith and the pair trotted from John Sibert's view .... The famous gang rode into town at half past nine. They left their horses in an alley and calmly strolled up to separate in the space before the town's two banks. Bob and Emmett plundered one bank. Grattan Dalton with the henchmen Bill Powers and Dick Broadwell attended to the other. Citizens grabbed the rifles with which the antecinemic West did its serious shooting and the fight began. Bright spires of glass toppled from frames of windows;

From Thomas Beer, *The Mauve Decade*. New York: Alfred A. Knopf, Inc., 1926, pp. 67–70. Vintage edition, 1961, pp. 41–43. Reprinted by permission.

smoke went in surges along the street as men fired busily from porches or through doorways. There are a hundred legends of what happened. Young John Sibert knelt beside the dying boy in the alley behind one bank and heard a man named Gump swearing in the pain of a shattered hand. Presently Broadwell rode wildly down the street with his hands gripped on the horn of his great Mexican saddle and fell dead from his mount a little way from the noisy town. Somebody killed Bill Powers. Grattan Dalton ran down the sidewalk with blood on his face and paused to rip the green handkerchief from his throat in full range of the batteries before he turned at the corner of a stable and fired back, killing the city's marshal with a superb shot from the hip. His shoulder was riddled so that he couldn't lift his rifle. He lurched from sight down the alley toward the tethered horses. Bob Dalton strolled into view, loading his rifle, and a hundred muzzles were aimed at his blue shirt. One ball caught him above the navel but he walked on and sat on a heap of stones beside a barn, firing again. A man named Kloehr ran from cover straight at the terrible rifle and shot the gang's captain in the lungs, then whirled and sent a bullet through Grattan Dalton's throat as the youngest brother crawled toward the plunging horses. Firing stopped. Men hurried up and a thick group formed around Bob Dalton in his carmine puddle on the clay. The body heaved in its blood but he kept yelling: "Ride!" Then someone howled and the crowd saw Emmett Dalton struggling among the horses. He was wounded four times when he got into his saddle and sat huddled with his gloves clasped on his groin. Men lowered their rifles, expecting him to fall, as men shot in the groin do, generally. But all the brothers were valiant. He spurred his horse down the alley and swung from the stirrups to seize Bob's arm. Politeness ended. Carey Seaman blew in his side with a fast shot. The last Dalton slid across his brother's body. It was now ten minutes to ten. Sightseers poured from trains before noon and the corpses of Lord Tennyson's escort to Walhalla were photographed so that it could be proved the Dalton gang was out of business after five years of graceful, even endearing performance. Unlike the James and Younger gangs, they didn't blow unarmed children to rags nor did they kill their mistresses in farewell as did the unlovable Tumlinson, once something of a hero. They were amiable and rather mannerly bandits, on the whole, and yet no ballad bears their name. The great tradition of Sturdevant, Murrel of "the mystic clan" in Andrew Jackson's reign, Boone Helm, Billy the Kid and Jesse James ended here in an alley on the crackling sound of Carey Seaman's shotgun. Jay Gould died eight weeks later in civilized New York, and in his bed. . . .

WESTERN POVERTY:
THE GOVERNMENTAL ATTITUDE

In the years following the Civil War the pioneers settled the Great Plains too rapidly. The wet side of the climatic cycle ended abruptly, and drought, blizzards, hail, and grasshoppers brought misery to the inhabitants of the lonely homesteads. Added to these woes were the ever-continuing mortgages, the excessive charges for patented machinery, the high railway rates, and the grain elevator charges that fluctuated according to need. Many farmers had settled with too little money, no reserves, and very little knowledge of the dynamics of plains agriculture. As a consequence, these settlers suffered from extreme poverty, malnutrition, and even starvation.

Gradually they found their political power and made their demands. At first these were modest requests, such as appropriations for seed or for mortgage relief. But America's statesmen still thought in the rigorous terms of the Protestant Ethic, and still acted from the viewpoint of a small nation, with a small population, with but small areas of hardship, where good-neighborliness could give succor to the destitute. President Cleveland's veto of a bill to provide seed to drought-stricken farmers is an excellent example of the kind of thinking that resisted the farmer's pleas for relief, and drove the people of the plains into Populism.

GROVER CLEVELAND, *Veto Message for the Seed Distribution Bill*

Executive Mansion, February 16, 1887

To the House of Representatives:

I return without my approval House Bill No. 10203, entitled: "An act to enable the Commissioner of Agriculture to make a special distribution of

---

Grover Cleveland, Veto of "An Act to Enable the Commissioner of Agriculture to Make a Special Distribution of Seeds in the Drought-Stricken Counties of Texas, and Making an Appropriation Therefor," in James D. Richardson, ed., *Messages and Papers of the Presidents* (Washington: Bureau of National Literature and Art, 1903), Vol. VIII, pp. 557, 558.

seeds in the drought-stricken counties of Texas, and making an appropriation therefor."

It is represented that a long-continued and extensive drought has existed in certain portions of the State of Texas, resulting in a failure of crops and consequent distress and destitution.

Though there has been some difference in statements concerning the extent of the people's needs in the localities thus affected, there seems to be no doubt that there has existed a condition calling for relief; and I am willing to believe that, notwithstanding aid already furnished, a donation of seed grain to the farmers located in this region, to enable them to put in new crops, would serve to avert continuance or return of an unfortunate blight.

And yet I feel obliged to withhold my approval of the plan, as proposed by this bill, to indulge a benevolent and charitable sentiment through the appropriation of public funds for that purpose.

I can find no warrant for such an appropriation in the Constitution, and I do not believe that the power and duty of the General Government ought to be extended to the relief of individual suffering which is in no manner properly related to the public service or benefit. A prevalent tendency to disregard the limited mission of this power and duty should, I think, be steadfastly resisted, to the end that the lesson should be constantly enforced that though the people support the Government the Government should not support the people.

The friendliness and charity of our countrymen can always be relied upon to relieve their fellow-citizens in misfortune. This has been repeatedly and quite lately demonstrated. Federal aid in such cases encourages the expectation of paternal care on the part of the Government and weakens the sturdiness of our national character, while it prevents the indulgence among our people of that kindly sentiment and conduct which strengthens the bonds of common brotherhood.

It is within my personal knowledge that individual aid has to some extent already been extended to the sufferers mentioned in this bill. The failure of the proposed appropriation of $10,000 additional to meet their remaining wants will not necessarily result in continued distress if the emergency is fully made known to the people of the country.

It is here suggested that the Commissioner of Agriculture is annually directed to expend a large sum of money for the purchase, propagation, and distribution of seeds and other things of this description, two-thirds of which are, upon the request of Senators, Representatives, and Delegates in Congress, supplied to them for distribution among their constituents.

The appropriation of the current year for this purpose is $100,000, and it will probably be no less in the appropriation for the ensuing year. I understand that a large quantity of grain is furnished for such distribution, and it is supposed that this free apportionment among their neighbors is a privilege which may be waived by our Senators and Representatives.

If sufficient of them should request the Commissioner of Agriculture to send their shares of the grain thus allowed them to the suffering farmers of Texas, they might be enabled to sow their crops, the constituents for whom in theory this grain is intended could well bear the temporary deprivation, and the donors experience the satisfaction attending deeds of charity.

IV / POLITICS
AND FOREIGN POLICY

INTRODUCTION

For many decades following the Gilded Age there was a stereotyped description of its politics that went something like this: From Ulysses S. Grant to Theodore Roosevelt, both major political parties represented nearly the same ideals. Issues were superficial, and politicians were likely to be physically obese, personally corrupt, intellectually shallow, and morally sterile. They catered to every whim of the vested interests, smoked big, black cigars, drank expensive bourbon whiskey, and shared in boodle at the city, state, and national levels. Even the Presidents partly fit this description, for they were at best naive mediocrities. Because neither party took action to ameliorate the unrest brewing among large segments of the electorate, a strong third party, the Populists, arose toward the end of the age and forced the Republicans and Democrats once more to bow to the wishes of the people.

Such a simple description would then be followed by some account of the major issues: the demonetization of silver, the tariff, "waving the bloody shirt" (stirring up old Civil War emotions to harm the Democrats), civil service reform, and possibly the railroad land grants or the fraudulent sales of the public lands. To try to maintain lagging interest, the textbook writer would include some comments about Stalwarts, Half-Breeds, and Mugwumps, and liven up the text for a few minutes' reading with some sinister statements about Grover Cleveland's private life, or Blaine's fatal acceptance of the phrase "Rum, Romanism, and Rebellion." Yet for all this, politics in the Gilded Age was portrayed as dull and unimportant.

Recent studies have upset this simple treatment. First of all, they point out that politics was very serious to the politicians at the time, because the two major parties were so evenly divided that any given election could result in a reversal of party fortunes. Second, despite the precarious balance of the two parties, it is clear now—and it was clear then to some of the master politicians—that of the two, the Republican party was below the Democratic party in registered members. Thus every election challenged the astuteness of the Republican campaign managers. Third, the emergence of an industrially and economically linked nation presented a growing need for some kind of new governmental policies toward labor, big business, and agriculture. The new policies must be introduced, defended or denounced in state legislatures, in Congress, and in executive chambers. This was the task of the politicians.

That the Interstate Commerce Act was passed under the Democrat Grover Cleveland, and the Sherman Antitrust Act under the Republican

Benjamin Harrison, is sufficient indication of the awareness of changed conditions, and of the new directions of governmental endeavor which were to be brought about by the democratic process under both Republican and Democratic leadership. That both parties lagged seriously behind national needs and ignored certain elements (the western farmers, for example) is obvious. They were hardly ignorant of the conditions, but were too slow and too dominated by reactionary elements to end the discontent.

Still, as the earlier textbook writers recorded, it was a crass age politically, an age of easy-flowing money, of supercilious morality, of corruption that "good men" accepted as a part of the rights of holding elected office. In essence, the politics and politicians of the age remind us perhaps too much of many elements of our politics of today.

The last two readings in this book pose the moralistic question of what justifies the use of power in foreign relations. This nation has always manifested a moralistic concern about its wars, something alien and incomprehensible to Europeans. With the coming of the Spanish-American War the issue was raised again, and it has remained with us in unbroken continuity ever since.

INTERPRETATION

Professor Vincent P. De Santis of the University of Notre Dame is an authority on the post-Civil War period and 20th-century American history. His penetrating analysis of the Republican Party in the Gilded Age is the result of several thousand hours of meticulous research on the subject. His larger study is entitled, Republicans Face the Southern Question: The New Departure Years, 1877–1897.

VINCENT P. DE SANTIS, The Republican Party Revisited, 1877–1897

Lord Bryce discovered that describing the American party system in *The American Commonwealth* was more difficult than explaining our Constitution and government. "Hitherto we have been on comparatively firm ground, for we have had definite data to rely upon, and the facts set forth have been mostly patent facts which can be established from books and documents," he wrote. "But now we come to phenomena for a knowledge of which one must trust to a variety of flying and floating sources, to newspaper paragraphs, to the conversation of American acquaintances, to impressions found on the spot from seeing incidents and hearing stories and anecdotes, the authority for which, though it seemed sufficient at the time cannot always be remembered. Nor have I the advantage of being able to cite any previous treatises on the subject," continued Bryce, "for though the books and articles dealing with the public life of the United States may be counted by hundreds, I know of no author who has set himself to describe impartially the actual daily working of that part of the vast and intricate political machine which lies outside the Constitution."

Yet for all his apologies and obstacles Bryce left a classic commentary on the parties of the Gilded Age that has influenced every historian's thinking about them. He believed that the two major parties of these years were in danger of losing their functional usefulness because they failed to offer the electorate an opportunity to vote on issues and because they used

"The Republican Party Revisited, 1877–1897," by Vincent P. De Santis. From H. Wayne Morgan, ed., *The Gilded Age: A Reappraisal*, pp. 91–110. Copyright © 1963 by Syracuse University Press, Syracuse, New York. Reprinted by permission, without footnotes.

public office to reward party workers. According to Bryce, "Neither party has any principles, any distinctive tenets. Both have traditions. Both claim to have tendencies. Both have certainly war cries, organizations, interests enlisted in their support. But these interests are in the main the interests of getting or keeping the patronage of the government. . . . All has been lost except office or the hope of it." The two major parties in this period "were like two bottles. Each bore a label denoting the kind of liquor it contained, but each was empty."

Other thoughtful observers of the political life of the Gilded Age agreed with Bryce. "One might search the whole list of Congress, Judiciary, and Executive during the twenty-five years 1870–1895 and find little but damaged reputations," wrote Henry Adams. "The period was poor in purpose and barren in results." The impulse to spring to the aid of the underdog has brought forth champions of the cultural, literary, and technological achievements of the Gilded Age, but none to defend its political record. "Even among the most powerful men of that generation," said Adams, speaking of the politicians, there were "none who had a good word for it." While present-day historians have had the benefit of more sources and perspective than either Bryce or Adams, they have usually subscribed to their conclusions. They have vied with each other to censure the political life of the Gilded Age for its barrenness, dreariness, and monotony. They have felt that at no other period in American history was the moral and intellectual tone of political life so uniformly low or were political conflicts so concerned with patronage rather than with principles. Charles Beard has called it the "age of negation," and Morison and Commager have described it as the dreariest chapter in American politics in which the titular leaders "contributed nothing of lasting importance to American politics or American life."

Because the Republican party occupied the presidency for most of these years, it has received the bulk of the criticism. It has become an historical convention to represent it as being conservative and to condemn it for evading issues, for dodging the responsibility of enacting major legislation, for not reflecting the mood and purposes of the American people, for deteriorating into a group of spoilsmen, for ignoring the needs of the farmer, the laborer, and the consumer in the industrial age, and for best serving the ends of business as it was itself best served by business collaboration. It is no wonder then that historians have pictured the eras of President Wilson and the two Roosevelts as times when America struggled out of the darkness into the light.

In the post-Civil War generation the Republican party possessed tremendous moral assets from which it profited immensely. It appeared as the savior of the Union and this allowed it to equate party loyalty with

national patriotism and to charge the Democrats with having fought under
the Confederate flag. The Republicans also offered the voters a surplus
of Civil War veterans. With the exception of James G. Blaine, all Republican nominees for the presidency from Rutherford B. Hayes to William
McKinley had an enviable Union war record, in sharp contrast to the only
one the Democrats could produce in the person of General Winfield Scott
Hancock in 1880. There was also the magic tradition of Lincoln. Americans
hailed him as the Great Emancipator, and Republicans capitalized on their
role as the party of liberation. They were so successful in emphasizing this
point that the Democrats were unable to show that the Republicans had
spurned the question of emancipation in 1860 and had accepted it only as
a war measure.

If the Republican party had assets it also had liabilities. Probably the
most important of these was a severe limitation upon its power. Contrary
to popular belief the post-Reconstruction period was not one of Republican
supremacy. It was an era of party stalemate and equilibrium in which a
bitter fight developed between the two major parties for control of the
government. And while the Republicans prevented the Democrats from
having charge of it, except for a few years, they could not direct it themselves. In the five presidential elections from 1876 to 1892 the Republicans,
while winning three of them, failed to carry a majority of the popular
vote in any one of them, and in only one, that of 1880, did they receive a
plurality—but even that plurality was less than one-tenth of one per cent.
In three of these elections the difference between the popular votes for the
two major party candidates was less than one per cent, although in the
electoral college votes, majorities ranged from 1 in 1876 to 132 in 1892.
Throughout much of this period the Republicans depended for victory
upon the very small majorities they received in such key states as Indiana
and New York, and they never once won a plurality of the counties in the
nation as a whole.

Added to the struggle to win the presidency was that to gain command
of Congress. Between 1877 and 1897 the Republicans controlled the presidency and Congress at the same time for only four years, in 1881–83 and
again in 1889–91. Only in the latter instance did they have a working
majority. On the first occasion they had a margin of but one in the House,
and only the cooperation of William Mahone, the readjuster from Virginia,
enabled them to organize the Senate. In contrast the Democrats held the
presidency and Congress at the same time for only two years, 1893–95.

The Republican party of the Gilded Age has invariably been described
as conservative, and the Republican presidents from Hayes to McKinley
have generally been characterized as respectable mediocrities who in their
social and political thinking were convinced that their party's support of

American individualism was in accord with some prearranged plan. Many of these judgments have resulted from treating the period in terms of present-day concepts about liberals and conservatives. In retrospect the achievements of the political leaders of the Gilded Age often seem few and meaningless. But though they lacked the boldness and imagination of Wilson and the two Roosevelts, they were clearly wholly different personalities; and there was an entirely different political situation and set of circumstances in the seventies and eighties than there has been in the twentieth century. A more fruitful study would measure the standards and ideas that prevailed in the Gilded Age and try to discover how the period actually looked to contemporaries who took part in its events.

The men who served in the presidency and Congress in the post-Reconstruction years knew little, if anything, about the major problem of their time—the adjustment of American politics to the great economic and social changes that came to the United States with the rise of industrial capitalism and urbanism. They were not educated for reform as were their successors in the Progressive era by muckrakers. In terms of prevailing ideas today about the relationship of government to the economy, the Republican leaders of the Gilded Age were conservatives. They believed governmental interference with economic natural laws impeded progress; thus government regulation should be limited to the barest minimum. To them, taxation hurt the economy and must be kept at a minimum. But in their own minds and in those of many contemporaries, they were not conservatives. They were not committed to lessening federal power. They did not oppose spending public money for special interests, as their support of national subsidy programs shows, especially the protective tariff. In this the Republican leaders differed markedly from the conservative Democrats, sometimes called Bourbons, who believed that the protective tariff and subsidies to special interest groups violated natural law.

Political studies of the last quarter of the nineteenth century emphasize the corrupt alliance between the Republican party and the business interests and the dominant role of the latter in shaping party policy. From this view, the party leaders were business hirelings. If this be true, how does one explain voter acquiescence in the arrangement? It is interesting to note not so much that this supposed combination was corrupt, but that it lasted so long without interference from the voters. E. L. Godkin in the *Nation* of May, 1873, put his finger on the situation when he wrote: "All being corrupt together, what is the use of investigating each other?" While writers have noted that the Republican party of the Gilded Age differed from that of Fremont and Lincoln, they overlook the shift in the character of political thought and democracy that followed the Civil War. Professor Robert McCloskey has set forth the idea that American politics of the post-Civil War generation was a product of perversion of democracy. A general deterioration of standards and ideals took place in these decades under the impact of an expanding capitalism, and it would be strange if this widespread debasement were not reflected in the age's political attitudes, and if it had not changed some of the assumptions of American democracy. Democracy became perverted when capitalism was welded to the democratic creed and when aims of democracy and business became indistinguishable. With democracy identified with property rights, it was harder to secure social reforms. For while the reformers called for some curtailment of economic freedom, they were also troubled by their attacks upon the democratic faith. If this bothered reformers it likewise disturbed politicians.

It is true that business dominated, but the bulk of Americans were sympathetic to business. The ideas of Social Darwinism and laissez faire prevailed, and most Americans regarded government intervention as unnecessary, unjust, and even immoral. Even reformers confined government regulation of business to those cases where it was clearly necessary and where a careful study had been made. Private enterprise and free competition without government interference, except to maintain law and order and to protect property rights, was held as an ultimate truth by a great majority of Americans. The Republican leaders of the Gilded Age were nothing more than the products of their time, and if we indict them for their conservatism and for their subservience to the business interests, then we must indict an overwhelming portion of effective and vociferous public opinion. Above all we must not read into this period of American politics the ideas about conservatism and liberalism and the relationship of the government to the economy that have grown up since the Progressive movement.

One of the most serious charges leveled against the Republican party of the Gilded Age is its failure to deal with the problems created by the industrial expansion of the post-Civil War years. It is customary to say that politics in these years became the fine art of avoiding issues. Not that there was any lack of important issues, for the problems arising out of the recurrent industrial crises and depressions of the period demanded vigorous government action. But the Republicans, and the Democrats too, so runs the charge, preferred to shun these new issues and to revive the old ones. The problems of the new economic order thus failed to get a hearing in the political arena except through the third parties, and the political battles of these years appear to have been fought over superficial issues.

The customary explanation for this shortcoming is that no important differences existed between the two major parties on the vital issues. The Democrats differed in no significant respect from the Republicans in outlook and achievement. Neither one of the old parties wished to disturb the status quo, and neither one believed that there was anything fundamentally wrong with American life. This is why Beard calls this period the "age of negation." But the critics have neglected to take into account the fact that the government in the post-Reconstruction years rarely concerned itself with economic and social matters as it has done in the twentieth century. The predominant feeling among Americans in the closing decades of the nineteenth century was simply that the government should not handle them.

But a number of other factors help to explain the legislative inactivity of the Republican party. Perhaps the most important of these was the sharp contest for power between the parties and the failure of either one to dominate the national government for any length of time. The struggle between a Republican president and a Democratic Congress, or vice versa, affected legislative achievement in the post-Reconstruction years as it did in any period in American history when political power has been thus divided. The case of President Hayes illustrates how these liabilities hampered the development of effective party leadership. He worked under severe handicaps that have not been fully appreciated. He held office with a disputed title, and Republicans and Democrats alike referred to him as "the de facto President," "His Fraudulency," and "Old Eight to Seven." His program for the South and for civil service reform along with his show of independence caused such a deep split to develop within his own party that at one time he had but three supporters in the Senate, and one of them, Stanley Matthews of Ohio, was a lifelong friend and relative. Moreover, the Democrats controlled the House throughout the whole of Hayes's administration and the Senate for the last two years of his term. Under these circumstances it is amazing that Hayes could accomplish anything.

Further crippling effective Republican leadership were the great factional feuds that plagued the party throughout the Gilded Age. Stalwart, Half-Breed, and Mugwump were pitted against each other in a naked grab for control of the party. The real leaders of the party like Blaine, Roscoe Conkling, John Logan, William E. Chandler, and others wasted their talents and energies in bitter personal rivalries rather than using them in the solution of the period's most pressing problems. The achievements of these men are few and insignificant. Their names are not associated with any major legislation.

The seat of national political power for most of these years was in Congress and not in the presidency. By 1877 a group of arrogant Republican leaders, who had dominated the federal government for nearly a decade, sat in the Senate. They had largely made the Republican party, and in a sense they were the party. They had overthrown President Andrew Johnson, had gained nearly complete possession of Grant, and they strove to put the succeeding presidents from Grant to McKinley at their mercy. The bitter struggle between the executive and legislative branches that had begun with Johnson and Congress, especially over the Tenure of Office Act, instead of dying down, continued to harass most of the presidents of this period. Added to this was the fact that the office of president in these years was at low ebb in power and prestige. Senator John Sherman, Republican leader of Ohio, himself a perpetual aspirant to the office, wrote, "The executive department of a republic like ours should be subordinate to the legislative department. The President should obey and enforce the laws, leaving to the people the duty of correcting any errors committed by their representatives in Congress." Republican leaders acted on these principles. "The most eminent Senators," wrote George F. Hoar of Massachusetts, "would have received as a personal affront a private message from the White House expressing a desire that they should adopt any course in the discharge of their legislative duties that they did not approve. If they visited the White House, it was to give, not to receive advice." Henry Adams agreed with this when he commented, "So far as the President's initiative was concerned, the President and his Cabinet might equally well have departed separately or together to distant lands."

Sectionalism also accounted for much of the legislative inactivity of the period. An analysis of the voting and debates in Congress clearly reveals the sectionalism of the country on issues of national importance and the fact that both major parties were split into sectional wings. The sectionalism of the seventies and eighties resulted from two movements, expansion of the West, particularly in the trans-Mississippi West, and the growth of industrialism in the Northeast.

Sectional alliances in this period proved to be flexible and shifted with changing economic conditions. For example the East North Central states (Ohio, Indiana, Illinois) which usually voted with the West North Central (Michigan, Wisconsin, Minnesota, Iowa) and southern states in the 1870's, by 1890 had joined hands with the Northeast. This change probably resulted from the growth of industry in the East North Central areas which affiliated them economically with the East.

Political personalities in the post-Reconstruction years played a subordinate role to an adjustment between the interests of the sections and party allegiance in determining the outcome of the vote on national policies. The leading issues of the country as indicated by the party platforms and congressional action were currency and banking, tariff, public lands, internal improvements, railroad and trust regulation, and immigration. While all these produced strong sectional feeling, they manifested one common feature—opposition of the agricultural regions to the industrial centers of the country.

More sectional voting occurred in the periods of depression and more party voting in the years of prosperity. Those sections hardest hit during a depression broke party ranks and combined with other hard-hit sections to redress their grievances. The vagueness of party platforms until 1888 also stimulated sectional divisions, since it allowed discontented sections to interpret the planks to suit their own interests without being accused of party disloyalty.

Much of the Republican voting in Congress on the leading issues of the seventies and eighties followed sectional lines. During the depression of the seventies, 70 per cent of the Republican vote was sectional. The New England wing, which remained consistently conservative on economic matters, opposed the North Central faction. In 15 per cent of the votes a majority of Republicans in all parts of the country sided with the radical minority located primarily in the North Central regions. In 15 per cent of the votes the party acted as a unit. In the years of prosperity, 1879–82, the Republican sectional voting fell to 41 per cent. Again New England and the West were on opposite sides. In 23 per cent of the votes the party acted almost as a unit, although a small radical minority existed in the West Central states, and 36 per cent was a purely party one. But in the slump of the mid-eighties the Republican sectional voting rose to 60 per cent only to drop to 33 per cent in the more prosperous years of the later eighties. In the seventies men like James A. Garfield, William McKinley, and Joseph Cannon, who later became influential Republican leaders, voted for radical financial legislation because their sections demanded it. McKinley's record on this matter was a source of embarrassment to the Republican party in 1896 when he campaigned on the gold standard plank.

Sectional voting was also more pronounced in Congress when both houses were divided between two parties than when one party was in control. This was equally true for both depression and prosperity years in the seventies and eighties. Thus not only did Republican presidents have to deal with Democratic congresses for most of the time in the post-Reconstruction years but with congresses in which their own party members did more sectional than party voting.

Much has been made also of the meaninglessness and futility of the platform upon which the Republican party campaigned in these years. But those who wag their heads about this matter fail to take into consideration certain factors. Theoretically, political parties offer to voters a distinctive set of principles or programs, and theoretically the public rewards the party whose principles it approves by voting for it. From this reasoning it follows that the necessity of competing for votes will cause the parties to vie with one another in giving the electorate a program it wants.

This is theory: practice is another matter. The major parties have had, or have at least professed principles, but the principles have appeared to be the same. Each generation has had its Bryce commenting on the empty bottles of American politics. Party contests cannot settle matters of vital importance, because a minority will not submit to an adverse majority vote on a question which it regards as essential to its security. Those who hold to this view point to the refusal of the South to acquiesce in the election of Lincoln. The point has also been made that party competition works best when parties have reached an implicit agreement on general principles.

The theory of party competition apparently breaks down in the Gilded Age if one accepts Edmund Burke's definition of party as a body of men united for promoting by their joint endeavor the national interest upon some particular principle on which they agree. But students of American politics believe that the only groups in this country that would come close to meeting this description have been those third parties fatally dedicated to forwarding limited interests or specific panaceas.

Perhaps the significance of our political system is not the alignment of voters pro and con in purely intellectual terms but rather in the maintenance of institutions which keeps key political power contingent and provides alternative sets of rulers. In practice our major parties have not been primarily concerned about drafting a distinctive program with a distinctive set of issues, but rather they have tried to find some way of bringing together into a reasonably harmonious relationship as large a proportion of the voters as possible. The methods used to achieve this end have been dictated by the times, the circumstances, and the kind of men in control of the party. Principles and issues have generally remained relative and subordinate to these conditions.

The Republicans faced the necessity of holding together the various elements that made up the party—businessmen, farmers, Negroes, federal officeholders, Union war veterans, and labor. They also had to combat the Democrats in the very closely contested elections of the period. Because of this the Republicans found it inexpedient and unwise to commit themselves in advance to a definite program. They could not in all probability have secured agreement among their ranks for it, nor could they have won general support for it. Yet the very lack of agreement allowed a degree of personal freedom for individual candidates that would have been impossible under other conditions. The Republican leadership labored to achieve the goal of any party, a working combination of sections, interests, and of liberals and conservatives. For this effort the Republicans must be credited with some degree of group diplomacy in politics. Professor H. Wayne Morgan has described the Republican party of the post-Civil War era as a classic coalition in American politics. It offered lands to the West, tariff protection to the East, some sort of controlled inflation to the Midwest, pensions to veterans, "and the moral rhetoric of the original anti-slavery crusade. The party built its success on a program rather than on corruption."

Even though the Republican party was labeled as conservative and the protector of business interests, it enjoyed a highly diversified group and broad geographical support. True, the Republican party remained sectional in a sense, for it had little visible support in the South, but outside this section a number of different elements voted for it. In these years the Republicans were strong in the small northern cities and in the rural districts. They were strong in the New England mill towns, the mining districts of Pennsylvania, everywhere on the farms and especially in the Old Northwest, among the small farmers and "poor whites" in the mountain districts of West Virginia, eastern Kentucky and Tennessee, and western Virginia and North Carolina, and the mining camps of the mountain and Pacific coast states. In spite of their reputation as the champions of the corporations and as having their special preserve in the East, the Republicans had their strongest congressional districts in the North Central and Central states. The Republicans were able to confine Democratic strength largely to the South, New York City and vicinity, and to parts of the Central states which had been settled by southerners.

The matter of spoils and patronage remains. If Bryce's view is accepted that the use of public office to reward party workers is wrong then it would certainly follow that the Republican party in the Gilded Age had degenerated into a group of spoilsmen and had failed in some of the functions for which it had come into existence. But it must also be remembered that the spoils system served a necessary purpose. Parties must be financed. Under the spoils system the government financed them in large measure. Sometimes incompetent persons received office, and at times, there were no duties to perform, for the usual requirement for obtaining the appointment was not fitness for office but partisanship. All this aroused at the time, and ever since, considerable protest. But the spoils system did provide a method for financing political parties. Unless men became suddenly virtuous and altruistic so that they were prepared to do party service at their own expense, some legal method of furnishing the party organization with funds had to be found. The spoils system was open and subject to much publicity and was in sharp contrast to the secret system, whereby large corporations, with special interests, supplied the money in exchange for favors. If for no other reason than that it was public, the spoils system was to be preferred.

While the Republicans dominated the presidency in the last quarter of the nineteenth century and appeared to have political supremacy, both in the national government and the country at large, their party, as we have seen, suffered from a sectional and minority status that seemed impossible to overcome. The loss of the South by 1877, the presence of a large bloc of doubtful voters in some of the Eastern and Central states, and the insecure hold of the Republicans upon the North are fundamental to the explanation of their failure to keep a complete and uninterrupted grip upon the national government after their great victory of 1872 in which they gathered 57 per cent of the popular vote in the North and West while in the South and the nation as a whole they polled 55.8 per cent. These developments along with the sharply contested elections of the post-Reconstruction years produced a series of major efforts by Republican strategists to find more recruits for the party. In their attempt to gain a more secure footing in the North they intensified their waving of the bloody shirt, twisted the tail of the British lion to please the Irish-Americans, and ingratiated themselves with the northeastern business community through favorable legislation. To win votes in the doubtful states the Republicans made concessions in the form of taking their presidential and vice-presidential nominees from these areas and by naming congressmen from these districts to important committee assignments. The Democrats matched them in their strategy in the doubtful states and among the businessmen.

But how to appeal to the South remained a major problem for the Republicans. They had not been able to maintain the Republican state governments set up in the South during Reconstruction. One by one they had fallen to the Democrats in spite of Force Bills and President Grant's efforts to uphold them with the use of the military. Even the most vigorous wavers of the bloody shirt realized this fact. "Gen. Grant held up the Southern Republican administration by main force for more than four years, and they got no stronger on their legs, but rather weaker and weaker," observed the *New York Tribune*. "We cannot continue that policy after experience has so fully demonstrated its futility." The *National Republican* pointed out, "The Republican party in the South has heretofore tried to rule by force of arms and Federal bayonets, and it failed."

The loss of the South was a bitter disappointment to the Republicans, for they were painfully aware of the severe handicap they had in the struggle to win control of the federal government when the Democrats had most of the 90 representatives and all of the 22 senators and 112 electoral votes in the South. Not only was it nearly impossible to make sufficient gains elsewhere to compensate for this loss, but it was illogical and poor strategy to allow the situation to continue without an attempt to remedy it. With their vote concentrated in the northern and western states, Republicans could expect to maintain their majority in the Senate. They could hope to battle for the presidency with the Democrats on fairly even terms, but without success in the South their prospects for gaining complete control of the national government were slim.

Because the South has been overwhelmingly Democratic since the Compromise of 1877 it has generally been assumed that the Republicans, apart from Reconstruction, have never really been seriously interested or active in building a strong party in this section. Furthermore, the belief has prevailed that with the removal of the troops, the Republicans gave up the fight in the South as hopeless and unprofitable and wrote off this part of the country as a possible area to contend for. All this has helped to foster one of the great myths of American politics, for Republican failure in the South did not come from lack of effort. Republican leaders worked constantly to break up the Democratic South and to rebuild their party in these states on a strong and permanent basis. They had no intention of permitting the South to go Democratic by default. They needed the South, and they needed it badly if they wished to become the majority party in all major sections of the country as they had done in 1872, and if they wanted to retain their grip on the federal government.

To coax southern Democrats out of their party and into the Republican fold involved a changeover from a policy of military interference to one of nonintervention in the South. Such a turnabout was a revolution in Republican policy, and the whole matter was debated privately and publicly toward the end of Reconstruction and was eventually adopted. Above all, Republicans hoped to benefit from Democratic cleavages in the South. They knew that a large number of Democrats in the South were dissatisfied with their party organization and leaders. Republicans also witnessed further Democratic discontent in the South in the rise of agrarian radicals. This led to the formation of independent movements which gathered strength in the late seventies and which reached their zenith in the Populist revolt of the nineties.

The Republicans launched their new policy in the South with the removal of the last of the federal troops from this section. Over the next twenty years they sought in a variety of ways to win over southern Democrats to the Republican party. But the Republican performance in the South in this period was so inept that it led many Republicans outside the South to conclude that their southern party was hopeless, and it caused many contemporaries and later generations to believe that the Republicans had permitted the South to go Democratic by default. Although this was clearly not the case these two notions, largely based upon faulty or erroneous history, grew up about the Republican party and the South and still persist in many quarters in spite of the evidence to the contrary.

The Republicans failed in the South not through any lack of interest or action on their part but because of the almost insuperable obstacles confronting their new venture. Southern white hostility toward the Republican party and fear of Negro supremacy did not give way before Republican blandishments. Republicans could afford to stand up for the rights of their southern brethren, but they could not afford to support their wrongs. The carpetbagger Negro governments had not won the respect of the country. "Carpet bag governments had not been successful," President Hayes told the editor of the *New Orleans Times.* "The complaints of the southern people were just in this matter." Neither had these radical governments in the South reflected a Republican sentiment based on a political conviction and sympathy growing among southern whites. In the main they had portrayed political shrewdness, skill in manipulating political machinery, and personal greediness. The one fatal defect of Republican policy since the Civil War, said the *New York Tribune,* was that of giving opportunity for "adventurers, who were utterly without standing or consideration in any Northern community, and who if not propped up by United States bayonets could not have been elected to any office by colored men of the South, to fasten themselves upon the party and the country as the representative Republicans of reconstructed States." "All other blunders put together," continued the *Tribune,* "have not cost the Republican party as many votes as the single fact that it was represented and controlled in reconstructed States by unworthy men."

Factional disputes also interfered with the attempted rejuvenation of the Republican party in the South. The problem was to find a formula, to bring together large numbers of whites and Negroes in the same party. But factionalism and splits between "black-and-tan" and "lily-white" groups undermined such attempts. Factionalism turned out to be the bane of southern Republicanism, and every Republican president since Grant has wrestled with it. Finally, the ability of Democrats to keep southern Republicans from the polls or to nullify their vote drastically reduced Republican strength in all the southern states after Reconstruction and nearly eliminated it entirely in some parts. The success of the whites in excluding the Republican vote as an important factor in southern politics contributed significantly to national Democratic victories.

By the end of these two decades the Republicans still had little support in the South. Twenty years of planning, maneuvering, and fusing still left them without electoral votes in this section. They were yet a sectional party without any great appeal for southern whites, and their party in the

South faced a greater problem of rejuvenation than it had in 1877. But the Republicans had not allowed the South to go Democratic by default. They had not written it off as hopeless. They had fought for it. They had tried to Republicanize it, and while the fruits of their effort seem small, they prepared themselves for a fresh try in the twentieth century.

One of the most controversial, tragic, and least understood aspects of the history of the Republican party of the Gilded Age is its relationship to the southern Negro. The Republican party emerged from the Civil War as the champion and protector of the southern Negro. It had emancipated and enfranchised him and had provided him with the same political and civil rights as the white man. And by joining hands with the Negro the Republicans were able to gain temporary political control of the South. While this Republican-Negro alliance produced fruitful political results in the beginning it also created a problem that still vexes both sides. In order to understand the nature of this problem it is necessary to recall what each side wanted from the other. The Republicans desired the votes of the Negro, and the freedman sought protection for his newly acquired rights and asked for the enforcement of the Fourteenth and Fifteenth amendments. He also wished to have greater political recognition and a larger share of the patronage for delivering his vote to the party of liberation.

In the last quarter of the nineteenth century the Republican party, through its official statements, gave every appearance of being the best friend that the Negro had. In their platforms from 1876 through 1896 the Republicans solemnly pledged themselves to enforce the Fourteenth and Fifteenth amendments, to secure to "every American citizen of whatever race and color complete liberty and exact equality in the exercise of all civil, political, and public rights," to protect "honest voters" against terrorism, violence, and fraud, and never to relax their efforts "until the integrity of the ballot and purity of elections . . . be fully guaranteed in every state." They demanded that every citizen, white or black, be allowed to cast one free unrestricted ballot and to have it counted and returned. They denounced the "continuous inhuman outrages" perpetrated upon American citizens for political reasons, and the "fraud and violence practiced by the Democracy in the Southern States." In Congress, Republicans moved investigations of fraud and violence in elections in the South, accused southern Democrats of holding their seats illegally and of exercising a disproportionate voting influence, and focused attention upon indiscreet statements by southern leaders and the press such as the editorial of the *Times-Democrat* of New Orleans which exclaimed, "The aim and desire of every white citizen of Louisiana is to eliminate the Negro from politics."

But the Republican party turned out to be among the poorest of friends that the southern Negro had after Reconstruction. For while the Republicans talked much about safeguarding the vote of the colored man and loudly lamented the state of political affairs in the South, they took few steps to remedy the situation or to meet their obligations to the freedmen. Instead of looking after the Negro as the ward of the nation, they deserted him and left him as the ward of the dominant race in the South. On three major occasions over these decades, the Republicans abandoned the Negro ally: when President Hayes removed the troops; when President Chester Arthur chose to work with southern independents; and when President Benjamin Harrison and a Republican Congress backed away from the Force Bill of 1890 to regulate federal elections.

In part this abandonment was beyond the control of the Republicans, for throughout most of this period they lacked the political power to enforce the Fourteenth and Fifteenth amendments. But the abandonment was also part of the new policy that Republicans had inaugurated in the South in 1877. These new plans called for a shift in Republican appeals in the South from Negroes to whites in the hope such strategy would result in the building of a Republican party in the South that could command the respect and support of southern conservative whites. This is not to say that the Republicans had lost interest in the Negro vote. On the contrary they wished to maintain, and even increase, their Negro support, but they also wanted to swell their ranks with white recruits. Thus Hayes forsook the Negro when he recalled the troops because he hoped this would reconcile North and South, conciliate southern whites, and ingratiate the Republican party with them. Arthur cast off the colored man when he joined hands with the white Independents in the South, because he believed that in order to exploit the Democratic cleavages in the South, which he had concluded was the only path to Republican success in this section, it was necessary to subordinate the freedman. In 1890 the Republicans abandoned the Negro when they failed to pass the Force Bill, because they had a greater interest in tariff and silver measures, although there was considerable opposition to the elections scheme in party ranks.

It must also be remembered that the Republican abandonment of the Negro was only a part of the general desertion of the freedman by northerners. By the end of Reconstruction the North had significantly changed its mind about the Negro. The *Nation*, one of his staunch northern champions, following the decision to take the troops out of the South, declared, "The negro will disappear from the field of northern politics. Henceforth the nation, as a nation, will have nothing more to do with him." Except for the Republican party interest in the Negro vote, there was not much concern among northerners for the colored man in the South. After 1877, northerners were, for the most part, in substantial agreement with southerners that the Negro was not prepared for equality and that the South should be allowed to deal with him in its own way. The North had come to believe that the elimination of the Negro from politics must be recognized to give more meaning to the reunion of North and South. Northerners were coming to regard the Negro as a thorn in their flesh, and as standing in the way of a return to national solidarity and a development of trade relations between the two sections. They were coming to look upon the Negro as the American peasantry, and as being inferior in race stamina, and they were coming to believe that the only hope for good government in the South rested upon the assured political supremacy of the white race.

The Republicans in their drive for new recruits from among southern whites had subordinated and even forsaken their Negro allies. In turn the Negro became suspicious and critical of the Republican party. Yet for all his misgivings and hostility the Negro preferred Republicans to Democrats and was reluctant to adopt the strategy of independent action. During the controversy over the new policy President Hayes had launched in the South, a Negro Republican from Baltimore in an open letter said that the defense of Horace Greeley in 1872 was child's play compared with efforts to defend Hayes among Republicans. This Negro had not met a Republican in weeks who attempted to disguise his disgust with Hayes's policy. Yet in all this he saw nothing to encourage the Negro except the prospect of their vindication by the defeat of the Republican party in 1880. "This would be a questionable satisfaction," wrote the Negro correspondent, "and as a remedy is worse than the disease." At the end of this period, in 1895, just before he died, Frederick Douglass pointed out that although the Republican party had become indifferent toward the Negro, "still we have a chance of getting a better man from the Republicans than from the Democrats." Whether this was a wise decision is surely debatable, for in our own time when the Negro has divided his political loyalty, both major parties have eagerly sought his vote.

The manner in which historians have treated the Republican party of the Gilded Age is reminiscent of a story of the mining country of the old West. In one of the mining camps there was a bully who cheated everyone he knew. He lied, he swore, he killed, and finally he died with his boots on. Now the miners wanted to give him some sort of religious service, but did not know how to do it. So they sent two of their group to a neighboring camp where they heard there was an old-time itinerant preacher prospecting for gold. They found him and asked him to preach a sermon over the dead man's remains. When he asked the character of the dead man, the two miners replied, "We can say nothing good for him. He is guilty of every crime on the calendar and had no conscience, no sympathy, no honor." When the preacher answered "all right," they asked, "You mean you are going to preach the sermon over his remains in spite of what we said." "Oh, yes." "What will you say?" they asked. "Well, I shall speak of the great times in which he lived."

The point is well made concerning the decades following the Civil War. It is a period in which the United States became the greatest industrial nation of the world. The chief actors on the American scene were businessmen. Americans witnessed a vast change in politics as the country became industrialized. Historians have called it the political triumph of business achieved through a corrupt alliance of business and government. Against such a background American historians have produced a stereotyped picture of a Republican party composed of ever needy and worthless Union veterans, greedy monopolists, and corpulent businessmen who made their corrupt senators and representatives dance to the tunes of enormously high protective tariffs, the gold standard, easy pensions, and extravagant river and harbor bills. This traditional description has been overdone as the authors of general histories and the most commonly used textbooks have competed with each other to find suitable disparaging phrases with which to describe the Republicans of the Gilded Age. Most certainly the Republican party must be judged in late nineteenth-century political terms. Those judgments must fit the situation as it actually was and not as we might like to have it be or suppose it was.

POLITICAL HYPOCRISY

From the novel The Gilded Age, by Charles Dudley Warner and Samuel L. Clemens (Mark Twain), we obtain the name that has been given first to the Grant years and finally to the entire era, 1865–1900.

Much of the novel is insipid; it is hardly worth reading in entirety. But some of the characters have lasting interest and a few of the situations are amusing. Colonel Sellers and Senator Dilworthy are realistic, and one of the delightful incidents is the one reprinted below. The hypocrisy of Senator Dilworthy, his unmitigated gall, his massive ego, remind us of a political type that emerged in the Gilded Age and has been with us ever since.

CHARLES DUDLEY WARNER
AND SAMUEL L. CLEMENS (MARK TWAIN),
Dilworthy at Saint's Rest, Prepares for Re-election

The session was drawing toward its close. Senator Dilworthy thought he would run out West and shake hands with his constituents and let them look at him. The legislature whose duty it would be to re-elect him to the United States Senate was already in session. Mr. Dilworthy considered his re-election certain, but he was a careful, painstaking man, and if, by visiting his state, he could find the opportunity to persuade a few more legislators to vote for him, he held the journey to be well worth taking. The University bill was safe, now; he could leave it without fear; it needed his presence and his watching no longer. But there was a person in his state legislature who did need watching—a person who, Senator Dilworthy said, was a narrow, grumbling, uncomfortable malcontent—a person who was stolidly opposed to reform, and progress and him—a person who, he feared, had been bought with money to combat him, and through him the commonwealth's welfare and its political purity.

"If this person Noble," said Mr. Dilworthy, in a little speech at a dinner-party given him by some of his admirers, "merely desired to sacrifice me,

From Charles Dudley Warner and Samuel L. Clemens, The Gilded Age. New York: Harper & Brothers, 1873. Quoted from Author's National Edition, 1915, Vol. II, pp. 213–221, 262.

I would willingly offer up my political life on the altar of my dear state's weal, I would be glad and grateful to do it; but when he makes of me but a cloak to hide his deeper designs, when he proposes to strike *through* me at the heart of my beloved state, all the lion in me is aroused—and I say, Here I stand, solitary and alone, but unflinching, unquailing, thrice armed with my sacred trust; and whoso passes, to do evil to this fair domain that looks to me for protection, must do so over my dead body."

He further said that if this Noble were a pure man, and merely misguided, he could bear it, but that he should succeed in his wicked designs through a base use of money would leave a blot upon his state which would work untold evil to the morals of the people, and *that* he would not suffer; the public morals must not be contaminated. He would seek this man Noble; he would argue, he would persuade, he would appeal to his honor.

When he arrived on the ground he found his friends unterrified; they were standing firmly by him and were full of courage. Noble was working hard, too, but matters were against him; he was not making much progress. Mr. Dilworthy took an early opportunity to send for Mr. Noble; he had a midnight interview with him, and urged him to forsake his evil ways; he begged him to come again and again, which he did. He finally sent the man away at three o'clock one morning; and when he was gone, Mr. Dilworthy said to himself:

"I feel a good deal relieved now, a great deal relieved."

The Senator now turned his attention to matters touching the souls of his people. He appeared in church; he took a leading part in prayer-meetings; he met and encouraged the temperance societies; he graced the sewing-circles of the ladies with his presence, and even took a needle now and then and made a stitch or two upon a calico shirt for some poor Bibleless pagan of the South Seas, and this act enchanted the ladies, who regarded the garments thus honored as in a manner sanctified. The Senator wrought in Bible classes, and nothing could keep him away from the Sunday-schools—neither sickness nor storms nor weariness. He even traveled a tedious thirty miles in a poor little rickety stagecoach to comply with the desire of the miserable hamlet of Cattleville that he would let its Sunday-school look upon him.

All the town was assembled at the stage office when he arrived, two bonfires were burning, and a battery of anvils was popping exultant broadsides; for a United States Senator was a sort of god in the understanding of these people, who never had seen any creature mightier than a country judge. To them a United States Senator was a vast, vague colossus, an awe-inspiring unreality.

Next day, everybody was at the village church a full half-hour before time for Sunday-school to open; ranchmen and farmers had come with their families from five miles around, all eager to get a glimpse of the great man —the man who had been to Washington; the man who had seen the President of the United States, and had even talked with him; the man who had seen the actual Washington Monument—perhaps touched it with his hands.

When the Senator arrived the church was crowded, the windows were full, the aisles were packed, so was the vestibule, and so, indeed, was the yard in front of the building. As he worked his way through to the pulpit on the arm of the minister and followed by the envied officials of the village, every neck was stretched and every eye twisted around intervening obstructions to get a glimpse. Elderly people directed each other's attention and said, "There! that's him, with the grand, noble forehead!" Boys nudged each other and said, "Hi, Johnny, here he is! There, that's him, with the peeled head!"

The Senator took his seat in the pulpit, with the minister on one side of him and the superintendent of the Sunday-school on the other. The town dignitaries sat in an impressive row within the altar railings below. The Sunday-school children occupied ten of the front benches, dressed in their best and most uncomfortable clothes, and with hair combed and faces too clean to feel natural. So awed were they by the presence of a living United States Senator, that during three minutes not a "spit-ball" was thrown. After that they began to come to themselves by degrees, and presently the spell was wholly gone and they were reciting verses and pulling hair.

The usual Sunday-school exercises were hurried through, and then the minister got up and bored the house with a speech built on the customary Sunday-school plan; then the superintendent put in his oar; then the town dignitaries had their say. They all made complimentary reference to "their friend, the Senator," and told what a great and illustrious man he was and what he had done for his country and for religion and temperance, and exhorted the little boys to be good and diligent and try to become like him some day. The speakers won the deathless hatred of the house by these delays, but at last there was an end and hope revived; inspiration was about to find utterance.

Senator Dilworthy rose and beamed upon the assemblage for a full minute in silence. Then he smiled with an access of sweetness upon the children and began:

"My little friends—for I hope that all these bright-faced little people are my friends and will let me be their friend—my little friends, I have traveled much, I have been in many cities and many states, everywhere in our great and noble country, and by the blessing of Providence I have been permitted to see many gatherings like this—but I am proud, I am truly proud to say that I never have looked upon so much intelligence, so much grace, such sweetness of disposition as I see in the charming young countenances I see before me at this moment. I have been asking myself, as I sat here, Where am I? Am I in some far-off monarchy, looking upon little princes and princesses? No. Am I in some populous center of my own country, where the choicest children of the land have been selected and brought together as at a fair for a prize? No. Am I in some strange foreign clime where the children are marvels that we know not of? No. Then where am I? Yes—where am I? I am in a simple, remote, unpretending settlement of my own dear state, and these are children of the noble and virtuous men who have made me what I am! My soul is lost in wonder at the thought! And I humbly thank Him to whom we are but as worms of the dust, that He has been pleased to call me to serve such men! Earth has no higher, no grander position for me. Let kings and emperors keep their tinsel crowns, I want them not; my heart is here!

"Again I thought, Is this a theater? No. Is it a concert or a gilded opera? No. Is it some other vain, brilliant, beautiful temple of soul-staining amusement and hilarity? No. Then what is it? What did my consciousness reply? I ask you, my little friends, What did my consciousness reply? It replied, It is the temple of the Lord! Ah, think of that, now. I could hardly keep the tears back, I was so grateful. Oh, how beautiful it is to see these ranks of sunny little faces assembled here to learn the way of life; to learn to be good; to learn to be useful; to learn to be pious; to learn to be great and glorious men and women; to learn to be props and pillars of the state and shining lights in the councils and the households of the nation; to be bearers of the banner and soldiers of the cross in the rude campaigns of life, and ransomed souls in the happy fields of Paradise hereafter.

"Children, honor your parents and be grateful to them for providing for you the precious privileges of a Sunday-school.

"Now, my dear little friends, sit up straight and pretty—there, that's it —and give me your attention and let me tell you about a poor little Sunday-school scholar I once knew. He lived in the Far West, and his parents were poor. They could not give him a costly education, but they were good and wise and they sent him to the Sunday-school. He loved the Sunday-school. I hope you love your Sunday-school—ah, I see by your faces that you do! That is right.

"Well, this poor little boy was always in his place when the bell rang, and he always knew his lesson; for his teachers wanted him to learn and he loved his teachers dearly. Always love your teachers, my children, for they love you more than you can know, now. He would not let bad boys persuade him to go to play on Sunday. There was one little bad boy who was always trying to persuade him, but he never could.

"So this poor little boy grew up to be a man, and had to go out in the world, far from home and friends, to earn his living. Temptations lay all about him, and sometimes he was about to yield, but he would think of some precious lesson he learned in his Sunday-school a long time ago, and that would save him. By and by he was elected to the legislature. Then he did everything he could for Sunday-schools. He got laws passed for them; he got Sunday-schools established wherever he could.

"And by and by the people made him governor—and he said it was all owing to the Sunday-school.

"After a while the people elected him a Representative to the Congress of the United States, and he grew very famous. Now temptations assailed him on every hand. People tried to get him to drink wine, to dance, to go to theaters; they even tried to buy his vote; but no, the memory of his Sunday-school saved him from all harm; he remembered the fate of the bad little boy who used to try to get him to play on Sunday, and who grew up and became a drunkard and was hanged. He remembered that, and was glad he never yielded and played on Sunday.

"Well, at last, what do you think happened? Why the people gave him a towering, illustrious position, a grand, imposing position. And what do you think it was? What should you say it was, children? It was Senator of the United States! That poor little boy that loved his Sunday-school became that man. *That man stands before you!* All that he is, he owes to the Sunday-school.

"My precious children, love your parents, love your teachers, love your Sunday-school, be pious, be obedient, be honest, be diligent, and then you will succeed in life and be honored of all men. Above all things, my children, be honest. Above all things be pure-minded as the snow. Let us join in prayer."

When Senator Dilworthy departed from Cattleville, he left three dozen boys behind him arranging a campaign of life whose objective point was the United States Senate.

When he arrived at the state capital at midnight Mr. Noble came and held a three hours' conference with him, and then as he was about leaving said:

"I've worked hard, and I've got them at last. Six of them haven't got quite the backbone enough to slew around and come right out for you on the first ballot to-morrow, but they're going to vote against you on the first for the sake of appearances, and then come out for you all in a body on the second—I've fixed all that! By supper-time to-morrow you'll be re-elected. You can go to bed and sleep easy on that."

After Mr. Noble was gone, the Senator said:

"Well, to bring about a complexion of things like this was worth coming West for."

[Senator Dilworthy appears 41 pages further on in the novel, but barely 24 hours later in the time sequence, in the following news item.]

Tremendous sensation! Startling news from Saint's Rest! On first ballot for U.S. Senator, when voting was about to begin, Mr. Noble rose in his place and drew forth a package, walked forward and laid it on the Speaker's desk, saying, "This contains seven thousand dollars in bank bills and was given me by Senator Dilworthy in his bed-chamber at midnight last night to buy my vote for him—I wish the Speaker to count the money and retain it to pay the expense of prosecuting this infamous traitor for bribery." The whole legislature was stricken speechless with dismay and astonishment. Noble further said that there were fifty members present with money in their pockets, placed there by Dilworthy to buy their votes. Amidst unparalleled excitement the ballot was now taken, and J. W. Smith elected U.S. Senator; Dilworthy receiving not one vote! *Noble promises damaging exposures concerning Dilworthy and certain measures of his now pending in Congress.*

POLITICAL HYPERBOLE

Robert Green Ingersoll was a highly successful lawyer who distinguished himself in American life as the "great agnostic." Not only did he question the basic tenets of the Christian religion, but he lectured widely on the subject. Had he adhered to more orthodox religious beliefs he could probably have enjoyed a successful political career.

One of his greatest orations was his nominating speech for James G. Blaine at the Republican National Convention of 1876. "He swayed and moved and impelled and restrained and worked in all ways with the mass before him as if he possessed some key to the innermost mechanism that moves the human heart," reported the Chicago Times, "and when he finished, his fine, frank face as calm as when he began, the overwrought thousands sank back in an exhaustion of unspeakable wonder and delight." From that time on Blaine was known by a phrase Ingersoll used in the speech, "the Plumed Knight."

ROBERT GREEN INGERSOLL, *Speech at Cincinnati, June 15, 1876*

... The Republicans of the United States demand as their leader in the great contest of 1876 a man of intelligence, a man of integrity, a man of well-known and approved political opinions. They demand a statesman; they demand a reformer after, as well as before, the election. They demand a politician in the highest, the broadest, and best sense—a man of superb moral courage. They demand a man acquainted with public affairs —with the wants of the people—with not only the requirements of the hour, but with the demands of the future. They demand a man broad enough to comprehend the relations of this government to the other nations of the earth. They demand a man well versed in the powers, duties, and prerogatives of each and every department of this government. They demand a man who will sacredly preserve the financial honor of the United States—one who knows enough to know that the national debt must be paid through the prosperity of this people; one who knows enough to know that all the financial theories in the world cannot redeem a single dollar; one who knows enough to know that all the money must be made, not by law, but by labor; one who knows enough to know that the people of the United States have the industry to make the money and the honor to pay it over just as fast as they make it.

The Republicans of the United States demand a man who knows that prosperity and resumption, when they come, must come together; that when they come they will come hand in hand through the golden harvest fields; hand in hand by the whirling spindles and turning wheels; hand in hand past the open furnace doors; hand in hand by the flaming forges; hand in hand by the chimneys filled with eager fire—greeted and grasped by the countless sons of toil.

This money has to be dug out of the earth. You cannot make it by passing resolutions in a political convention.

The Republicans of the United States want a man who knows that this government should protect every citizen at home and abroad; who knows that any government that will not defend its defenders and protect its protectors is a disgrace to the map of the world. They demand a man who believes in the eternal separation and divorcement of church and school. They demand a man whose political reputation is spotless as a star; but they do not demand that their candidate shall have a certificate of moral

Robert Green Ingersoll, "Speech at Cincinnati, June 15, 1876" in C. P. Farrell, ed., *The Works of Robert G. Ingersoll* (New York: The Ingersoll Publishers, Inc., 1900), Vol. XI, pp. 55–60.

character signed by a Confederate Congress. The man who has in full, heaped and rounded measure, all these splendid qualifications is the present grand and gallant leader of the Republican party—James G. Blaine.

Our country, crowned with the vast and marvelous achievements of its first century, asks for a man worthy of the past and prophetic of her future; asks for a man who has the audacity of genius; asks for a man who is the grandest combination of heart, conscience, and brain beneath her flag. Such a man is James G. Blaine.

For the Republican host, led by this intrepid man, there can be no defeat.

This is a grand year; a year filled with the recollections of the Revolution, filled with proud and tender memories of the past, with the sacred legends of liberty; a year in which the sons of freedom will drink from the fountains of enthusiasm; a year in which the people call for a man who has preserved in Congress what our soldiers won upon the field; a year in which we call for the man who has torn from the throat of treason the tongue of slander—for the man who has snatched the mask of Democracy from the hideous face of Rebellion—for the man who, like an intellectual athlete, has stood in the arena of debate and challenged all comers, and who, up to the present moment, is a total stranger to defeat.

Like an armed warrior, like a plumed knight, James G. Blaine marched down the halls of the American Congress and threw his shining lance full and fair against the brazen foreheads of the defamers of his country and the maligners of his honor. For the Republicans to desert this gallant leader now is as though an army should desert their general upon the field of battle.

James G. Blaine is now, and has been for years, the bearer of the sacred standard of the Republican party. I call it sacred, because no human being can stand beneath its folds without becoming and without remaining free.

Gentlemen of the convention, in the name of the great Republic, the only republic that ever existed upon this earth; in the name of all her defenders and of all her supporters; in the name of all her soldiers living; in the name of all her soldiers dead upon the field of battle; and in the name of those who perished in the skeleton clutch of famine at Andersonville and Libby, whose sufferings he so vividly remembers, Illinois—Illinois nominates for the next President of this country that prince of parliamentarians, that leader of leaders, James G. Blaine.

POLITICAL CHICANERY

In the Gilded Age, even as today, there was sometimes a glaring difference between the salary received by an elected official and the expensive life he lived. In the case of James G. Blaine, the "Plumed Knight," the shoddy transactions that brought him his wealth cost him dear in other ways. Even with a tarnished reputation he almost received the Republican presidential nomination in 1876, easily did win it in 1884, and nearly won the election. Had the populace possessed a little more faith in Blaine's personal integrity, he would certainly have been one of our Presidents.

On the morning of June 5, 1876, just nine days before the Republican National Convention, Blaine staved off the presentation of an anticipated devastating report from a subcommittee of the House Judiciary Committee by presenting a self-justification. The matter concerned a bundle of letters, the so-called "Mulligan Letters," which implicated him with shady dealings concerning $75,000 worth of bonds of the Little Rock and Fort Smith Railroad. It was alleged that Blaine, who had possessed the bonds, sold them at an inflated value to the Union Pacific Railroad in exchange for an assumption that he would look after its interests in Congress. As Speaker of the House, he could easily carry out his end of such a bargain.

Part of Blaine's defense and the resulting ridicule from Mr. Hunton, a Democrat from Virginia and Chairman of the investigating subcommittee, are given below. It should be stated, however, that Blaine was oratorically triumphant in his defense before the House, and the pro-Blaine galleries cheered him lustily as he left the Chamber, while Mr. Hunton and Mr. Knott, his opponents, cringed before their hostility. It was the sober second thoughts of the Republican delegates that denied him the Republican nomination to the Presidency that year.

JAMES G. BLAINE
AND ADVERSARIES, *Debate on the Mulligan Letters*

Mr. Blaine. Mr. Speaker, on the 2d day of May this resolution was passed by the House:

Congressional Record, 44th Congress, 1st Session (Washington: Government Printing Office, 1876), pp. 3602–3617.

Whereas it is publicly alleged, and is not denied by the officers of the Union Pacific Railroad Company, that that corporation did, in the year 1871 or 1872, become the owner of certain bonds of the Little Rock and Fort Smith Railroad Company, for which bonds the said Union Pacific Railroad Company paid a consideration largely in excess of their actual or market value, and that the board of directors of said Union Pacific Railroad Company, though urged, have neglected to investigate said transactions: Therefore,

Be it resolved, that the Committee on the Judiciary be instructed to inquire if any such transaction took place, and, if so, what were the circumstances and inducements thereto, from what person or persons said bonds were obtained and upon what consideration, and whether the transaction was from corrupt design or in furtherance of any corrupt object; and that the committee have power to send for persons and papers.

That resolution, on its face, and in its fair intent, was obviously designed to find out whether any improper thing had been done by the Union Pacific Railroad Company; and of course, incidentally thereto, to find out with whom the transaction was made. The gentleman who offered that resolution offered it when I was not in the House, and my colleague [Mr. Frye], after it was objected to, went to the gentleman and stated that he would have no objection to it, as he knew I would not have if I were present in the House. The gentleman from Massachusetts [Mr. Tarbox], to whom I refer, took especial pains to say to my colleague that the resolution was not in any sense aimed at me. The gentleman will pardon me if I say that I had a slight incredulity upon that assurance given by him to my colleague.

No sooner was the subcommittee designated than it became entirely obvious that the resolution was solely and only aimed at me. I think there had not been three questions asked until it was obvious that the investigation was to be a personal one upon me, and that the Union Pacific Railroad or any other incident of the transaction was secondary, insignificant, and unimportant. I do not complain of that; I do not say that I had any reason to complain of it. If the investigation was to be made in that personal sense, I was ready to meet it.

The gentleman on whose statement the accusation rested, Mr. Harrison, was first called. He stated what he knew from rumor. Then there were called Mr. Rollins, Mr. Morton, and Mr. Millard from Omaha, a Government director of the Union Pacific road, and finally Thomas A. Scott. The testimony was completely and conclusively in disproof of the charge that there was any possibility that I could have had anything to do with the transaction.

I expected . . . that I should have an early report; but the case was prolonged and prolonged and prolonged. . . .

When the famous witness Mulligan came here loaded with information in regard to the Fort Smith road, the gentleman from Virginia drew out what he knew had no reference whatever to the question of investigation. He then and there insisted on all of my private memoranda being allowed to be exhibited by that man in reference to business that had no more connection, no more relation, no more to do with that investigation than with the North Pole.

And the gentleman tried his best, also, though I believe that has been abandoned, to capture and use and control my private correspondence. This man had selected out of correspondence running over a great many years letters which he thought would be peculiarly damaging to me. He came here loaded with them. He came here for a sensation. He came here primed. He came here on that particular errand. I was advised of it, and I obtained those letters under circumstances which have been notoriously scattered throughout the United States, and are known to everybody. I have them. I claim I have the entire right to those letters, not only by natural right, but upon all the precedents and principles of law, as the man who held those letters in possession held them wrongfully. The committee that attempted to take those letters from that man for use against me proceeded wrongfully. They proceeded in all boldness to a most defiant violation of the ordinary private and personal rights which belong to every American citizen, and I was willing to stand and meet the Judiciary Committee on this floor. I wanted them to introduce it. I wanted the gentleman from Kentucky and the gentleman from Virginia to introduce that question upon this floor, but they did not do it.

Mr. Knott [of Kentucky—Ed.] (in his seat). I know you did.

Mr. Blaine. Very well.

Mr. Knott. I know you wanted to be made a martyr of. [Laughter]

Mr. Blaine. ... I would like any gentleman on this floor—and all gentlemen on this floor are presumed to be men of affairs, whose business has been varied, whose intercourse has been large—I would like any gentleman to stand up here and tell me that he is willing and ready to have his private correspondence scanned over and made public for the last eight or ten years. I would like any gentleman to say that. Does it imply guilt? Does it imply wrongdoing? Does it imply any sense of weakness that a man will protect his private correspondence? No, sir; it is the first instinct to do it, and it is the last outrage upon any man to violate it. ...

... But, sir, having vindicated that right ... I am not ashamed to show them. There they are [holding up a package of letters]. There is the very original package. And with some sense of humiliation, with a mortification that I do not pretend to conceal, with a sense of outrage which I think any man in my position would feel, I invite the confidence of 44,000,000 of my countrymen while I read those letters from this desk. [Applause] ...

[Blaine then read the correspondence, though many believed it was altered, not in chronological order, with some parts excised. He included additional explanatory comments. Subsequently, Mr. Hunton of Virginia, Chairman of the subcommittee, rose to defend his committee. He denied that the aim was to malign Mr. Blaine and insisted that postponement had been purely in deference to Mr. Blaine's requests. Mr. Hunton was a Democrat, of course, and while he may have been fair, he was also partisan.—Ed.]

Mr. Hunton. ... During the present session of this House two resolutions were adopted, each of which ordered an investigation, each of which was referred to the Committee of the Judiciary of this House, and each of which was referred to a subcommittee consisting of Mr. Ashe of North Carolina, Mr. Lawrence of Ohio, and myself as chairman of the committee, and before the committee has finished the taking of testimony, before that committee has reached a conclusion, an effort is made by the gentleman supposed to be most concerned in these investigations to take the consideration of these questions from the organ of the House and report upon them in person. I need not remind the House what sort of a report would come from that committee if it were allowed to be made by the gentleman from Maine. But I say that after this House has ordered an investigation and has committed that investigation to a committee of the House, it is not only unexampled, but entirely against legislative proceedings for a gentleman to rise and undertake to anticipate what the conclusion of that committee shall be and to state what the action of that committee has been. ...

[Mr. Hunton then elaborated upon the committee's relations with Mr. Mulligan.—Ed.]

Mr. Hunton. ... In the course of his examination the first day Mr. Mulligan was testifying very quietly; there was no excitement in the committee room at all when he happened to mention that he had in his possession certain letters written by Mr. Blaine to Warren Fisher, Jr. The mention of these letters seemed to have a remarkable effect upon Mr. Blaine, for in a moment or two afterward he whispered to Mr. Lawrence, the Republican member of that committee, "Move an adjournment." It so happened that I heard the suggestion. Mr. Lawrence got up with great solemnity on his countenance and said, "Mr. Chairman, I am very sick and I hope the committee will adjourn." [Laughter]

[Mr. Lawrence then rose and reminded Mr. Hunton that he had informed him of his illness earlier, when the committee convened.—Ed.]

Mr. Hunton. The gentleman has stated the matter exactly as it occurred. He did come in the morning sick.

Mr. Lawrence. Yes, sir.

Mr. Hunton. But he went to work in a most vigorous style for two hours.

Mr. Lawrence. But I became exhausted.

Mr. Hunton. When these letters were mentioned the gentleman became sick, and somebody else sicker. [Laughter] And the motion to adjourn was made at his suggestion. ...

The committee adjourned until the next morning at ten o'clock; and when we met, James Mulligan was put upon the stand again to complete his examination. ... He said, "Mr. Chairman ... I desire to make a personal explanation painful to myself."

I will commence at the beginning of his personal explanation. ... Upon the evening of his first arrival in the city of Washington, before I knew he was in the city, he and Warren Fisher were waited on by Mr. Blaine. They were invited to the house of Mr. Blaine. Mr. Mulligan said, "Mr. Blaine I decline to go to your house; I do not want to talk about what I have been brought here for. I desire to take the stand tomorrow untrammeled by conversation of any kind with anybody. Warren Fisher went to the house of Mr. Blaine. Twice Mr. Blaine sent a messenger down to induce Mulligan to come to his house. Mr. Mulligan still declined, and presently Mr. Blaine and Warren Fisher came into the hotel where Mulligan stopped in the city of Washington (the Riggs House). Mr. Mulligan was in the barber-shop undergoing the pleasant operation of shaving, or about to undergo it, and Mr. Blaine followed him into the barber-shop and commenced to entreat and earnestly to request that Mulligan would give up those letters which Blaine had addressed to Warren Fisher. Mulligan declined to do it. ... Mr. Blaine entreated him. I give you now the substance of the language of the witness. He entreated him with tears in his eyes, going down on his knees, or almost on his knees—

Mr. Frye. In the barber-shop?

Mr. Hunton. I did not say in the barber-shop. I do not care where it was. It was in his room, I believe; but he made this entreaty. The witness said, "with tears in his eyes, almost, if not quite, on his knees"; " 'if you do not deliver those letters to me, I am ruined and my family disgraced.' " Of course I mean to understand here that the witness meant that Blaine's family would be disgraced through the ruin of Mr. Blaine. He also threatened to commit suicide. Mr. Mulligan refused to deliver the letters. ... Mr. Blaine then tried politics on him, and he asked the witness: "Are you content with your station?" To this Mulligan said he would like to improve it if he could. Mr. Blaine said: "Would you like a political office?" Mulligan replied he did not like politics, and did not care about it. Mr. Blaine then asked how he would like a foreign consulship? He said he would not like it; and after that Blaine said: "Let me see the letters to peruse them." ... He read them over once or twice, and returned them to the witness. ... He asked the witness to let him see the letters again ... and when Mr. Blaine had read them and kept them a short time he refused to deliver them. ...

POLITICAL LITERATURE OF PROTEST

As the Gilded Age approached its end, the politics that accepted chicanery and hypocrisy, boodle and spoils, gave way to something far more meaningful—the politics of protest. The Grangers had protested against excessive railroad and grain elevator charges in the 1870's, but population increases in nearby urban areas restored much of their prosperity. The protesters of the late 1880's and the early 1890's were further from markets, however, and theirs tended to be a single crop economy. These were the farmers of the destitute South or the Middle Border country (western Minnesota, Dakota, Nebraska, Kansas, and on down into Texas). After years of hardships these agrarians turned to radicalism in every sense of the word; they held protest meetings at country school houses and Grange halls, and began sending men to Congress.

Their grievances were real (though often nature-made rather than man-made), their bitterness extreme, their sense of persecution alarming. Their demands for change were phrased like the slogans for a military crusade.

One of their periodicals was The National Economist, published in Washington, D.C., from 1889 until 1892. It was the sounding board for the Farmer's Alliance, which had originated in Texas, but it quoted news and editorial items from farm papers throughout the United States. The pitch of the agrarian's feelings is indicated in the following excerpts from this paper.

Excerpts from THE NATIONAL ECONOMIST

March 29, 1890, p. 7
"Why Farming Does Not Pay," by Lynn Tanner of Cheneyville, Louisiana

... What vocation in life at the present time requires the most toil, the greatest amount of patience, the most skillful management directed by brains and forethought, the answer would [be] farming. ...

... He [the farmer] is called upon to endure the inclemencies of winter,

---

The National Economist, Vol. 3 (Washington, D.C., 1890).

the rains of spring, the heats of summer, and to encounter an intermingling of all the seasons during the autumn months. ...

Why are the farmers so illy paid for their labor? [Because of] ... the great want of money. Who is to blame for the people not having money? The two g.o.p.'s of this nation known as Democratic and Republican. For what are they to be blamed? For legislating at all times in the interests of commerce and capital, and to the total neglect of agriculture. ...

How would Judas Iscariot compare with all such? He would be a gentleman; though, if living, the American politician would denounce him, not for his crime, but because he accepted so small a bribe. ...

April 12, 1890, p. 64
"The Good the Alliance Has Done," by J. A. Tetts of Ruston, Louisiana

Many members and ex-members have asked the question, "What good has the Alliance done?" ...

There are men foolish enough to want an equal distribution of the wealth of this country, but you will not find many of them foremost in the ranks of any farmers' organization. What we want distributed equally to all men, "regardless of race, color, or previous condition of servitude," is the opportunity for the pursuit of happiness. Some men, who do not look below the surface, will say, "Why, you have that now; you can be a millionaire ... you can be a banker now if you have the spundulix [sic]; the chance is open to you." Yes, this is true, the chance is open to me ... there is no law prohibiting me from trying; but it is the privileges of the classes I am objecting to, and not the classes themselves. It is the privileges of the ins that makes it so easy for them to stay in and hard for the outs to get in. If the classes had less privileges and individuals more it would be better for the country, and it can be brought about only by the united effort of the underprivileged classes. So long as they remain divided in sentiment and undisciplined in purpose, so long the workingmen will be the outs and the privileged classes the ins. Organization has taught us the weak places in human nature. It is generally believed in my section that the average composition of the genus homo is one part man and three parts dog. This is why there are·so many falling away from the organization ... when many of them are confined together there is generally a considerable amount of snarling, if not some fighting. This, of course, accounts for so many who say the Alliance has done them no good; these are no doubt the ones who got bitten and failed to get a bone.

Taking a surface view of the Alliance, many who have not studied it might conclude that it was going into a decline; but I can assure its friends ... "it sleepeth" only, and will awaken like Sampson and turn upon its enemies. The seeds that have been falling for the last five years have fallen on some fertile soil and are taking deep root; and they will develop into plants of liberty that will so occupy the ground as to overshadow and choke out the noxious weeds of ignorance, lethargy, selfishness, and humble submission. ... The Alliance has brought careless and uneducated men together under the same roof with men who have studied the history of dead nations and can read the handwriting on the wall, and these [groups] have assimulated [sic] and now through a labor press, established and maintained by them together, are sending out into the world facts and theories that will yet bring gladness to the toiler and hope to the heart of the father of poor children.

The Alliance has done what the sword, the press, and the pulpit have failed to do, and if it had died without accomplishing more, it might have claimed a monument with this inscription "I am mightier than all," for after twenty-four years of political reconstruction, forty years of philanthropy, and a hundred years of preaching, it was left to the Alliance to blot out the Mason and Dixon line—that imaginary line on which the bloody shirt was hung every four years—and to unite the working, mortgage-hunted farmer of the Northwest with the half Ku-Klux and half desperado cotton-planter of the South. The horns of the Ku-Klux were knocked off ... and the shirt that has been waved so faithfully has been torn up ... and cast into the Mississippi, and by this time no doubt [is] in the maw of some cat-fish, or making a nest for some mud-turtle of a politician who will have to crawl into his shell when he sees the result of the next election.

April 19, 1890, p. 4

In the early settlement of this country people had few conveniences, as compared with the present time, and yet their situation in life was far more happy and prosperous. ... Then they were enjoying the blessings of a new and unpolluted government. ... But in later years those whom you have entrusted to make the laws and act as your guardians, have sold your birthright to the scheming gold changers, land sharks, and transportation kings. The Congress of these United States has become a cesspool of cringing servitude to the wiles of the money power. ... Oh, God! how long will the patience and long suffering of a crushed people endure? Freemen, you have nine votes out of every ten; you can elect every law-maker in this nation from your own ranks. Will you do it before this land is baptised in the red hot blood of a vindictive people? May God help you.

July 26, 1890, p. 322

There is a determination on the part of machine politicians to whip into line the Alliance members, which to some degree will succeed. ... There are men whose children are debarred from school, growing up tramps and prostitutes, who at elections will fall into line and cast their votes for political tricksters ... who will drag them down lower and lower, and the multitude with them. There are men with education and intelligence who will shut their eyes to the acts and spurious opinions of their political leaders, and on election day will be found voting ... for a system that will drag themselves down to a level with the serfs they vote with, all for lack of manly independence and vigilance, which is the price of liberty. ... There never was a time when the common people were studying the principles of economical government as they are now. Necessity has finally driven them to think and act for themselves. ... [*Southern Agriculturalist,* Homer, La.]

POLITICAL ORATORY OF PROTEST

The discontent reflected in the farm literature increased with the depression years of the 1890's, and by convention time in the summer of 1896, the protest had reached alarming proportions. The Democratic party adopted most of the Populist platform, even including the faulty plank, Free Silver at 16 to 1. It nominated William Jennings Bryan, but the money raised for the rival party by Mark Hannah, the fear of Free Silver engendered by a conservative press, the ending of hard times, and the "secure" image of the Republican nominee, William McKinley, all combined to defeat the "radicals."

Yet from this time until the decade of the 1920's the Federal Government was more sensitive to the nation's ills, more hostile to monopoly and private interest, and less amenable to corruption than it had been in the Gilded Age. Changes were rapidly taking place; an age was coming to an end.

William Jennings Bryan, so agrarian and midwestern in face, body, and mind as to constitute an "everyman" type, was the leader who listened to the complaints of the discontented and rose to represent them. Bryan's moment of glory came at the Democratic National Convention of 1896. His oration, known as the "Cross of Gold" speech, is famous the world over. Excerpts are given below.

WILLIAM JENNINGS BRYAN,
Speech Concluding Debate on the Chicago Platform

Mr. Chairman and Gentlemen of the Convention: I would be presumptuous, indeed, to present myself against the distinguished gentlemen to whom you have listened if this were a mere measuring of abilities; but this is not a contest between persons. The humblest citizen in all the land, when clad in the armor of a righteous cause, is stronger than all the hosts of error. I come to speak to you in defense of a cause as holy as the cause of liberty—the cause of humanity. ...

Never before in the history of this country has there been witnessed such a contest as that through which we have just passed. ... With a zeal approaching the zeal which inspired the crusaders who followed Peter the Hermit, our silver Democrats went forth from victory unto victory until they are now assembled, not to discuss, not to debate, but to enter up the judgment already rendered by the plain people of this country. In this contest brother has been arrayed against brother, father against son. The warmest ties of love, acquaintance and association have been disregarded; old leaders have been cast aside when they have refused to give expression to the sentiments of those whom they would lead, and new leaders have sprung up to give direction to this cause of truth. Thus has the contest been waged, and we have assembled here under as binding and solemn instructions as were ever imposed upon representatives of the people. ...

The gentleman who preceded me (ex-Governor Russell) spoke of the State of Massachusetts; let me assure him that not one present in all this convention entertains the least hostility to the people of the State of Massachusetts, but we stand here representing people who are the equals, before the law, of the greatest citizens in the State of Massachusetts. When

---

William Jennings Bryan, "Speech Concluding Debate on the Chicago Platform," in W. J. Bryan, *The First Battle: A Story of the Campaign of 1896* (Chicago: W. B. Conkey Co., 1896), pp. 199–206.

From *Leslie's Illustrated Weekly*, Vol. 83, No. 2135 (August 13, 1896).

"Tempted."

you (turning to the gold delegates) come before us and tell us that we are about to disturb your business interests, we reply that you have disturbed our business interests by your course.

We say to you that you have made the definition of a business man too limited in its application. The man who is employed for wages is as much a business man as his employer; the attorney in a country town is as much a business man as the corporation counsel in a great metropolis; the merchant at the cross-roads store is as much a business man as the merchant of New York; the farmer who goes forth in the morning and toils all day—who begins in the spring and toils all summer—and who by the application of brain and muscle to the natural resources of the country creates wealth, is as much a business man as the man who goes upon the board of trade and bets upon the price of grain; the miners who go down a thousand feet into the earth, or climb two thousand feet upon the cliffs, and bring forth from their hiding places the precious metals to be poured into the channels of trade are as much business men as the few financial magnates who, in a back room, corner the money of the world. We come to speak for the broader class of business men.

Ah, my friends, we say not one word against those who live upon the Atlantic coast, but the hardy pioneers who have braved all the dangers of the wilderness, who have made the desert to blossom as the rose—the pioneers away out there (pointing to the West), who rear their children near to Nature's heart, where they can mingle their voices with the voices of the birds—out there where they have erected schoolhouses for the education of their young, churches where they praise their Creator, and cemeteries where rest the ashes of their dead—these people, we say, are as deserving of the consideration of our party as any people in this country. It is for these that we speak. We do not come as aggressors. Our war is not a war of conquest; we are fighting in the defense of our homes, our families, and posterity. We have petitioned, and our petitions have been scorned; we have entreated, and our entreaties have been disregarded; we have begged, and they have mocked when our calamity came. We beg no longer; we entreat no more; we petition no more. We defy them.

The gentleman from Wisconsin has said that he fears a Robespierre. My friends, in this land of the free you need not fear that a tyrant will spring up from among the people. What we need is an Andrew Jackson to stand, as Jackson stood, against the encroachment of organized wealth. ...

Mr. Carlisle said in 1878 that this was a struggle between "the idle holders of idle capital" and "the struggling masses, who produce the wealth and pay the taxes of the country"; and, my friends, the question we are to decide is: Upon which side will the Democratic party fight; upon the side of "the idle holders of idle capital" or upon the side of "the struggling masses"? That is the question which the party must answer first, and then it must be answered by each individual hereafter. The sympathies of the Democratic party, as shown by the platform, are on the side of the struggling masses who have ever been the foundations of the Democratic party. There are two ideas of government. There are those who believe that, if you will only legislate to make the well-to-do prosperous, their prosperity will leak through on those below. The Democratic idea, however, has been that if you legislate to make the classes prosperous, their prosperity will find its way up through every class which rests upon them.

You come to us and tell us that the great cities are in favor of the gold standard; we reply that the great cities rest upon our broad and fertile prairies. Burn down your cities and leave our farms, and your cities will spring up again as if by magic; but destroy our farms and the grass will grow in the streets of every city in the country.

My friends, we declare that this nation is able to legislate for its own people on every question, without waiting for the aid or consent of any other nation on earth; and upon that issue we expect to carry every State in the Union. I shall not slander the inhabitants of the fair State of Massachusetts nor the inhabitants of the State of New York by saying that, when they are confronted with the proposition, they will declare that this nation is not able to attend to its own business. It is the issue of 1776 over again. Our ancestors, when but three millions in number, had the courage to declare their political independence of every other nation; shall we, their descendants, when we have grown to seventy millions, declare that we are less independent than our forefathers? No, my friends, that will never be the verdict of our people. Therefore, we care not upon what lines the battle is fought. If they say bimetallism is good, but that we cannot have it until other nations help us, we reply that, instead of having a gold standard because England has, we will restore bimetallism, and then let England have bimetallism because the United States has it. If they dare to come out in the open field and defend the gold standard as a good thing, we will fight them to the uttermost. Having behind us the producing masses of this nation and the world, supported by the commercial interest, the laboring interests, and the toilers everywhere, we will answer their demand for a gold standard by saying to them: You shall not press down upon the brow of labor this crown of thorns, you shall not crucify mankind upon a cross of gold.

THE CHRISTIAN USE OF POWER

On the 25th day of April, 1898, a sensitive, Christian, humane President, William McKinley, led his nation into a brief and successful little war with Spain. Before the year was out the war had ended and, for better or for worse, America had acquired an overseas empire.

In his capacity as Commander in Chief, McKinley set the moral tone of the war, and he insisted that America's actions had been and must continue to be on the highest moral and humanistic plane. Such assurances of high motives met with great approval from the American people, and McKinley became one of the most popular of Presidents.

In a speech delivered on October 12, 1898, at the Trans-Mississippi Exposition at Omaha, he elaborated upon the Christian, moral, and humanistic virtues of the war. "President McKinley probably never received a more enthusiastic greeting," wrote the reporter for the St. Louis Post-Dispatch. "Hardly one sentence was spoken by him which did not evoke from the people cheer upon cheer."

Yet his remarks were in glaring contrast to the thoughts expressed in the next reading by Theodore Roosevelt. Taken together, they present the terrible question that confronts a powerful country: when is the use of the raw military might of a great power justified in world affairs?

PRESIDENT WILLIAM MCKINLEY, *Speech at Omaha, October 12, 1898*

... One of the great laws of life is progress, and nowhere have the principles of this law been so strikingly illustrated as in the United States. A century and a decade of our national life have turned doubt into conviction; changed experiment into demonstration; revolutionized old methods and won new triumphs which have challenged the attention of the world. This is true not only of the accumulation of material wealth and advance in education, science, invention and manufactures, but above all in the opportunities to the people for their own elevation which have been secured by wise, free government.

Excerpts from speech of President William McKinley at Omaha, Nebraska, October 12, 1898. St. Louis *Post-Dispatch*, October 12, 1898, p. 1.

Hitherto in peace and war, with additions to our territory and slight changes in our laws, we have steadily enforced the spirit of the constitution secured to us by the noble self-sacrifice and far-reaching sagacity of our ancestors. We have avoided the temptations of conquest in the spirit of gain. With an increasing love for our institutions and an abiding faith in their stability, we have made the triumphs of our system of government in the progress and prosperity of our people an inspiration to the whole human race. Confronted at this moment by new and grave problems, we must recognize that their solution will affect not ourselves alone, but others of the family of nations.

In this age of frequent interchange and mutual dependency, we cannot shirk our international responsibilities if we would. They must be met with courage and wisdom, and we must follow duty even if desire opposes. No deliberation can be too mature, or self-control too constant, in this solemn hour of our history. We must avoid the temptation of undue aggression, and aim to secure only such results as will promote our own and general good.

It has been said by someone that the normal condition of nations is war. That is not true of the United States. We never enter upon war until every effort for peace without it has been exhausted. Ours has never been a military government. Peace, with whose blessings we have been so singularly favored, is the national desire and the goal of every American.

On the 25th of April, for the first time for more than a generation, the United States sounded the call to arms. The banners of war were unfurled; the best and bravest from every section responded; a mighty army was enrolled; the North and the South vied with each other in patriotic devotion; science was invoked to furnish its most effective weapons; factories were rushed to supply equipment; the youth and the veteran joined in freely offering their services to their country; volunteers and regulars and all the people rallied to the support of the republic.

There was no break in the line, no halt in the march, no fear in the heart, no resistance to patriotic impulse at home, no successful resistance to the patriotic spirit of the troops fighting in distant waters or on a foreign shore. What a wonderful experience it has been from the standpoint of patriotism and achievement. ...

... And above and beyond all, the valor of the American army and the bravery of the American navy and the majesty of the American name stand forth in unsullied glory, while the humanity of our purpose and the magnanimity of our conduct have given to war, always horrible, touches of noble generosity, Christian sympathy and charity, and examples of human grandeur which can never be lost to mankind. Passion and bitterness formed no part of our impelling motive, and it is gratifying to feel that humanity triumphed at every step of the war's progress. ...

The faith of a Christian nation recognizes the hand of Almighty God in the ordeal through which we have passed. Divine favor seemed manifest everywhere. In fighting for humanity's sake we have been signally blessed. We did not seek war. To avoid it, if this could be done in justice and honor to the rights of our neighbors and ourselves, was our constant prayer. The war was no more invited by us than were the questions which are laid at our door by its results. Now, as then, we will do our duty. The problems will not be solved in a day. Patience will be required; patience, combined with sincerity of purpose and unshaken resolution to do right, seeking only the highest good of the nation and recognizing no other obligation, pursuing no other path but that of duty.

Right action follows right purpose. We may not at all times be able to divine the future; the way may not always seem clear; but if our aims are high and unselfish, somehow and in some way the right end will be reached. The genius of the nation, its freedom, its wisdom, its humanity, its courage, its justice favored by divine providence, will make it equal to every task and the master of every emergency.

THE ARROGANCE OF POWER

During most of the nineteenth century the United States appeared bois-terous, haughty, and even insolent in her relations with the rest of the world. Possibly her behavior in the realm of foreign affairs had acquired some sophistication or maturity by the Gilded Age, but still very present was that expansive, pugnacious, lick-your-weight-in-wildcats arrogance. While the frontier was drawing to a close, the energy and enthusiasm that had conquered the wilderness continued unabated. To Spain, Chile, England, and Germany we were a problem, and it took a measure of patience on their part to put up with us.

If great leaders are the products of the times in which they live, if they reflect the ideals and aspirations of their people, then Theodore Roosevelt fit the pattern of a great leader indeed. A moralistic, clean-living, sports-loving, wealthy, energetic American, he thought their thoughts when he spoke, wrote, or established policy. As he matured in the Gilded Age, he acquired certain ideas about America's role in world affairs and how she should act. Millions shared his bold, warlike, manly attitudes.

THEODORE ROOSEVELT, Two Letters

TO ALFRED THAYER MAHAN

Personal and Private   Washington, May 3, 1897

My dear Captain Mahan: This letter must, of course, be considered as entirely confidential, because in my position I am merely carrying out the policy of the Secretary and the President. I suppose I need not tell you that as regards Hawaii I take your views absolutely, as indeed I do on foreign policy generally. If I had my way we would annex those islands tomorrow. If that is impossible I would establish a protectorate over them. I believe we should build the Nicaraguan canal at once, and in the meantime that we should build a dozen new battleships, half of them on the Pacific Coast; and these battleships should have large coal capacity and a consequent increased radius of action. I am fully alive to the danger from Japan, and I know that it is idle to rely on any sentimental good will toward us. I think President Cleveland's action was a colossal crime, and we should be guilty of aiding him after the fact if we do not reverse what he did. I earnestly hope we can make the President look at things our way. Last Saturday night Lodge pressed his views upon him with all his strength. I have been getting matters in shape on the Pacific coast just as fast as I have been allowed. My own belief is that we should act instantly before the two new Japanese warships leave England. I would send the *Oregon,* and, if necessary, also the *Monterey* (either with a deck load of coal or accompanied by a coaling ship) to Hawaii, and would hoist our flag over the island, leaving all details for after action. I shall press these views upon my chief just so far as he will let me; more I cannot do.

As regards what you say in your letter, there is only one point to which I would take exception. I fully realize the immense importance of the Pacific coast. Strictly between ourselves, I do not think Admiral Beardslee quite the man for the situation out there, but Captain Barker, of the *Oregon,* is, I believe, excellent in point of decisions, willingness to accept responsibility, and thorough knowledge of the situation. But there are big problems in the West Indies also. Until we definitely turn Spain out of those islands (and if I had my way that would be done tomorrow), we will always be menaced by trouble there. We should acquire the Danish Islands, and by turning Spain out should serve notice that no strong European power, and especially not Germany, should be allowed to gain a foothold by supplanting some weak European power. I do not fear England; Canada is a hostage for her good behavior; but I do fear some of the other powers. I am extremely sorry to say that there is some slight appearance here of the desire to stop building up the Navy until our finances are better. Tom Reed, to my astonishment and indignation, takes this view, and even my chief, who is one of the most high-minded, honorable and upright gentlemen I have ever had the good fortune to serve under, is a little inclined toward it.

I need not say that this letter must be strictly private. I speak to you with the greatest freedom, for I sympathize with your views, and I have precisely the same idea of patriotism, and of belief in and love for our country. But to no one else excepting Lodge do I talk like this.

As regards Hawaii I am delighted to be able to tell you that Secretary Long shares our views. He believes we should take the islands, and I have just been preparing some memoranda for him to use at the Cabinet meeting tomorrow. If only we had some good man in the place of John Sherman as Secretary of State there would not be a hitch, and even as it is I hope for favorable action. I have been pressing upon the Secretary, and through him on the President, that we ought to act now without delay, before Japan gets her two new battleships which are now ready for delivery to her in England. Even a fortnight may make a difference. With Hawaii once in our hands most of the danger of friction with Japan would disappear.

The Secretary also believes in building the Nicaraguan canal as a military measure, although I don't know that he is as decided on this point as you and I are; and he believes in building battleships on the Pacific slope. *Faithfully yours*

TO JOHN DAVIS LONG

Washington, September 30, 1897

Sir: The steady growth of our country in wealth and population, and its extension by the acquisition of non-contiguous territory in Alaska, and at the same time the steady growth of the old naval powers of the world, and the appearance of new ones, such as Germany and Japan, with which it is possible that one day we may be brought into contact, make me feel that I should respectfully, and with all possible earnestness, urge the advisability of the Navy Department doing all it can to further a steady and rapid upbuilding of our Navy. We cannot hope to rival England. It is probably not desirable that we should rival France; while Russia's threefold sea front, and Italy's peculiar position, render it to the last degree improbable that we shall be cast into hostile contact with either of them. But Japan is steadily becoming a great naval power in the Pacific, where her fleet already surpasses ours in strength; and Germany shows a tendency to stretch out for colonial possessions which may at any moment cause a conflict with us. In my opinion our Pacific fleet should constantly be kept above that of Japan, and our naval strength as a whole superior to that of Germany. It does not seem to me that we can afford to invite responsibility and shirk the burden that we thus incur; we cannot justify ourselves for retaining Alaska and annexing Hawaii unless we provide a Navy sufficient to prevent all chance of either being taken by a hostile power; still less have we any right to assert the Monroe Doctrine in the American hemisphere unless we are ready to make good our assertion with our warships. A great navy does not make for war, but for peace. It is the cheapest kind of insurance. No coast fortifications can really protect our coasts; they can only be protected by a formidable fighting navy. If through any supineness or false economy on our part, we fail to provide plenty of ships of the best type, thoroughly fitted in every way, we run the risk of causing the nation to suffer some disaster more serious than it has ever before encountered—a disaster which would warp and stunt our whole national life, for the moral effect would be infinitely worse than the material. We invite such a disaster if we fail to have a sufficiency of the best ships, and fail to keep both our matériel and personnel up to the highest conditions.

I believe that Congress should at once give us six (6) new battleships, two (2) to be built on the Pacific and four (4) on the Atlantic; six (6) large cruisers, of the size of the *Brooklyn,* but in armament more nearly approaching the Argentine vessel *San Martin;* and seventy-five (75) torpedo boats, twenty-five (25) for the Pacific and fifty (50) for the Atlantic. I believe that we should set about building all these craft now, and that each one should be, if possible, the most formidable of its kind afloat.

We should at once build new dry docks. With the additions which are outlined above we should need to have one more dry dock for the largest battleships on the Pacific coast, and three more on the Atlantic coast; that is, four extra, although we probably could get along with only two extra.

Many of our cruisers and battleships are armed, in part, with the slow-fire six-inch gun, a weapon which is now obsolete. It would be cruel to pit these vessels against hostile vessels nominally of the same type, but armed with modern rapid-fire guns. The vessels could be doubled in effectiveness by substituting the converted rapid-fire six-inch guns for the old style guns as rapidly as possible. There are ninety-five of these old style guns in the service. The conversion would cost about $1,000 per gun. We should have guns for auxiliary cruisers; we now have almost none. The greatest need at the moment is smokeless powder. Smokeless powder would greatly increase the power and rapidity of the fire, and would be of great tactical advantage. We should get two million pounds at once, in order to completely outfit our ships. This would probably cost $1,500,000. For $100,000 all our armor-piercing shell should be capped, loaded and fused. We should provide a reasonable reserve supply of projectiles (about nine thousand in all) so as to permit a complete refill of all the ships.

If we stop building up the Navy now it will put us at a great disadvantage when we go on. The greatest difficulty was experienced when we began our work on the new Navy in 1883. We had to train the workmen and the designers; we had to build factories, and make tools. The difference between such a vessel as the *Texas* and such a vessel as the *Indiana* will illustrate the cost to the country of carrying on such an experiment. We are now in a situation to build up a navy commensurate with our needs, provided the work is carried on continuously, for the era of experiment has passed, and we possess designs suitable for our own use, with types of vessels equal to those of any other power. But if the work is interrupted, and new vessels are not begun, we shall soon find it necessary to start all over again, as we did in 1883, and to reinstruct the men and manufacturers and re-educate the officers and designers and re-experiment with the designs. It would be difficult to calculate the course we should incur by such a proceeding; and meanwhile we should be exposing the country to the possibility of the bitterest humiliation. *Very respectfully*